"*The Extra Mile* takes a careful look at the life virtues Jesus emphasizes in his Sermon on the Mount. These glimpses into the core virtues of discipleship are a helpful reminder of who Jesus calls us to be as his followers. Reflecting on these characteristics can help us grow and mature into being the people God made us to be."

—**Darrell L. Bock**
Executive Director for Cultural Engagement
Howard G. Hendricks Center for Christian
Leadership and Cultural Engagement
Senior Research Professor of New Testament Studies

"Dr. Cody Wallace loves the lost and is passionate about seeing believers go past the point of salvation, becoming disciples of Christ. You may not agree with the interpretation of every passage by Dr. Wallace, but any believer who reads this book will be challenged to grow as a Christian and in following after Christ be every inch the disciple God wants them to be."

—**Dr. R. Larry Moyer**
Founder and CEO, Chairman of the Board
Evantell

"Dr. Cody Wallace has done an excellent job of explaining free grace theology. The discussion is thorough, irenic, and well-written."

—**Dr. Joseph Dillow, ThD**
Author of *Final Destiny: The Future Reign of the Servant Kings*

"*The Extra Mile* is a compelling read of Jesus's profound teachings as presented in Matthew 5-7. For someone like me seeking to blend my faith with the demands of professional life, Dr. Cody Wallace has crafted a remarkable work that transcends the traditional boundaries of religious texts, offering timeless wisdom that resonates not only with individuals but also with business professionals alike. His insightful analysis of Jesus's character provides a stellar model for personal growth and professional integrity. This book is not just a guide for spiritual discipleship but a beacon for ethical leadership in any arena. Cody's passionate style and deep understanding make *The Extra Mile* a key resource for anyone seeking to navigate the complexities of modern life with grace and conviction."

—**Ronell Rivera**
President and Founder, El-Gibhor International
President, SED International de Colombia

"Jesus presented his yoke as easy and light. Sadly, many Bible teachers leave new disciples feeling discouraged over their law-based instructions which weigh God's people down. Dr. Wallace helps the reader to understand how Jesus's yoke truly is easy and light in his latest book on how to walk with Christ.

In a church filled with demoralizing calls to be better and do better, he provides the reader with a grace-focused study on the Sermon on the Mount. Follow grace in a spirit of grace and mercy, not burdensome striving and effort."

—**Shawn Wilson**
Pastor of Grace Community Bible Church
Host of "Rev Reads"

"Countless works have delved into Jesus's renowned sermon recorded in Matthew 5–7. Dr. Cody Wallace, drawing from his pastoral experience, offers unique insights in his book, approaching the Sermon on the Mount with a heart devoted to Christ. Through practical wisdom, Wallace guides pastors and church leaders in nurturing disciples who embody the teachings of Jesus, fostering a kingdom-focused life among those who bear His name."

—**Al Fernandez**
Regional Catalyst-Southern Region
Florida Baptist Convention

"*The Extra Mile* is the most thorough discipleship tool I have read on Matthew 5–7, the Sermon on the Mount. Dr. Cody Wallace combines his scholarship with his pastoral heart to lead the reader into the depths of what it means to be a disciple of Jesus. As Dr. Wallace makes his way through this famous sermon by Jesus, he explains how this teaching by Jesus is supported in the broader context of the New Testament. I appreciate how Dr. Wallace does not shy away from some of the difficult and controversial teachings of Jesus (e.g., Matthew 5:22 and 7:20) but hits them head on with solid exegetical explanations. I was also engaged by his captivating illustrations he used to explain, prove, or apply the biblical truths.

The main thrust of the book comes out clearly for those who want to follow Jesus: 'Don't lose sight of the goal—to be like Christ,' or, more broadly, he says to 'live for a higher calling' and 'hailed as faithful,' to Him. I highly recommend *The Extra Mile*."

—**Jeremy Vance, MDiv, DMin**
President of the Free Grace Alliance
Senior Pastor of Faith Church, Manitowoc, WI

"Dr. Cody Wallace has given an excellent, biblically-sound treatment of the subjects of discipleship and kingdom-mindedness from the Sermon on the Mount. Dr. Wallace gives excellent insights, but the core teaching is ultimately the Lord's, from His incredible sermon recorded in Matthew 5–7. This book will be a tremendous blessing to those who learn this material and put this teaching into practice, and it will bless those around them, too!"

—**Grant Hawley**
Bold Grace Ministries

"In a world that cries out for meaning and purpose, Dr. Cody Wallace has composed a vital work pointing us to find our identity and hope in Christ. As a military officer, continual training, study, and growth are requirements to be effective in our profession of arms. These same principles apply to those who fight the spiritual war on the side of Christ. Dr. Wallace provides a valuable resource to equip growing disciples with timeless wisdom from Christ's Sermon on the Mount in a manner that is comprehensible and relevant to the layman."

—**Major James Carraway**
United States Air Force

THE EXTRA MILE

LIVING CHRIST'S LEGACY

DR. CODY A. WALLACE

The Extra Mile: Living Christ's Legacy
Copyright © 2024 by Dr. Cody Wallace

Published by Grace Theology Press in Houston, TX
www.GraceTheology.org

All rights reserved. No part of this publication may be reproduced, stored in a retrieval system, or transmitted in any form by any means, electronic, mechanical, photocopy, recording, or otherwise, without the prior permission of the publisher, except as provided for by USA copyright law.

Unless otherwise indicated, scripture quotations are taken from (NASB®) New American Standard Bible®, Copyright © 1960, 1971, 1977, 1995, 2020 by The Lockman Foundation. Used by permission. All rights reserved. www.lockman.org

eISBN: 978-1-957202-08-2
ISBN: 978-1-957202-07-5

Special Sales: Most Grace Theology titles are available in special quantity discounts. Custom imprinting or excerpting can also be done to fit special needs. Contact Grace Theology Press.

TABLE OF CONTENTS

Foreword	ix
Introduction	1
Chapter 1: Poor in Spirit	13
Chapter 2: Those Who Mourn	19
Chapter 3: The Gentle	25
Chapter 4: Hunger & Thirst	31
Chapter 5: Merciful	37
Chapter 6: Pure Heart	45
Chapter 7: Peace Makers	53
Chapter 8: Persecuted	59
Chapter 9: Because of Me	67
Chapter 10: Salt	73
Chapter 11: Light	85
Chapter 12: Fulfill	91
Chapter 13: Great in the Kingdom	101
Chapter 14: Righteousness	107
Chapter 15: Make Friends	115
Chapter 16: Eye Makes You Stumble	129
Chapter 17: Your Statement	137
Chapter 18: Go The Extra Mile	145

Chapter 19:	Be Perfect	151
Chapter 20:	Give	157
Chapter 21:	When You Pray	169
Chapter 22:	Your Will Be Done	185
Chapter 23:	Earth & Heaven	191
Chapter 24:	Pray for Your Daily Bread	195
Chapter 25:	Pray for Forgiveness	203
Chapter 26:	Pray for Deliverance From the Evil One	213
Chapter 27:	Fast	221
Chapter 28:	Treasures of the Heart	229
Chapter 29:	Clear Eyes	235
Chapter 30:	Worry	243
Chapter 31:	Seek	253
Chapter 32:	Judging	265
Chapter 33:	Pearls of Wisdom	275
Chapter 34:	Ask	283
Chapter 35:	The Golden Rule	291
Chapter 36:	The Gate	299
Chapter 37:	Fruit of Falseness	307
Chapter 38:	Lord, Lord!	313
Chapter 39:	The Wiseman Builds	321
Chapter 40:	Our Response	329

FOREWORD

When I first met Dr. Cody Wallace, I discovered his fervent dedication to nurturing disciples both within his church and throughout the world. His theology, rooted in grace, underscores the importance of genuine motivations for discipleship, stemming from a response to God's boundless grace and love. This book encapsulates his earnest desire to witness individuals closely following Jesus, embodying true righteousness in their lives as a testament to the world.

Wallace has penned a profound exploration of the Sermon on the Mount (Matthew chapters 5–7), delving into the depths of authentic spirituality that guides individuals in their earthly journey and prepares them for an enriched eternity. He posits that the Sermon on the Mount speaks directly to believers, particularly those committed to the path of discipleship and following the teachings of Jesus Christ. Through meticulous analysis, he illuminates how Jesus's teachings provide clear directives for living according to His principles in the present age, with a promise of a more fulfilling existence in the forthcoming kingdom. Wallace envisions this kingdom as a tangible, earthly realm where King Jesus reigns from Jerusalem.

The book offers insightful exposition and elucidation of each section of the sermon. Not only does Wallace provide cultural and biblical context for each passage, but he also interweaves Jesus's teachings with other biblical passages, providing a comprehensive understanding of the topic and its practical implications. Additionally, I found Wallace's illustrations to be enlightening, shedding further light on the examined passages.

Written in a relatable tone accessible to any Christian, the book is underpinned by rigorous scholarship and diligent research. It serves as a valuable resource for individuals seeking to deepen their commitment to following Jesus in a life of discipleship, as well as for those guiding others on this journey. Readers will emerge with a heightened desire and deeper insight into the essence of following Jesus in this world, thereby better preparing for the future kingdom. With characteristics akin to a commentary on the sermon, the book is poised to resonate with Bible students and ministry practitioners alike.

The Extra Mile stands as a beacon, urging Christians to embody righteousness amidst the challenges of a fallen world. It motivates, exhorts, and enlightens its readers toward this noble pursuit. Yet, Wallace's vision extends beyond the temporal, directing attention towards the future and imparting essential guidance for a more fulfilling experience in the kingdom to come. I am profoundly appreciative of the invaluable contribution this book makes to our understanding and practice of discipleship.

Charles C. Bing, ThM, PhD
Founder and Director of GraceLife Ministries

INTRODUCTION

A believer in Jesus should harbor a fervent desire for growth in Christ, aspiring to mirror His character both on earth and in the heavenly realm. Essential to this aspiration is a deep understanding of His nature, desires, actions, and teachings.

Jesus, in His earthly ministry, handpicked a group of disciples whom He mentored and equipped to carry forward the mission of reaching the lost (Luke 19:10). He imparted to them the goal of aligning their thoughts, actions, and teachings with His own (Matthew 10:24-25), and before His departure, He entrusted them with the task of spreading the message of His death, burial, and resurrection to both the dispersed Jewish nation and the Gentiles, with discipleship as a central focus (Matthew 28:16-20). Across generations, the gospel has been transmitted, and the wisdom and guidance of God's word have been passed down to us.

As children of God through Christ (John 1:12), we are charged with the responsibility of growing as followers and responding to the Master's call to "follow Me." Answering this call entails a commitment to discipleship, necessitating a thorough examination of His teachings to understand the essence of discipleship—embracing the character, actions, thoughts, prayer life, speech, practices, and mindset of a disciple. This book ventures to lay the groundwork for this understanding by expounding upon the Master's teachings within their original context while also acknowledging the contemporary context of modern-day followers. While the entirety of the Gospel provides insight into Jesus's instructions to His followers, our focus will be on the Sermon on the Mount (Matthew 5–7). It is my hope that upon engaging with this book, readers will undergo a transformative journey, gaining a deeper understanding of the Sermon on the Mount and allowing its principles to shape their lives as they follow Jesus and live according to His teachings. The aim of this book is to equip readers with a comprehensive understanding of the character, thoughts, and actions befitting a modern-day disciple of Jesus.

AN ABUNDANT LIFE NOW AND IN THE KINGDOM

In Matthew 5–7, Jesus delineates the blueprint for an abundant life in Him for His ambassadors on earth, representing His kingdom. He is instructing them to refine their minds, character, and actions, promising rich rewards, elevated positions, and an inheritance in the future kingdom. Throughout the teachings and writings of the apostles, including figures like John, Paul, and Peter, one can discern the recurring themes of Jesus's summons to live according to kingdom principles and its profound implications on one's position, rewards, and triumphant entry into the kingdom. This emphasis stems from their intimate association with Jesus, where they grasped the paramount importance of discipleship aimed at perpetuating the kingdom's influence.

Because the Sermon on the Mount is replete with ethical and moral teachings, some individuals mistakenly perceive it as a checklist for earning salvation. However, Jesus is not advocating for a works-based salvation; rather, He imparts His instructions to a group of believers who have already committed to following Him—the twelve disciples. Jesus is guiding them on how to redefine their understanding of entering into the kingdom. True righteousness, He teaches, does not stem from mere actions or works. Instead, it is a deeper transformation of the heart and soul.

INTRODUCTION

I would propose that Jesus's teachings in Matthew 5–7 are in reference to the forthcoming Millennial Kingdom (Revelation 2:26–27; 20:6). He illuminates how His followers can navigate their present circumstances with a view toward the future kingdom. The concept that Matthew 5–7 outlines a lifestyle not only for the future Millennial Kingdom or for what some believe to be an offering of the Kingdom during the first coming of Christ, but also for believers to pursue presently is often referred to by theologians as an Interim Approach.

As Stanley Toussaint states, "Those who come to the Sermon on the Mount with the interim interpretation see in it as an ethic for the time preliminary to the establishment of the kingdom."[1] In essence, Jesus is providing guidance for His followers on how to live while awaiting the establishment of His kingdom.

The kingdom, as prophesied, was always anticipated as a future state, irrespective of the Jewish nation's acceptance of Jesus. Even Jesus instructs His disciples to pray for the coming of the kingdom (Matthew 6:10)—a prayer uttered in the future tense, mirroring the predominantly future-oriented references to the kingdom in His sermon. However, the actions and sufferings described in His teachings are portrayed as current realities. One might question why they were instructed to pray for a kingdom they were in the process of establishing. Yet, prophecies such as Daniel 9:26–27 and Psalm 118:22 foretold of the Messiah's rejection and suffering, events that Jesus Himself claimed to fulfill (Matthew 21:33–46), as corroborated by Peter in Acts 4:1–12 and his epistle (1 Peter 2). The rejection of Jesus by His own people was an inevitable part of the divine plan.

Moreover, Jesus emphasized the everlasting validity of His words, transcending dispensational boundaries. Though He offered the kingdom, He wasn't immediately ushering it in. He asserted His kingship unequivocally, with no higher delegate or representative.

---

1. Stanley Toussaint, *Behold the King* (Portland, OR: Multnomah Press, 1980), 91.

In Scripture, when a kingdom's delegate or the king is present, they represent the kingdom, speaking and acting on its behalf. Therefore, the notion of the "kingdom at hand" aligns with Jesus already being the reigning king from the line of David. This concept is epitomized in Luke 11:20, where Jesus declares that His kingdom has come. John the Baptist echoed this urgency, urging people to prepare for the king's arrival (Matthew 3:2).

However, as foretold in Isaiah 53, Jesus had to endure rejection and suffering for the sake of humanity. Despite His earthly ministry, the events foretold in Daniel 7 regarding the establishment of His kingdom did not occur. This ultimate consummation of the kingdom, depicted as Christ coming on the clouds (Daniel 7:13-14; Zechariah 12:9-12; Revelation 1:7), was yet to be realized. John the Baptist's proclamation of Jesus as the Lamb of God further underscores His mission to seek and save humanity (Luke 19:10). Jesus indeed spoke of His kingdom-building project during His earthly ministry, setting the stage for the fulfillment of prophecy and the ultimate establishment of His reign.

> Jesus answered, "My kingdom is not of this world. If My kingdom were of this world, My servants would be fighting so that I would not be handed over to the Jews; but as it is, My kingdom is not of this realm." Therefore Pilate said to Him, "So You are a king?" Jesus answered, "You say *correctly* that I am a king. For this *purpose* I have been born, and for this I have come into the world: to testify to the truth. Everyone who is of the truth listens to My voice (John 18:36-37).

His first coming was centered on securing humanity's salvation, while His second coming is anticipated to inaugurate a kingdom characterized by peace and perfection. Understanding this framework, readers can readily discern Jesus's emphasis on the rewards awaiting those who devote their lives to Him in the kingdom. Equally significant is the theme of character and actions that His followers must embody in their daily lives.

THE CALL TO DISCIPLESHIP

The "beatitudes" listed in Matthew 5 outline the characteristics that Jesus affirms His followers are blessed to possess and live by in the present tense, with the reward in the Kingdom spoken in the future tense. "The Sermon involves teaching which is to be understood and acted upon by men. The interpretation and application of it is much more closely related..."[2] However, embodying qualities such as 'meekness,' 'gentleness,' and being 'poor in spirit' poses a challenge, doesn't it? What's crucial to grasp about this teaching is the call Jesus issued to His disciples when He stood at the shore and said, "Follow me." Though this concept might be lost in today's terms, His disciples were intimately familiar with it. "'Come, follow Me.' 'Follow me,' LECH AHARAI (literally, 'walk after me'), was a technical term in Hebrew for becoming a disciple."[3] Jesus, operating as a rabbi in ancient settings, employed this phrasing to beckon His followers into a similar role. Paul echoed this call in his writings, extending it to all readers, including us (1 Corinthians 11:1). Notably, Jesus never required His followers to do things He hadn't done Himself. The attitudes listed in Matthew 5, the actions depicted in Matthew 6, and the mindset outlined in Matthew 7 were all facets of His own life.

The commitment He demanded entailed a renunciation of familial ties (Luke 14:26), a detachment from material provisions (Luke 9:3, 58-62), and a denial of self (Luke 9:23). However, this wasn't to cultivate a robotic army of uniform individuals; that was far

---

2. Harry A. Sturz, "The Sermon on the Mount and its Application to the Present Age," Grace Journal Fall, 4:3 (Fall 1963): 5.
3. Robby Gallaty, *Rediscovering Discipleship: Making Jesus' Final Words Our First Work* (Grand Rapids, MI: Zondervan, 2015), 34.

from His intention. Instead, He intentionally selected individuals and harnessed their unique personalities in His mission. Jesus aimed to mold His followers into His likeness in nature, mindset, and speech.

"The decision to follow a rabbi meant total commitment. They would have to memorize His words and replicate His lifestyle."[4] Jesus applied a similar approach with His disciples, yet as evident in the Sermon on the Mount, His teachings diverged from those of contemporary rabbis. Jesus sought more than mere adherence to a religious merit system; He aimed for a transformation of the mind. He rebuked the modern rabbis for burdening their followers with rules, laws, and traditions that they themselves couldn't uphold (Matthew 23:4). The Jewish people were tasked with adhering to 613 laws, and depending on a rabbi's interpretation, additional traditions, and rules could be imposed. Jesus cautioned against following these leaders, labeling them as unjust hypocrites incapable of meeting their own standards or bearing their yoke (Matthew 23:6–14).

In Jewish culture, when someone became a disciple of a rabbi, they adopted the rabbi's interpretation of Old Testament Law, symbolized by taking on the yoke of the rabbi. Dave Earley notes, "the term was adapted to apply to a disciple placing himself under the yoke of his rabbi's instruction."[5] Jesus described these as heavy burdens on the shoulders of men, yet He described His yoke of teaching as "… easy and My burden is light" (Matthew 11:30). His call was to release themselves of the other rabbis' unobtainable teachings (Matthew 11:28) and "Take My yoke upon you and learn from Me" (Matthew 11:29).

Discipleship was designated to individuals following a rabbi's or Pharisee's particular interpretation of law and Scripture. It all had to do with learning and application rather than salvation.

---

4. Dave Earley and Rod Dempsey, *Disciple Making Is* (Nashville, TN: B&H, 2013), 78.
5. Ibid., 73.

[D]isciples could attach themselves to individual Pharisees in order to study with them and to become involved in their projects. [...] If a person was a disciple of the Pharisees, then that one was an adherent of the teachings of the Pharisees, was in training to become a part of that group, and possibly even belonged to one of the academic institutions. The disciples of the Pharisees, therefore, would have centered their activities on traditional interpretations that would lead to a more complete understanding and personal application of Torah.[6]

Jesus's teaching was a new application of Scripture, not for religious service, not for merit to earn salvation, but God's original intention to be an example of speech, life, action, and behavior so others see the difference Yahweh makes in one's life.

BACKGROUND AND SETTING

To grasp the depth of Jesus's teachings in Matthew chapters 5-7, it's crucial to consider the context surrounding this pivotal moment of imparting wisdom on character, action, and mindset. Matthew 4 provides a backdrop: Jesus had already confronted temptation and undergone baptism by His cousin John (Matthew 3). Particularly noteworthy is Matthew 4:12, which mentions John's arrest by Herod—a grim event that ultimately led to John's execution (Matthew 14). This timing aligns with John's account, where he indicates that John the Baptist had not yet been imprisoned following Jesus's conversation with Nicodemus (John 3:24).[7]

---

6. Michael Wilkins, *Following the Master* (Grand Rapids, MI: Zondervan, 1992), 85.
7. In his book, *Grace in Eclipse*, Zane Hodges comes to a similar conclusion as to the timeline of the Sermon on the Mount stating, "In Matthew, in Mark and apparently in Luke, our Lord's public ministry commences after the Baptist is imprisoned...." Though his book was not used as a reference for the research of this book, it is essential to recognize the similar findings and stance as Zane's works have influenced many. Zane Hodges, *Grace In Eclipse* (Dallas, TX: Rendencion Viva, 1987), 19.

This sequence aligns with Luke's Gospel account, where the Sermon on the Mount is placed in Luke 6. It follows significant events such as the calling of the twelve disciples, Jesus's temptation in the wilderness (Luke 4), and John's baptism (Luke 3).

Why is this sequencing important? Some believe Jesus taught a works-based salvation to the Jews prior to their rejection of Him, and the main evidence they use is Matthew 5-7 seeing it as salvific rather than discipleship based. Yet, this timeline indicates the Sermon on the Mount took place after Jesus offers salvation to Nicodemus through belief in Him (John 3:16). Additional evidence supporting this includes the healing of the centurion's servant, which Luke places after the Sermon on the Mount (Luke 7), consistent with Matthew's account (Matthew 8), and following Nicodemus's encounter in John's Gospel (John 4). This suggests that the Sermon on the Mount took place between these two events.

This timeline highlights Jesus's consistent message of salvation through belief leading to eternal life before and after the Sermon on the Mount (e.g., John 3:16–18, 36; 5:24; 6:40, 47). To attain eternal life is to gain entrance into the kingdom of God, taking on roles as members (Hebrews 12:28), ambassadors (2 Corinthians 5:20), and heirs (Romans 8:17). Admission into the kingdom hinges on trusting Christ as Savior.

> Jesus answered, "Truly, truly, I say to you, unless someone is born of water and *the* Spirit, he cannot enter the kingdom of God. That which has been born of the flesh is flesh, and that which has been born of the Spirit is spirit" (John 3:5–6).

Matthew 5-7 is being looked at not in a context of living perfectly to receive eternal life but as a discipleship manual for His followers. "'It should be kept clearly in mind that the incentive for "observing all things whatsoever He has commanded" is not that by doing so one becomes a disciple, or earns salvation, or wins eternal life, for this is the "free gift of God ... through Jesus Christ our Lord." The motivation force or incentive is the desire (wrought in the Christian by the Holy Spirit) "to walk even as He walked" (I Jn. 2:6), to "walk and to please God" (I Thess. 4: 1)."[8]

"Truly, truly, I say to you, he who believes has eternal life" (John 6:47). The verb "has" is a present tense indicative active. The person in the action of belief is given eternal life in that precise moment. In other words, everyone that has believed already has eternal life even though they are not dead or raptured; their admittance is already theirs, they instantly become kingdom representatives, inheritors, and members.[9] But as inheritors, members, and representatives, the Lord wants and expects to see those claiming His name act, live, walk, and talk in a manner becoming of their stature.

Matthew 5:1 suggests that Jesus ascended the mountain to find solitude from the pressing crowd and to impart teachings specifically to His disciples. Similarly, Luke 6:20 implies that, though the crowd remained, Jesus directed His focus and words toward His disciples. Luke's narrative in chapter 6 encompasses the selection of the twelve apostles, Jesus retreating to the mountain for seclusion, rest, and prayer, and the subsequent formation of crowds around the flat area where Jesus chose to instruct His disciples.

The language employed throughout the teaching is inclusive, indicating that the disciples are integral to God's mission. Jesus speaks of their persecution similar to the prophets (Matthew 5:12) and their elevated status as teachers in the kingdom (v. 19). Moreover, the metaphor of being salt and light (Matthew 5:13–16) underscores the disciples' responsibility to share the Gospel and teachings of Jesus with others.

---

8. Harry A. Sturz, "*The Sermon on the Mount and its Application to the Present Age*," Grace Journal Fall, 4:3 (Fall 1963): 12.
9. Colossians 1:14–18.

Therefore, when Jesus began His teaching by opening His mouth (Matthew 5:2), He was addressing the disciples who had drawn near (Matthew 5:1), emphasizing their vital role in spreading the message of the kingdom. In Luke's account preceding the Sermon on the Mount, he provides additional contextual details about the events and the address compared to Matthew.

> And *then* Jesus came down with them and stood on a level place; and *there was* a large crowd of His disciples, and a great multitude of the people from all Judea and Jerusalem, and the coastal region of Tyre and Sidon, who had come to hear Him and to be healed of their diseases; and those who were troubled by unclean spirits were being cured. And all the people were trying to touch Him, because power was coming from Him and healing *them* all. And He raised His eyes toward His disciples and *began* saying…(Luke 6:17–20a).

Even though admirers surrounded Jesus, the text suggests that His admonitions in the passage were aimed at His followers. Note that Jesus's gaze and address is fixed on His disciples in the above passage as He leads into the teaching of the Sermon on the Mount.

His disciples were already believers before fully committing to follow Jesus as His learners. Consider Peter and Andrew: Andrew had been a disciple of John (John 1:35–40) and upon recognizing Jesus as the Messiah, he urged his brother Peter to investigate for himself (John 1:41–42). However, even after witnessing and believing, Andrew and Peter returned to their occupation as fishermen. It took Jesus calling them to discipleship twice for them to fully dedicate themselves to learning from Him and following Him (Matthew 4:18–22; Luke 5:1–11).

Matthew's account distinguishes these two occasions. In the first instance, there is no mention of a miraculous catch, nor is Jesus present in the boat with them. Luke recounts that after a long day of fishing, as they were washing their nets, Jesus, pressed by a crowd, asked to be taken out to fish, resulting in a bountiful catch. However, it wasn't until the later event described by Luke that the disciples answered the call to follow and become disciples.

Understanding the timeline of events surrounding the Sermon on the Mount, including instances of Jesus offering salvation before and after His preaching, provides insight into the nature of Jesus's offer of eternal life through belief. However, it also highlights the distinction between accepting salvation and responding to the call to discipleship, which involves a deeper, more sacrificial relationship with Jesus.

The Sermon on the Mount primarily serves as a teaching on discipleship, urging followers to embody the principles outlined therein. While salvation remains a free gift accessible only through faith in Jesus, becoming a disciple entails a commitment to nurturing a growing relationship with Him, often at a personal cost.

In essence, while salvation secures eternal life, discipleship involves actively living out the teachings of Jesus, striving to align one's life with His example and teachings. This may involve sacrifices, obedience, and a willingness to prioritize God's kingdom above personal desires and comfort.

WHAT ABOUT YOU?

So how should a believer approach Matthew 5-7? First, we should view Jesus's teaching here as illustrating what true righteousness looks like, and thus as a moral compass for those growing in Him. We recognize that Jesus is certainly not indicating a works salvation--when Jesus offers salvation, He says to believe in Him. In Chapter 3 of the Gospel of John, John describes Jesus's interaction with Nicodemus, which precedes the Sermon on the Mount and does not mention obedience to a moral code, is the most apparent evidence of God and Jesus's intention of saving grace.

After the Sermon on the Mount, Jesus maintains the same call to believe (as seen in John 6:47). Matthew 8 and John 4 are interlocking timelines for the healing of the official's son and Matthew 14 and John 6 for the feeding of the five thousand.

What can we glean from this? While obedience is vital for nurturing relationships, bearing fruit, and earning rewards, it isn't a prerequisite for eternal salvation. Jesus desires us to adopt a kingdom mentality and live accordingly. Therefore, Matthew 5–7 should be regarded as Jesus's instruction on what it means to follow Him—a disciple's thoughts, actions, and attitude. Richard C. H. Lenski points out, although the address is aimed at the disciples, "The imperfect 'began to teach' invites us, too, as we read, to follow this teaching."[10] The use of the imperfect tense is a technical Greek term indicating that Jesus didn't solely intend for the twelve disciples to hear and live by this teaching, but He invited all who were present and all who would read it in the future to strive to live as disciples. Part of the reason the people were astonished at Jesus's teaching (Matthew 7:28–29) as He concluded the Sermon on the Mount is because it starkly contrasted with the teachings of the day, which focused on a checklist approach to obtain salvation. Instead, Jesus presented a lifestyle rooted in relationship, serving as a guide for growth and a roadmap for citizens of the kingdom.

Therefore, as you engage with and study this book, keep your Bible handy to reference the verses, maintain an open mind, and approach it prayerfully. Ask the Lord to reveal to you how He desires you to live a Spirit-led, kingdom-minded, and application-rich life.

---

10. R. C. H. Lenski, *Commentary on the New Testament: The Interpretation of Matthew* (USA: Hendrickson, 1998), 183.

CHAPTER 1
POOR IN SPIRIT

"Blessed are the poor in spirit, for theirs is the kingdom of heaven."

—Matthew 5:3

Do you find yourself blessed in your present condition? In the Sermon on the Mount, Jesus presents eight statements about being blessed. However, these blessings are not associated with receiving material wealth, fame, or worldly success. Instead, they focus on those who exhibit contentment even amidst challenging circumstances. Being blessed is not merely a fleeting moment of happiness; rather, it reflects an individual's outlook on life—a state chosen regardless of the circumstances.

Where the "holy" groups of Jesus's day--Pharisees, Sadducees, scribes, and priests--may look down at someone poor, or meek as struggling in life, Jesus shows how one's outlook and perspective is what is important. The Beatitudes, in Matthew 5, are not conditions of salvation; they are the characteristics of those who realize they have all they need in Jesus.

Likewise, Philippians 4:12 says the way of content living lets Paul, and us, know how to get along in any instance because of holding an attitude of blessing. This is why verse 13 beautifully follows verse 12 and lets the reader know that contentment in all things can be achieved in Christ.

> I know how to get along with little, and I also know how to live in prosperity; in any and every *circumstance* I have learned the secret of being filled and going hungry, both of having abundance and suffering need. I can do all things through Him who strengthens me (Philippians 4:12–13).

In Matthew chapters 5–7, Jesus sat His followers down on a mountainside and delivered in one hundred and eleven verses what it looks like to pray, fast, and live in love with God in true righteousness. On a mountainside, as crowds drew near, Jesus instructs His followers about what it means to have a life, character, heart, mind, and soul that loves God and people, and how the life of following God needs to become a lifestyle and action rather than a pharisaical act lacking heart.

THE POINT OF HIS ADDRESS

The Beatitudes describe the character of God's kingdom rulers--people who devoted their lives to following Him as disciples and who would one day co-rule in His kingdom. As Jesus says, "for theirs is the kingdom" (Matthew 5:3), but the Beatitudes are not *conditions* of salvation. The Scripture here said He sat down and spoke to His disciples!

He said to them. "Them" are His followers. "Them" are those who had committed to His teaching and headship as Rabbi. He says blessed are those who are content in whatever circumstance and attitude they find themselves in. Jesus does not say, for example, "Only the pure in heart may enter the kingdom of heaven." This teaching on the mountainside is not a standard for salvation but the mark for Christlikeness.

The Bible says all fall short (Romans 3:23); this means saved and unsaved alike find themselves wanting. Instead, these are the footprints left behind for those who follow to place their feet in. It is a call to heart change for those He told in Matthew 4:19, "Follow Me." It is a manual to those He said to love Him above all others (Luke 14:26). It is a GPS for those He warned would lose their life, wealth, and have no home (Luke 9:3, 58–62). To those (not the lost looking for eternal salvation) He is saying this is the commitment and what it brings.

You see, Jesus talks about heaven--eternal life, which is given freely to all who believe (John 6:47). He speaks of an earthly kingdom for those who live as His disciples studying His word and living by it (2 Timothy 2:12, Revelation 20:6).

We should not assume everyone that says they are a Christian must be living for Jesus. The parables in Luke 15 demonstrate that believers can wander and live lives apart from Christ. We also should not assume that everyone living upstanding lives and doing good things are believers.

> Not everyone who says to Me, "Lord, Lord," will enter the kingdom of heaven, but he who does the will of My Father who is in heaven *will enter*. Many will say to Me on that day, "Lord, Lord, did we not prophesy in Your name, and in Your name cast out demons, and in Your name perform many miracles?" And then I will declare to them, "I never knew you; DEPART FROM ME, YOU WHO PRACTICE LAWLESSNESS." Therefore everyone who hears these words of Mine and acts on them, is like a wiseman who built his house upon the rock (Matthew 7:21–24).

Kingdom of heaven means kingdom from above; it distinguishes between Roman occupation, Herod's shaky kingdom, and any other earthly human-led kingdoms.

A person can call Jesus Lord but not listen and apply what He teaches. Calling Him Lord is a decision to let Jesus rule your life. The Pharisees occasionally called Jesus Rabbi and Lord, but that did not mean they followed Him or gave Him rule of their lives, and Judas did the same. None of these submitted their will to Him or His teaching. None of them did what He said or enacted what He showed them (John 13:13–15). A follower takes Jesus as Lord and does what He exemplified. And though they may not be successful in following every statement Jesus made, they wake each morning and try again (Luke 9:23).

Not everyone that has called Jesus Lord will enter the kingdom of heaven. Why? In Matthew 7:23, they do not follow His word. They had not truly made Him Lord or Rabbi because they did not follow His teaching. This passage is a kingdom passage, just like the Beatitudes are attitudes of a disciple looking to be part of Christ's kingdom. It is not a salvation verse for eternal life or heaven.

Ephesians 2:8–10 says heaven, eternal life, is a free gift to all who believe, but reigning, rewarding, and ruling in the kingdom has a cost: following Christ. This is why we pray for the kingdom to come, as in Matthew 6:9–10:

> Pray, then, in this way:
> "Our Father who is in heaven,
> Hallowed be Your name.
> Your kingdom come.
> Your will be done,
> On earth as it is in heaven."

We are praying that the will of God be done in our lives like it is in heaven, and that will be when His kingdom comes.

THE POOR

> When Jesus saw the crowds, He went up on the mountain; and after He sat down, His disciples came to Him. He opened His mouth and *began* to teach them, saying, "Blessed are the poor in spirit, for theirs is the kingdom of heaven" (Matthew 5:1–3).

In other words: Blessed are those who realize their contentment and fulfillment is in Jesus, for the kingdom is made of these people. To be blessed, content or happy means an individual is at peace with the events in life due to their overwhelming happiness in Christ.

Poor in spirit is a realization of a need. *Poor, ptōchoi*, suggests you are reduced to begging, but the beauty is you are begging at the grace, love, and mercy of abundance that Jesus has. Therefore, being poor in spirit means one depends on Jesus for spiritual well-being. Jesus declares that it is a blessing to recognize that our need is filled by God's grace. Consider Mark 2:16–17:

> When the teachers of the law, who were Pharisees, saw Him eating with the sinners and tax collectors, they asked His disciples: "Why does he eat with tax collectors and sinners?" On hearing this, Jesus said to them, "It is not the healthy who need a doctor, but the sick. I have not come to call the righteous, but sinners" (NIV).

Those who feel they are sinful or morally sick and so cry out to Jesus to be saved are poor in spirit; thus, they are the ones and only ones who inherit God's kingdom. On the other hand, those who are self-righteous are morally self-confident but yet are in spiritual poverty and will not obtain salvation because rather than believing in the One who can make them righteous, they thought they could obtain or grasp salvation based on their own righteous acts. This is why Jesus tells them they need to repent or change their mind. They needed to change their mind about how they could enter the kingdom.

It makes sense that Jesus would make this the first attitude of a Christian because it is by being poor in spirit or reduced to being a beggar that you actually begin the life of a disciple. The first Beatitude is: Be dependent. In Matthew 20, Jesus said that to be great in the kingdom is to be a humble servant. That means you are poor in spirit but will be great in His kingdom.

God will make happy or bless such people with inexpressible spiritual riches and joy in the kingdom.

> And you will be hated by all because of My name, but it is the one who has endured to the end who will be saved. But whenever they persecute you in one city, flee to the next; for truly I say to you, you will not finish *going through* the cities of Israel until the Son of Man comes. A disciple is not above his teacher, nor a slave above his master. It is enough for the disciple that he may become like his teacher, and the slave like his master (Matthew 10:22–25a).

This humble servant attitude is Jesus's (Philippians 2:7–11), and a disciple's goal is to be like the teacher.

Have you decided to live for Jesus and learn from Jesus--to be more like Jesus? Then, start building your house on the rock, being a doer of His word.

CHAPTER 2
THOSE WHO MOURN

"Blessed are those who mourn, for they shall be comforted."
—Matthew 5:4

I read a story about Queen Victoria going to a tea party with all the socialites of the day. She saw a woman sitting by herself and asked the other women who were happily talking and drinking what was wrong and one said, "Oh, she recently lost her baby." The queen got up and sat next to her, and after a time she got up. The grieving mother left her isolation and joined the other ladies. She was quickly asked what the queen had said to her. She said, "She told me nothing, but she held my hand and cried with me."

In Matthew 5:4, people who have committed a life and an attitude to following Jesus are told they will be comforted in their mourning. "Blessed are those who mourn, for they shall be comforted" (Matthew 5:4). Jesus holds our hand and weeps with us in our trials of pain, hurt, and grief. He comforts us in our mourning and weeping. He holds us in our realization of pain too deep for words.

> In the same way the Spirit also helps our weakness; for we do not know how to pray as we should, but the Spirit Himself intercedes for us with groanings too deep for words; and He who searches the hearts knows what the mind of the Spirit is, because He intercedes for the saints according to the will of God. And we know that God causes all things to work together for good to those who love God, to those who are called according to His purpose (Romans 8:26–27).

We do not know what to say. We do not have the words. The phrase "groanings too deep for words" means mute words. The pain is too deep to express in words. The phrase "cry out" is from the Greek word *krazo*, meaning to make an unintelligible noise, like a bird's caw or a frog's croaking. It is a cry. It is a literal crying on the shoulder of your Father who is holding you to His chest in comfort. All we can do is cry out, and say, "Father!" It is a weakness we have, and trust me, we all have it.

Romans 8:26–28 says we do not see, we do not know, but "God causes all things to work together for good to those who love God, to those who are called according to His purpose." God is working to build us, to build our dependency on Him, to grow our relationship with Him, and as a result, growing our faith, our families, our work, our marriages, and our relationships. Do you see how and why we can praise God in our struggle? Do you see how He is comforting in the midst of suffering? Blessed are the mourning for they will be comforted.

WE THE MOURNERS

The word *mourn* is from the Greek word *penthountes*. It means to be grief-stricken. Many times, it is used for someone experiencing the death of a loved one. It is an intense pain and grief so that your entire body feels it; you writhe and ache in grief. And in a weird twist, Jesus says these people are blessed. Why? Because the verse ties to the preceding verse: "Blessed are the poor in spirit, for theirs is the kingdom of heaven. Blessed are those who mourn, for they shall be comforted" (Matthew 5:3-4). They are poor in spirit, and realizing they are spiritually empty, they cry, realizing they are beggars spiritually. They mourn, realizing they are dependent on God's grace because they are sinners. They cry for the wrong they create. They cry because of separation from God because they are spiritually empty apart from Jesus. They cry because, as Paul says in Romans 7, they are wretched men on their own. Romans 8:18-23 says the earth and all creation groans (cries) because of sin.

Sin makes people groan. Death makes us weep, and pain makes us hurt. When we lose a loved one, it is painful. When people we love reject us, it is painful. When cancer attacks someone, it causes grief. Telling lies pains people. Due to all this, the earth and all its inhabitants groan.

You see, the weeping and mourning here is for people who feel pain and remorse for their own sin, for other's sin, and other's pain and losses. So this is a compassionate person--a disciple that rejoices with the rejoicing and weeps with the weeping (Romans 12:15).

JESUS THE MOURNER

Those who mourn are in good company. John 11:35 is one of the shortest Bible verses: "Jesus wept" (*edakrysen ho Iēsous*). Jesus shook with tears. He shook with compassion as He felt the pain of Martha and Mary over the loss of their brother Lazarus, even though He knew the miracle He would perform to bring Lazarus back from the dead.

When Jesus saw the brokenness of Jerusalem, *He wept over it* (Luke 19:41). When He retreated to the Garden of Gethsemane, Jesus *"began to be sorrowful and troubled"* and said, *"My soul is overwhelmed with sorrow to the point of death"* (Matthew 26:37-38). Consider that if you are sad, if you mourn the death of a friend, if you grieve over the brokenness of the world, you are not alone. Among "those who mourn" is Jesus Himself.

LEARNING TO MOURN

When Matthew penned, "Blessed are those who mourn" (Matthew 5:4), he used a special term for *mourn*. It is a term that declares deep pain and sincerity, concern, and grief for someone you deeply care for. A disciple cares for the burdens of others, and in the kingdom, they are comforted by the One who weeps with them.

You see, there are different people in this world. There are those who look at people's pain, suffering, and circumstance and judge, and those who look with compassion.

Jesus seems to be saying that those who mourn have special access to the Lord's healing power. This is because those who mourn get a direct line to the God who is present.

And much as it is with the poor in spirit, those who mourn have something in common with Christ Himself. Isaiah 53:3 says Jesus was a man of sorrows acquainted with grief.

John 8 says the scribes and Pharisees sought to test Jesus and brought to Him a woman they had caught in the act of adultery. As righteous people, as the teachers and keepers of law, they had the right to condemn her and stone her to death, but they brought her to Jesus, the righteous Rabbi. Jesus, you're holier than us. You judge her. Jesus's response in verse 7 shows why He speaks to His disciples about having an attitude of mourning.

> "He who is without sin among you, let him *be the* first to throw a stone at her." Again He stooped down and wrote on the ground. When they heard it, they *began* to go out one by one, beginning with the older ones, and He was left alone, and the woman, where she was, in the center *of the court*. Straightening up, Jesus said to her, "Woman, where are they? Did no one condemn you?" She said, "No one, Lord." And Jesus said, "I do not condemn you, either. Go. From now on sin no more" (John 8:7–11).

He felt compassion for her; she needed mercy and compassion, not condemnation for what she knew was wrong. The Pharisees wanted their brand of justice, which was stoning, but Jesus showed grace and mercy and comforted her instead.

Jesus was accused in Matthew 11:19 as being "a friend of tax collectors and sinners." He mourned with those in hurt and pain of sorrow, whether by their own accord or someone else's doing.

Blessed are those who mourn because their comfort comes from the friend of tax collectors and sinners. Let's keep in mind that if we are to live like the Savior, sin doesn't make Jesus sick; it makes Him sad.

Sin made the Pharisees furious and judgmental, "let's stone her to death!" But that was not the approach of the Master Rabbi. Jesus came alongside her. He peered into her tear-soaked eyes, and He forgave her.

Right now, people do not need judgment. People do not need fingers pointing at their pain. When someone is depressed, when they lose a loved one to cancer, depression, rejection, suicide, or old age, they do not need judgment; they need a Christ-follower to weep with (Romans 12:15).

People do not need rock throwers. They need Christ-followers. The world needs disciples who can be with them in their pain. People need someone to weep with, someone who feels their pain, holds their hand, and cries with them.

> For His anger is but for a moment,
> His favor is for a lifetime;
> Weeping may last for the night,
> But a shout of joy *comes* in the morning (Psalm 30:5).

Blessed are the disciples who feel pain because they hold the hand of the Comforter.

CHAPTER 3

THE GENTLE

"Blessed are the gentle, for they shall inherit the earth."
—Matthew 5:5

There's a tale about a wealthy industrialist who encountered a fisherman one day. He grew annoyed seeing the man lounging by his boat instead of being out at sea. The rich man asked, "Why aren't you out there fishing?"

The fisherman replied, "Because I've caught enough fish for today."

The rich man asked, "Why don't you catch more fish than you need? There's still more work to be done."

The fisherman responded, "What would I do with them once I caught them?"

"You could buy a better boat so you could go deeper into the sea and catch more fish," the rich man impatiently replied. "You could purchase nylon nets, catch even more fish, and make even more money. Eventually, you'd have a fleet of boats, people to do the work for you, and be rich like me."

After quietly contemplating, the fisherman asked, "Then what would I do?"

"You could sit down and enjoy life like I am," the industrialist said.

Looking placidly out to sea, the fisherman replied, "What do you think I'm doing now?"[11]

The fisherman was content in his circumstances. Jesus desires to see this quality in those who profess to follow Him. He wants His disciples to find contentment in His love and compassion rather than in their own capabilities. When Jesus uses the phrase blessed, content or happy, He is calling people toward realizing their peace in a difficult situation.

> When Jesus saw the crowds, He went up on the mountain; and after He sat down, His disciples came to Him. He opened His mouth and *began* to teach them, saying, "Blessed are the poor in spirit, for theirs is the kingdom of heaven. Blessed are those who mourn, for they shall be comforted. Blessed are the gentle, for they shall inherit the earth" (Matthew 5:1–5).

Gentle is used synonymously with the word *meek* depending on the translation of your Bible. Meekness is often a misunderstood term. We commonly perceive meekness as a quality of weakness and mildness, often labeled as 'soft' in today's lingo. The third Beatitude can perplex those who haven't witnessed it lived biblically, as they may not grasp its true essence.

MEEK IS NOT WEAK

"There's truth to the old bromide, *'Meekness isn't weakness.'* But meekness also *welcomes* weakness."[12] So, what does meekness mean? Meekness comes from the Greek word *praeis* that means strength under control. It gives us a picture of the wild horse that had become obedient to a bit and bridle. It could easily buck the rider off with its strength, but it is bridled power, bridled strength. Strength still there, just now controlled.

---

11. https://www.crosswalk.com/devotionals/seniors/senior-living-december-8-1455409.html.
12. Steve Elkins, *Keys to Kingdom Greatness*, (Coppell, TX: Allie Grace Publishing, 2014), 67.

Moses could have asserted his strength with Israel. He was a strong man and could have imposed his will, but he kept his want in check to God's plan. He had bridled strength.

In 2 Samuel 16, Shimei is cursing David and speaking evil of him, prompting one of David's mighty men to rise up to remove Shimei's head from his shoulders. However, David, acknowledging his kingship, refrains from such action. He reflects, 'Yes, I have the right to strike that man down, but God may have sent him to correct me. Jehovah may have brought him here to get my attention.' This episode illustrates the strength of a powerful king under the control of the King of kings.

There is nothing weak about being meek; indeed, the strongest people exemplify meekness. Jesus promised that they will inherit the earth. The meek aren't driven by personal gain, fame, or power-seeking. Why? Because they already possess it and have submitted it to the authority of Christ. They are blessed because they have harnessed their power, influence, and gains under the authority of Jesus.

The meek find happiness because they do not feel out of control; rather, they have surrendered their own spirit to God's control.

> For through the grace given to me I say to everyone among you not to think more highly of himself than he ought to think; but to think so as to have sound judgment, as God has allotted to each a measure of faith (Romans 12:3).

A meek person exhibits sound judgment, with their power kept in check and under control. They focus on how they can uplift, build, and assist others. This passage in Romans 12 transitions into the concept of the body of Christ. The church is not comprised of just one individual, but rather everyone ministering to one another, mutually edifying and supporting each other, harnessing their power for the collective benefit and upliftment of all.

BRIDLED UNDER CHRIST'S CONTROL

Meekness means spiritual humility. In practice, it is expressed in placing oneself at the feet of Jesus, under His teaching, under His guidance, under His yoke. Discipleship has long been a Jewish/Rabbinical approach to training since the beginning of the Law, with Aaron training his sons (Leviticus 8). Jesus described His yoke as light, because His yoke was based on faith and not outward obedience to rules, laws, and traditions. "For My yoke is easy and My burden is light" (Matthew 11:30). His call was to release themselves of the other rabbis' unobtainable teachings (Matthew 11:28) and "Take My yoke upon you and learn from Me, for I am gentle and humble in heart, and YOU WILL FIND REST FOR YOUR SOULS" (Matthew 11:29).

The yoke of Jesus, meaning His interpretation of the law, is love. In Mark 12:28-33, Jesus said love is greater than any sacrifice, oath, or ritual. Jesus's interpretation of the law was love. Love God, and love others. The Pharisees interpreted the law as rules or regulations that separated people from God. They singled out the elite, but Jesus said the law is love, meekness, bridled power--strength under God's control.

I admire how the Apostle Paul, once a Pharisee who persecuted Christians, illustrates the practical application of the teachings of Jesus, the Master Rabbi,

> Owe nothing to anyone except to love one another; for he who loves his neighbor has fulfilled *the* law. For this, "YOU SHALL NOT COMMIT ADULTERY, YOU SHALL NOT MURDER, YOU SHALL NOT STEAL, YOU SHALL NOT COVET," and if there is any other commandment, it is summed up in this saying, "YOU SHALL LOVE YOUR NEIGHBOR AS YOURSELF." Love does no wrong to a neighbor; therefore love is the fulfillment of *the* law (Romans 13:8-10).

The yoke, the correct interpretation of the law, of interaction, of putting yourself under God's control is LOVE. For those that have learned to be controlled by love, to those who have learned to put what

THE GENTLE

they *can* do under the submission of what they *should* do because of love, to those who have taken Jesus's gentle, meek, and loving teaching yoke, Jesus says: "Blessed are the gentle, for they shall inherit the earth" (Matthew 5:5). The meek, the gentle, or the bridled powerful will "inherit the earth."

Jesus called the Jewish nation to change their mind about how they could gain entrance into the kingdom. Instead of leaning on their own self-righteousness, He challenged them to humility of spirit finding their righteousness in Him. This humility in spirit was to be expressed in the ways Jesus commanded.[13]

The kingdom will crush other kingdoms (Daniel 2:44-45) and is made of all peoples and kingdoms, tribes, and nations (Daniel 7:14-15). It will be filled with young and old and the called back nation of Israel (Zechariah 8:1-8). It will be led by people that have remained faithful in Christ (2 Timothy 2:12). It is the inheritance of those that served the Master (Luke 19) and that loved others (Matthew 25:31-40). Jesus's rule and His followers' rule will put all people under subjection to Yahweh (1 Corinthians 15:20-28). It is a time of one thousand years that Jesus will sit on the throne of David and rule with His people.

The rule of the future kingdom is for those who are content to humbly and gently submit their power under the authority of Jesus. Let us all aspire to follow and be disciples, applying His teachings and the law of love to our lives. True contentment lies in harnessing our power under the rule of Jesus, for it is they who will inherit the kingdom on earth!

---

13. Matthew 5-7.

CHAPTER 4

HUNGER & THIRST

"Blessed are those who hunger and thirst for righteousness, for they shall be satisfied."

—Matthew 5:6

Hunger and thirst are profound desires. After a run, an intense workout, or spending hours working in the yard, the craving for a drink becomes intense. When dinner is cooking and its aroma wafts through the air, it triggers a response akin to Pavlov's law for dogs. You become hungry and won't be satisfied until you eat.

In the Beatitudes, Jesus wants the character of His followers to have a similar type of overwhelming desire. His followers who are learning from Him should have this same intensity in being like Him in attitude and behavior. "Blessed are those who hunger and thirst for righteousness, for they shall be satisfied" (Matthew 5:6). And this kind of desperate hunger, this kind of need for clean water and nourishing food, is what Jesus speaks of in Matthew 5:6. He wants His disciples to taste His covering of righteousness and want more; like a good meal, I want seconds! He wants you to hunger and thirst for His lifestyle, His way, and His righteousness.

Jesus is painting a desperate scene of an empty people seeking a holy filling. But let's break this down to understand it fully. What is righteousness? The Greek term *dikaiosunen* is when God approves of someone or something as upright or just in His eyes, when God sees you as meeting His standard of righteousness--His standard of right, blameless, and perfect.

> For if by the transgression of the one, death reigned through the one, much more those who receive the abundance of grace and of the gift of righteousness will reign in life through the One, Jesus Christ. So then, as through one offense the result was condemnation to all mankind, so also through one act of righteousness the result was justification of life to all mankind. For as through the one man's disobedience the many were made sinners, so also through the obedience of the One the many will be made righteous (Romans 5:17–19).

This verse conveys that I sinned in Adam. I was born into sin, and my life is entangled with it, but just as Adam marred my prospects of perfection, Jesus rectified my flaws. My life is sheltered in His righteousness, enveloped by His grace, and through His death, everyone is forgiven. Now, when the Father gazes upon us, He doesn't behold the imperfections of sin, nor does He see Adam's failure or our struggles; He sees the perfection of His Son. Why? Through our faith in the gospel, we now possess 'a righteousness from God'—Jesus's righteousness, His perfection, His grace, and His love and mercy. His righteousness envelops my struggles, my failure to be perfect, and my inability to always do what is right.

This covering of righteousness is what happens when someone trusts Jesus as Savior. They are covered by Him through His grace and love, so when the Father looks down, it is like He sees a cloak of Christ's goodness upon you. Now isn't that a beautiful thought!

HUNGRY FOR HIS STANDARD

In Matthew 5:1–2, Jesus addresses His disciples, His followers, those dedicated to Him. Matthew 5:6 urges us to hunger and thirst for righteousness. What is He conveying? Let's piece it together within the context of the Sermon on the Mount.

In Matthew 5:10, Jesus says, "Blessed are those who have been persecuted for the sake of righteousness, for theirs is the kingdom of heaven." The phrase "for the sake of" is translated from the Greek word *heneken*, meaning "because of" or "on account of." In other words, a follower is being persecuted because of their righteous way of living. They face abuse because of their commitment to emulate Jesus and the righteous acts they strive to live out in His likeness.

In Matthew 5:20 He says, "For I say to you that unless your righteousness surpasses *that* of the scribes and Pharisees, you will not enter the kingdom of heaven." Kingdom of heaven is referring to His millennial and subsequent eternal reign. The Pharisees' righteousness was what Matthew 6:1 warns about: "Beware of practicing your righteousness before men to be noticed by them; otherwise you have no reward with your Father who is in heaven." He explains they give money to be pat on the back for their charity and not to support the need (6:2); they pray not to God but to be heard by men (6:5); and when they fast, it's for the show of holiness not for the seeking of holiness (6:16). Their righteousness was a good outward show, but inside it was empty.

The people of the day witnessed their loud songs of prayer, their ostentatious donations, and observed their hunger for attention. It was a remarkable theatrical display, which is why Jesus labeled them hypocrites. Their aim was not spiritual fulfillment but rather seeking approval from people.

A disciple craves righteousness, actively pursuing the qualities of Jesus. Their every action is aimed at deepening their connection with Him. Let your hunger for Jesus exceed the superficial displays of the Pharisees.

Jesus depicted the disciple's condition as "to hunger" and "to thirst." These verbs are in the present tense participle form, signifying continuous action. So, they are consistently hungry and thirsty. Can you say the same about your own journey with Christ?

If you rush through the Beatitudes, you might overlook the character of the person Jesus praises and calls blessed or content. He emphasizes that if you are following Him while experiencing present hunger, thirst, or a need for spiritual fulfillment and righteousness, your future will be satisfaction in Him.

Future reward hinges on whether you feel content in seeking Him in the present. Are you content with your relationship with Him now? Or do you yearn for deeper growth? Are you satisfied with remaining a spiritual infant? Or do you desire to mature?

DISCIPLES STAY HUNGRY & THIRSTY

Some people hunger and thirst only for salvation; they just want to be saved from hell, and when they get salvation, their pursuit of Christ stops. That was me as a ten-year-old. I didn't want a relationship with Jesus; I wanted to be saved from hell. I was thirsty and hungry for saving, and once that need was met, I stopped pursuing.

But Matthew 5:6 says blessed are those who are continually hungering and thirsting. The follower doesn't stop hungering and thirsting for righteousness once he or she has experienced what Christ gives. They received salvation by trusting that Jesus died for them and rose again, and now they desire more. It's an ongoing pursuit to lead a righteous life, to continually strive to become more like Christ. Jesus emphasized that the goal of a disciple is to resemble their mentor (Matthew 10:25), illustrating the character of a disciple hungering and thirsting to emulate Jesus. Jesus is conveying that a disciple's attitude isn't satisfied with mere nibbles but craves the whole loaf.

Jesus saved them, covered them in His righteousness so they could enter heaven; it is a free gift of God (Ephesians 2:8–9). But now that they are saved, now that they are eternally secure, a disciple hungers for more Jesus, they thirst for more.

I like how Paul describes these same thoughts.

> But godliness *actually* is a means of great gain when accompanied by contentment. For we have brought nothing into the world, so we cannot take anything out of it either. If we have food and covering, with these we shall be content. But those who want to get rich fall into temptation and a snare and many foolish and harmful desires which plunge men into ruin and destruction. For the love of money is a root of all sorts of evil, and some by longing for it have wandered away from the faith and pierced themselves with many griefs. But flee from these things, you man of God, and pursue righteousness, godliness, faith, love, perseverance *and* gentleness (1 Timothy 6:6-11).

Paul says godliness, or being like Jesus in your thoughts and actions, is gain because it comes with reward. As we discussed earlier, we understand that part of that reward is found in Matthew 5:5—'the meek will inherit the earth.' So, be content, be joyful, or as Jesus puts it, 'happy are those'—who find joy in godliness. Why? Because our pursuits of fame, fortune, and material abundance do not endure in eternity. The pursuit of worldly gain only leaves us spiritually empty; it's a snare of the devil. However, 1 Timothy 6:11 urges us to seek righteousness and actively pursue it. Therefore, let us actively seek, chase, pursue, apply, and live out righteousness before God.

Jesus says don't seek men's praise, don't seek money, don't seek fancy clothing, "For the Gentiles (the word is *ethne*, meaning the unbelieving world, the pagans, or unbelievers) eagerly seek all these things; for your heavenly Father knows that you need all these things. But seek first His kingdom and His righteousness, and all these things will be added to you" (Matthew 6:32-33). Friend, we have been clothed in His righteousness at salvation, and now we are seen as good, right, and blameless because of Jesus. And Jesus says His disciples will live pursuing His likeness. They hunger and thirst to live like Jesus, for others, for His kingdom, and for His glory.

Prioritizing His kingdom and His righteousness—the divine standard—has a transformative effect on our lives. It has a way of rectifying our mistakes and overshadowing our past failures. It brings harmony to our marriages, friendships, parenting, and work relationships because it entails seeking Jesus in every aspect of our lives. Following Jesus and adhering to His standard, post-salvation, for growth and His glory in everything we do, fosters holistic personal development.

A righteous person lives by faith, meaning they embody their beliefs in Christ. Their faith isn't just internal; it bursts forth into action. What they hold within has manifested outwardly—an inside-out effect of Jesus in them. Jesus's righteousness resides within them, and they actively pursue it, live it, and grow in it.

Hunger and thirst are intense desires, as any hungry teenager waiting to raid their parent's fridge can attest. So, let us approach the Lord with that same intensity. Let us not be content with merely seeking righteousness. This is the mindset of a disciple.

CHAPTER 5

MERCIFUL

"Blessed are the merciful, for they shall receive mercy."
—Matthew 5:7

In a leper camp in Calcutta, a group of Bible college students dedicated themselves to bandaging the sick and tending to the infected, rotting flesh of those afflicted with the disease. In India's persisting caste system, lepers are deemed untouchable and shunned by society. Even in today's advancing civilization, any association with them renders one untouchable and an outcast.

Despite government provisions of supplies, food, and medicine to leper camps outside the cities, few are willing to risk infection and social ostracization to administer the much-needed care. Many of the afflicted lack fingers and hands, making it difficult for them to help themselves, resulting in aid often going unused.

The students resolved to demonstrate compassion and mercy, defying societal norms and risking their own well-being to offer comfort to those in need. This tangible display of mercy, regardless of personal discomfort, exemplifies what Jesus taught would distinguish His followers.

THE CHOOSING OF DISCIPLES OF MERCY

Consider the historical context while contemplating this "be attitude." In Luke 6, a parallel passage to Matthew 6, Jesus has selected His twelve disciples. He has deliberately chosen twelve individuals from various backgrounds, seemingly with modest resources, to sit under His guidance in a traditional learner-teacher relationship, akin to the Jewish model of disciple and rabbi. Typically, only those who were privileged, educated, or well-connected could aspire to become disciples of esteemed rabbis. However, in this instance, Jesus handpicks tax collectors, merchants, and fishermen, rather than those who might be considered the elite or top of their class.

None of the twelve disciples, including Peter, James, John, Andrew, Nathaniel, and others, were regarded as prospective rabbis. In fact, they found themselves in quite the opposite situation; they were essentially failed rabbinical students. "If a young man hadn't achieved a certain academic and social status by the time of his bar mitzvah at age thirteen, he would instead choose a life of farming, fishing, carpentry, or the like. The fact that Jesus and his followers were laborers explains why the religious establishment did not accept them."[14] "While most rabbis of the day would quiz prospective candidates, asking them difficult questions about various laws and customs to find out if they truly had what it takes to continue with a formal Jewish education, Jesus was busy eyeing four fishermen coming in from a lackluster shift at sea."[15] Jesus diverged from the conventional approach of selecting the academic cream of the crop to become His disciples, as was customary among the rabbis of His era. Instead, as the master rabbi, He intentionally chose twelve ordinary individuals from various walks of life. These were not esteemed scholars or religious elites; they were everyday people.

---

14. Bill Hull, *The Complete Book of Discipleship: On Being and Making Followers of Christ* (Colorado Springs, CO: NavPress, 2006), 63.
15. Robby Gallaty, *Rediscovering Discipleship: Making Jesus' Final Words Our First Work* (Grand Rapids, MI: Zondervan, 2015), 35.

In choosing these unlikely candidates, Jesus exemplified His mission to reach out to the marginalized and overlooked in society. He specifically selected those who were considered outcasts in the religious hierarchy to reach outcasts in the broader world. Then, He implores them to embody a new way of life encapsulated in the Beatitudes, diametrically opposed to the Pharisaic lifestyle.

The religious leaders of Jesus's time were proficient in theatrical displays of piety (Matthew 6), yet they often lacked genuine love for God and their fellow human beings. Their hearts were hardened toward the suffering and needy, prone to making snap judgments based on their perception of blessings and curses. They attributed the troubles of the less fortunate to divine judgment, failing to extend compassion and understanding.

In contrast, Jesus emphasizes the importance of having a tender heart toward both God and people. When He speaks of mercy, He emphasizes the active manifestation of meekness. This is perhaps why He handpicked seemingly insignificant individuals to carry His message and serve as His disciples. He knew they would possess the willingness to approach those whom higher society deemed untouchable or unworthy.

THE MERCY RULE

Jesus teaches that those who are merciful—those who embody meekness, mourn for wickedness and suffering, acknowledge their need for Christ's guidance, and strive for righteous living—demonstrate compassionate actions. When they live out this mercy, they will receive compassion from Christ.

The Pharisees propagated the notion that strict adherence to the law precluded them from showing mercy and compassion. They often disregarded individuals such as tax collectors, prostitutes, and sinners, viewing them as unworthy of kindness or assistance. Furthermore, they interpreted afflictions such as blindness as punishments for sin.

In contrast, Jesus instructed His disciples to cultivate hearts filled with mercy and to let their actions overflow with compassion.

He encouraged them to empathize with the suffering of others and to actively respond to it. By doing so, Jesus assured them that He would be present with them in their times of need.

> Then Jesus spoke to the crowds and to His disciples, saying: "The scribes and the Pharisees have seated themselves in the chair of Moses; therefore all that they tell you, do and observe, but do not do according to their deeds; for they say *things* and do not do *them*. They tie up heavy burdens and lay them on men's shoulders, but they themselves are unwilling to move them with *so much as* a finger. But they do all their deeds to be noticed by men; for they broaden their phylacteries and lengthen the tassels *of their garments*. They love the place of honor at banquets and the chief seats in the synagogues, and respectful greetings in the market places, and being called Rabbi by men. But do not be called Rabbi; for One is your Teacher, and you are all brothers. Do not call *anyone* on earth your father; for One is your Father, He who is in heaven. Do not be called leaders; for One is your Leader, *that is,* Christ. But the greatest among you shall be your servant. Whoever exalts himself shall be humbled; and whoever humbles himself shall be exalted. But woe to you, scribes and Pharisees, hypocrites, because you shut off the kingdom of heaven from people; for you do not enter in yourselves, nor do you allow those who are entering to go in (Matthew 23:1-13).

The Pharisees had little love, humility, and mercy which is at the heart of the message in the Old Testament.

God used Moses when he was at his lowest--an eighty-year-old murderer on the run and shepherding someone else's flocks in the desert. God worked through Rahab, a prostitute, and elevated her to be in the lineage of Messiah. God called humble, nomadic, wandering, and lying (lying when it came to his wife being his sister) Abraham and made him a nation out of one child. He made that nation, called Israel--small and weak as it was--great, and He blessed them. That is a message of mercy and love. It is a message of humility and grace.

But the rabbis, Pharisees, and scribes looked at God and didn't see love, humility, grace, and mercy; they saw law. Jesus said your failed interpretation of law keeps you and others out of the kingdom way of living and bound to the flesh.

THE YOKE OF RULES VERSUS THE YOKE OF MERCY

Their issue lay in their rigid interpretation of the Law, devoid of recognizing the love inherent in God's commandments. Instead of perceiving the Law as a framework for living in love, they reduced it to a set of rigid rules. Consequently, it became a burden to bear rather than a pathway to freedom and love. Jesus described the yokes of these hypocrites as heavy burdens on the shoulders of men, yet He described His yoke of teaching as "…easy and My burden is light" (Matthew 11:30). Jesus didn't bind people with the constraints of religion; rather, He liberated them through love. He would move from being the Master Rabbi to the Savior of the world by enacting the greatest example of love by fulfilling our death on the cross.

> Every priest stands daily ministering and offering time after time the same sacrifices, which can never take away sins; but He, having offered one sacrifice for sins for all time, SAT DOWN AT THE RIGHT HAND OF GOD, waiting from that time onward UNTIL HIS ENEMIES ARE MADE A FOOTSTOOL FOR HIS FEET. For by one offering He has perfected for all time those who are sanctified (Hebrews 10:11-14).

Where the religious leaders of the day took a harsh view that if people were sick it was their own fault or their parent's sin, they felt no compassion. No heart was given to the struggle of others.

> He entered again into a synagogue; and a man was there whose hand was withered. They were watching Him *to see* if He would heal him on the Sabbath, so that they might accuse Him. He said to the man with the withered hand, "Get up and come forward!" And He said to them, "Is it lawful to do good or to do harm on the Sabbath, to save a life or to kill?" But they kept silent. After looking around at them with anger, grieved at their hardness of heart, He said to the man, "Stretch out your hand." And he stretched it out, and his hand was restored (Mark 3:1–5).

The scribes and Pharisees did not receive God's mercy because they had become so self-satisfied with their own religious achievements that they did not see that they were so bankrupt of compassion they failed to see the needs of others.

In contrast, there is Jesus:

> Therefore, He had to be made like His brethren in all things, so that He might become a merciful and faithful high priest in things pertaining to God, to make propitiation for the sins of the people. For since He Himself was tempted in that which He has suffered, He is able to come to the aid of those who are tempted (Hebrews 2:17–18).

In Matthew 5, Jesus sets forth the blueprint for His followers, urging them to embody the same pattern He exemplified: mercy. He calls upon us to empathize with the pain of others, to be stirred to compassion, and to actively alleviate their burdens.

WHAT IS MERCY?

Merciful, translated from the Greek word *eleemon,* conveys an active thought or action of compassion. A merciful person demonstrates genuine concern for the well-being of others. They are characterized by being "mercy-full," meaning they abound with the compassion of Jesus, pouring it into the lives of those around them.

Jesus is conveying to those to whom He extends the offer of the kingdom that those who are moved to compassion here on earth will receive compassion in abundance in the future kingdom. This principle holds significance for us today as well, as citizens of the kingdom. When we stand by people in need on earth, Jesus promises to stand by our side in the kingdom to come.

Scripture says many times that Jesus would see the state of people, and it would move Him to action; it would rattle Him to the core to work to the point of exhaustion. He would spend hours healing, preaching, touching, and crying with people. Those that came were people that had been cast out and rejected, people seen as rejects and unworthy.

> Jesus was going through all the cities and villages, teaching in their synagogues and proclaiming the gospel of the kingdom, and healing every kind of disease and every kind of sickness. Seeing the people, He felt compassion for them, because they were distressed and dispirited like sheep without a shepherd. Then He said to His disciples, "The harvest is plentiful, but the workers are few. Therefore beseech the Lord of the harvest to send out workers into His harvest" (Matthew 9:35–38).

When pity, compassion, and mercy overwhelm you to act, you are following Jesus.

But mercy also implies that you show mercy in moments when you could exact punishment or judgment. Instead of giving the punishment or justice required, a tender heart shows forgiveness, not giving what is due. This is the stance of Christ displayed in you.

As we have seen and experienced God's mercy given in Jesus to us, we provide it to others. We become the overflow of Christ's mercy to others. We can't outgive His mercy to us. We give. He gives more. We show compassion. He shows more compassion.

Paul defines the actions and mind of a merciful person in Romans 12:

> Rejoice with those who rejoice, and weep with those who weep. Be of the same mind toward one another; do not be haughty in mind, but associate with the lowly. Do not be wise in your own estimation. Never pay back evil for evil to anyone. Respect what is right in the sight of all men. If possible, so far as it depends on you, be at peace with all men. Never take your own revenge, beloved, but leave room for the wrath *of God,* for it is written, "VENGEANCE IS MINE, I WILL REPAY," says the Lord. BUT IF YOUR ENEMY IS HUNGRY, FEED HIM, AND IF HE IS THIRSTY, GIVE HIM A DRINK; FOR IN SO DOING YOU WILL HEAP BURNING COALS ON HIS HEAD. Do not be overcome by evil, but overcome evil with good (Romans 12:15–21).

Those who are merciful will receive mercy. And yet Jesus is not saying that God's mercy depends on our mercy; He is saying mercy grows mercy, compassion grows compassion. When you weep with the weepers, and rejoice with the rejoicing, others will also share in your emotions, needs, and moments as well.

CHAPTER 6
PURE HEART

"Blessed are the pure in heart, for they shall see God."
—Matthew 5:8

In 1961, the Russian cosmonaut Yuri Gagarin was the first human to travel into Earth's orbit and successfully return. He was proud to declare to his Russian comrades (who were from Communist Soviet Union with Lenin's and Marxist's atheistic beliefs) that after being in space and looking into the vastness, he did not see God anywhere. A famous preacher at the time replied, "Let him step out of his spacesuit for just one second, and he'll see God quick enough."[16]

The pure in heart perceive the presence of the Lord in their lives. They recognize His guidance in the steps they take and discern His handiwork in the beauty of creation. Their hearts are centered on seeking the Lord and aligning their actions with His will.

---

16. https://www.preceptaustin.org/matthew_58.

> Therefore if you have been raised up with Christ, keep seeking the things above, where Christ is, seated at the right hand of God. Set your mind on the things above, not on the things that are on earth. For you have died and your life is hidden with Christ in God. When Christ, who is our life, is revealed, then you also will be revealed with Him in glory (Colossians 3:1–4).

Paul encourages us to seek what is above, to fix our gaze on our heavenly destination, and to continually direct our attention upward. Let's maintain our focus on Christ, who resides within us, and whose love, creation, redemption, and grace are evident all around us.

Jesus is addressing His disciples, urging them to adopt a perspective of grace and to recognize God's hand at work in all aspects of life.

He says blessed are the pure in heart. Let's pause for a moment and reflect on what it means to be pure in heart.

> Then some Pharisees and scribes came to Jesus from Jerusalem and said, "Why do Your disciples break the tradition of the elders? For they do not wash their hands when they eat bread." And He answered and said to them, "Why do you yourselves transgress the commandment of God for the sake of your tradition? For God said, 'HONOR YOUR FATHER AND MOTHER,' and, 'HE WHO SPEAKS EVIL OF FATHER OR MOTHER IS TO BE PUT TO DEATH.' But you say, 'Whoever says to *his* father or mother, "Whatever I have that would help you has been given *to God*," he is not to honor his father or his mother.' And *by this* you invalidated the word of God for the sake of your tradition. You hypocrites, rightly did Isaiah prophesy of you: 'THIS PEOPLE HONORS ME WITH THEIR LIPS, BUT THEIR HEART IS FAR AWAY FROM ME. BUT IN VAIN DO THEY WORSHIP ME, TEACHING AS DOCTRINES THE PRECEPTS OF MEN.'"

After Jesus called the crowd to Him, He said to them, "Hear and understand. *It is* not what enters into the mouth *that* defiles the man, but what proceeds out of the mouth, this defiles the man." Then the disciples came and said to Him, "Do You know that the Pharisees were offended when they heard this statement?" But He answered and said, "Every plant which My heavenly Father did not plant shall be uprooted. Let them alone; they are blind guides of the blind. And if a blind man guides a blind man, both will fall into a pit." Peter said to Him, "Explain the parable to us." Jesus said, "Are you still lacking in understanding also? Do you not understand that everything that goes into the mouth passes into the stomach, and is eliminated? But the things that proceed out of the mouth come from the heart, and those defile the man. For out of the heart come evil thoughts, murders, adulteries, fornications, thefts, false witness, slanders. These are the things which defile the man; but to eat with unwashed hands does not defile the man" (Matthew 15:1–20).

CEREMONY AND TRADITION RUIN RELATIONSHIP

In Matthew 15:1-2, the Pharisees confront Jesus, expressing their displeasure that His disciples were not adhering to the ceremonial hand-washing tradition. Jesus confronts the heart of the matter by highlighting their focus on outward appearances over genuine compassion. He points out their hypocrisy, as they prioritize rituals like Corban—setting aside items as consecrated for the Lord—while neglecting their duty to care for their parents. Rather than offering assistance to their families when needed, they would declare items as Corban, withholding them for religious reasons externally while harboring selfish motives internally.

Corban can still manifest today as an excuse for avoiding doing what is right. For instance, if your parents are facing eviction but you designate your spare room as a prayer space instead of offering it to them.

Just as we see today, the Pharisees were dishonoring God through the hardness of their hearts towards others. Jesus highlighted in Matthew 15:9, 11, and 18 how their teachings defiled them, as they contradicted the fundamental law of love decreed by the Lord. In Matthew 15:8–9, Jesus exposed their practice of using traditions to project an outward appearance of holiness, while their hearts lacked genuine love for others, leaving them hollow inside.

The disciples weren't required to perform ceremonies or uphold traditions to earn admiration for their holiness. Jesus emphasized the importance of seeking after God and remaining close to Him. It was having an inward heart devoted to God and sharing in His concerns that truly purified them. By striving to pursue what pleases God and aligning their hearts with His, they found true cleanliness.

Jesus indeed teaches in Matthew 5:20 that it is the condition of the heart that renders someone defiled. The term *defile* originates from the Greek word *koinounta*, which implies polluting or contaminating something that has been sanctified by God for everyday use. A polluted heart tends to harbor thoughts of evil, murder, hatred, gossip, slander, and all the other vices listed in verse 20.

Jesus teaches that it's not the omission of a ceremony that pollutes the heart, but rather closing one's heart to the needs of others, particularly to the needs of one's parents. Refusing to extend God's love to others and shutting oneself off from compassion is what truly pollutes the heart.

A PURE HEART IS BETTER THAN RELIGION

In Matthew 5:8, Jesus declares, "Blessed are the pure in heart." The term *pure* comes from the Greek word *katharos*, which denotes physical cleanliness or purity, suggesting that something is unblemished and untouched by external influences. Jesus is affirming that those who possess a heart free from the corruption of the world are truly blessed or content. Such individuals have their hearts firmly set on God and remain untainted by the worldly influences that seek to sway them.

The disposition of a pure heart is one devoid of impurity or wrongdoing, free from thoughts of evil, devoid of gossip, devoid of desires for harm towards a fellow believer, and completely devoid of selfishness. Such individuals possess a heart that is wholly dedicated and reserved for God's use.

While the Pharisees emphasized outward cleanliness to gain approval from others, God desires an inwardly pure heart. We shouldn't allow our hearts to be tainted by a mixture of self-love and love for God. Instead, let our hearts be solely and entirely devoted to Him.

> Woe to you, scribes and Pharisees, hypocrites! For you tithe mint and dill and cummin, and have neglected the weightier provisions of the law: justice and mercy and faithfulness; but these are the things you should have done without neglecting the others. You blind guides, who strain out a gnat and swallow a camel! Woe to you, scribes and Pharisees, hypocrites! For you clean the outside of the cup and of the dish, but inside they are full of robbery and self-indulgence. You blind Pharisee, first clean the inside of the cup and of the dish, so that the outside of it may become clean also. Woe to you, scribes and Pharisees, hypocrites! For you are like whitewashed tombs which on the outside appear beautiful, but inside they are full of dead men's bones and all uncleanness. So you, too, outwardly appear righteous to men, but inwardly you are full of hypocrisy and lawlessness (Matthew 23:23–28).

Jesus observes that outwardly, the Pharisees may appear clean, but inwardly they are spiritually dead (verse 27) and impure, *akatharos*—mixed up and lacking in purity. Despite their ability to read Scripture, they remain spiritually blind (verse 24), unable to discern the love, grace, and mercy that emanate from its pages.

King David, despite being described as a man after God's own heart in Acts 13 and 1 Samuel 13, wasn't free from sin; his life was marked by significant struggles. So, being pure in heart doesn't imply sinlessness but rather a steadfast commitment to seeking God's rule in one's heart and recognizing His hand in every aspect of life. King David wrote:

> The earth is the LORD'S, and all it contains,
> The world, and those who dwell in it.
> For He has founded it upon the seas.
> And established it upon the rivers.
> Who may ascend into the hill of the LORD?
> And who may stand in His holy place?
> He who has clean hands and a pure heart,
> Who has not lifted up his soul to falsehood
> And has not sworn deceitfully.
> He shall receive a blessing from the LORD
> And righteousness from the God of his salvation.
> This is the generation of those who seek Him,
> Who seek Your face—*even* Jacob (Psalm 24:1–6).

Having clean hands and a pure heart signifies integrity and a singular devotion. It reflects a commitment to loving the Lord with all aspects of one's being—heart, soul, mind, and strength—emanating from a genuine and wholesome place. This level of contentment doesn't arise merely from surface actions, akin to the Pharisees, but rather from a deep, overflowing love that permeates every facet of life.

The result of a life filled with this character or developing this character is seen in the second half of Matthew 5:8, "they shall see God." For my fellow Greek grammar geeks, it is a future indicative, a future continuous, with a middle reflexive. It means you will continually see God yourself.

In this context, *see*, derived from the Greek word *optánomai*, can indeed refer to appearing before or encountering. When God resides at the core of your being and is the driving force behind all your actions, you perceive His presence manifesting in every circumstance, discern His hand at work in every moment, and feel His constant presence surrounding you.

CHAPTER 7
PEACE MAKERS

"Blessed are the peacemakers, for they shall be called sons of God."
—Matthew 5:9

As we delve further into the traits every follower should strive for, we encounter the characteristic of possessing a peaceful nature and a calm demeanor. What sets this follower of Jesus apart is their ability to swiftly impart this calmness to others.

The seventh Beatitude presents a challenge to be peacekeepers, conflict resolvers, and peacemakers. It's undeniable that conflict is unavoidable in this fallen world. We won't always see eye to eye with everyone, and not everyone will have our best interests at heart. Even the purest individuals can unintentionally hurt others. In this passage, Jesus declares blessed are those who seek to uphold peace and content are those who can reconcile people in conflict.

Paul reiterates Christ's words in Romans:

> Never repay evil for evil to anyone. Respect what is right in the sight of all people. If possible, so far as it depends on you, be at peace with all people (Romans 12:18).

"PEACE-ED" TOGETHER

According to Scripture, peace ultimately depends on you. Why? Because as a disciple and God's representatives on earth, you have embraced the role and attribute of a peacemaker. Jesus restored peace with God for us, and now, as His followers, we are called to actively pursue peace in our interactions with others.

He left peace in our hearts (John 14:27). By choosing the path of peace, no matter how uncommon it may seem, and by living and sharing the way of peace, we embody the essence of Jesus's teachings and fulfill our calling as His followers.

High up in the Andes Mountains, directly center of the borders of Chile and Argentina, sits a depiction of Jesus holding a cross, standing on a globe, and raising a hand of blessing. For years, these two neighboring nations fought over the borderlands till Oliveira Cezar, who ran a school Bible study, persuaded the countries to place the statue in the middle of the lands as a monument to remind people of the peace brought through Christ. In 1902, the two nations agreed to peace, and the memorial was successfully rehomed by 1904, all because one woman believed in peace!

Collier's New Encyclopedia, V. 1 (1921) p. 154 Panel H

"Blessed are the peacemakers" refers to individuals dedicated to fostering, creating, sharing, and practicing peace. Their spiritual harmony with God enables them to live in peace with others in their physical lives.

Peacemaker is a composite of two Greek words: *eirēnē*, meaning peace, and *poieo*, meaning to produce or create. When combined, Jesus is affirming the blessedness of those who, amidst the conflicts, pain, and hardships of a fallen world, actively generate peace.

LET PEACE CALL THE SHOTS

But how does one become a peacemaker? How can you be a person that brings resolution between others and calms storms in people's lives?

> Let the peace of Christ rule in your hearts, to which indeed you were called in one body; and be thankful. Let the word of Christ richly dwell within you, with all wisdom teaching and admonishing one another with psalms *and* hymns *and* spiritual songs, singing with thankfulness in your hearts to God. Whatever you do in word or deed, *do* all in the name of the Lord Jesus, giving thanks through Him to God the Father (Colossians 3:15–17).

Paul says "whatever you do" multiple times. Whatever you do, do it heartily. "Whatever you do in word or deed, do in the name of the Lord" encompasses every action, intention, and endeavor you pursue. Whether you're setting deadlines for your dreams, establishing goals, planning accomplishments, speaking, or acting, ensure that everything aligns with bringing honor to the name of Christ and is achieved for His glory.

God is more interested in the intentions behind your plans than the plans themselves. He encourages you to take action and speak, but even more importantly, to embody a transformed being. He desires not merely mechanical actions, but actions rooted in gratitude, wisdom, diligence, joy, and praise. God seeks a change in your attitude, not just in the actions you undertake.

Here are actions outlined that can transform your life from simply doing tasks to embodying joy in your work if you allow them to permeate your day.

Consider that the word *rule*, derived from the Greek word *brabeueto,* is often used in the context of athletic competitions to denote the authority of officials such as referees, judges, or umpires. These individuals are responsible for ensuring proper conduct on the field of play. For instance, a referee might rule a player "out" due to poor performance or failure to adhere to the rules.

Living at peace (Romans 12:18) and letting peace call the shots in our lives (Colossians 3:15) will determine outcomes. In essence, when we allow God's peace to abundantly dwell within us, to the extent that it governs our thoughts, words, and actions, we are purposefully living for Christ while considering others. Christ's peace embodies the essence of the gospel, which is the redemption of humanity. Therefore, let the gospel reign supreme in our lives, guiding and directing us in all that we do.

Your boss, spouse, or parents don't have authority over your heart and mind; only you can make decisions about your day and who you live for. Allow God to guide your decisions, to protect your thoughts and emotions. Let Him bring completeness to your joy by governing and directing peace in your life. Ultimately, our daily experiences are shaped by who is in charge and umpiring our thoughts and actions.

"Let the word of Christ dwell." *Dwell* comes from the Greek word *enoikeito*, meaning settle and make domain and influence. Let the word of God influence your life. Do not just read it; live it! Let God's word be the loudest one you hear and the clearest one you obey and live by.

I know a police officer who seeks to live as an 'officer of peace', even in the midst of difficult situations like making an arrest. Not long ago, this officer had to process a man after an arrest. He had tragically become addicted to pain medication while grappling with a debilitating knee injury sustained during his professional athletic career.

One night, the combination of sleep deprivation due to pain and the medications in his system triggered a psychotropic episode for this former athlete. In his altered state, he believed the building was on fire and rushed outside, yelling "fire" and grabbing a woman, whom he believed he was rescuing from a non-existent fire.

As a result, he was arrested for causing a disturbance and holding someone against their will. However, during the process of fingerprinting him, the compassionate officer offered words of reassurance: "You are loved, and there is a purpose for everything. Though today may seem bleak, I believe that soon, you and I will be praising alongside each other in the house of the Lord."

Nearly a year later, during a church service, the officer and the former athlete's eyes met. They quickly made their way to each other, tears streaming down their faces as they embraced in the back of the church. The message of peace amid pain had indeed come true, and it was a beautiful moment of redemption and reconciliation that I was privileged to witness.

A peacemaker brings a message of peace, which Ephesians 6:15 says is the gospel. A peacemaker sees the way to bring peace and makes peace through Jesus.

> Depart from evil and do good;
> Seek peace and pursue it (Psalm 34:14).

Strive to cultivate a mindset of peace and let your life be characterized by it. Embrace the peace that surpasses all understanding and actively pursue it. As a follower of Jesus, make peace a central goal in your life journey.

Matthew 5:9 teaches us that embracing a life of peace brings one of the highest honors a person can receive—a designation from God Himself. The outcome of being a peacemaker is being recognized as a "child of God." Since God is the epitome of peace, when we actively embody this divine attribute, we become positive ambassadors of His family.

In ancient times, being called a "son" was a significant honor. It signified inheritance, parental blessings, and the rights to conduct business associated with the family name at the city gates. Moreover, it meant representing the family, as mentioned in Galatians 3:26–29. This is the honor that God bestows upon those who represent Him well as peacemakers.

God calls you His child because He acknowledges you, whether you are a man or a woman, as an inheritor of His kingdom, clothed in the image of His Son Jesus. It signifies that He sees Christ reflected in you. As Matthew 5:9 declares, "Blessed are the peacemakers, for they shall be called sons of God."

CHAPTER 8

PERSECUTED

"Blessed are those who have been persecuted for the sake of righteousness, for theirs is the kingdom of heaven."
—Matthew 5:10

Do you believe that the Lord is both just and gracious? Understanding discipleship involves recognizing the Lord's grace in forgiving sin and acknowledging His justice in rewarding righteousness. One aspect of this just reward is often borne through hardship. The Lord promises reward amidst pain. As Paul articulates in 2 Timothy 2, farmers labor through adverse conditions such as scorching sun, persistent weeds, and unforgiving soil, all for the eventual yield of fruit. Soldiers sacrifice their safety and home comforts to secure a land of freedom. Athletes forsake indulgent foods and luxuries, committing themselves to early mornings, strict diets, and rigorous training, all in pursuit of a coveted medal. Similarly, disciples endure trials and tribulations in anticipation of their ultimate prize.

Blessed are those who endure persecution—those who are belittled, reviled, hated, and despised for their commitment to Christ. They may face discrimination, overlooked for advancement, and ostracized for their righteous actions.

The term *persecute* originates from the Greek word *dediōgmenoi*, signifying being driven to flee, run, or seek cover from malevolent intentions. Originally, it is used to describe a hunter's pursuit of prey, forcing them to flee from mortal danger.

Jesus teaches that when people harbor intense hatred towards you, actively oppose you, and make it their mission to stand against you, it is a profound blessing.

A LIFE WELL LIVED--NOT ALWAYS WELL LIKED

"Keep your behavior excellent among the Gentiles, so that in the thing in which they slander you as evildoers, they may because of your good deeds, as they observe *them,* glorify God in the day of visitation" (1 Peter 2:12). In these passages, the focus is on your life lived as a disciple of Jesus, closely scrutinized by others. People may unjustly, maliciously, and hatefully judge you based on their own perceptions. They might suggest someone is only kind because they seek favor with their boss, or assume another person's reluctance to engage in inappropriate behavior stems from a sense of superiority. However, they are actually reacting to the good deeds you do. You're pursued and slandered for your acts of kindness, hunted for your benevolent actions. Despite this, you endure criticism and persecution for the love and grace you extend to others.

As Peter advises, continue to engage in these righteous deeds, motivated by the promise of eternal glory rather than seeking recognition from people. You are living in anticipation of Christ's return, not seeking validation from others. This aligns with the promise Jesus makes in Matthew 5:10, where those whose righteous actions are despised, criticized, and hated will ultimately inherit the kingdom. Their reward transcends mere entrance; it encompasses the fullness of God's eternal inheritance. Their inheritance extends far beyond earthly possessions like beat-up cars, run-down houses, or jars of coins hidden away. Instead, they will receive a share in the rule of Jesus the King. "And without faith it is impossible to please *Him,* for the one who comes to God must believe that He exists, and *that* He proves to be One who rewards those who seek Him" (Hebrews 11:6). Indeed, as a rewarder of the faithful, Jesus is promised to return, as Revelation 22:12 attests, bringing with Him rewards for His people, especially for those who endured persecution for righteousness' sake. His reward includes reigning, ownership, and being honored in the kingdom.

> Then Jesus said to His disciples, "If anyone wants to come after Me, he must deny himself, take up his cross, and follow Me. For whoever wants to save his life will lose it; but whoever loses his life for My sake will find it. For what good will it do a person if he gains the whole world, but forfeits his soul? Or what will a person give in exchange for his soul? For the Son of Man is going to come in the glory of His Father with His angels, and WILL THEN REPAY EVERY PERSON ACCORDING TO HIS DEEDS. Truly I say to you, there are some of those who are standing here who will not taste death until they see the Son of Man coming in His kingdom (Matthew 16:24–28)."

Revelation 19:8 emphasizes that we are clothed in righteous acts for the wedding of Christ, signifying the importance of our eternal focus over temporary pain. Our minds should remain steadfast on His return. In Matthew 16:28, Jesus promises that when He comes, *erchomenon,* we will also come. Therefore, let us maintain our focus on our part in this divine promise.

YOUR PART IS TO GROW IN HIM

> Therefore we do not lose heart, but though our outer man is decaying, yet our inner man is being renewed day by day. For momentary, light affliction is producing for us an eternal weight of glory far beyond all comparison, while we look not at the things which are seen, but at the things which are not seen; for the things which are seen are temporal, but the things which are not seen are eternal (2 Corinthians 4:16–18).

The struggles, persecutions, afflictions, and discomforts endured for the sake of Jesus, as Paul describes, serve to build glory for you in the eternal realms. In contrast, the hypocrite seeks recognition and elevation from people (Matthew 6), but the disciples' earthly reward lies in deepening their relationship with Jesus and growing in likeness to Him as they live as citizens of the kingdom today. But they also have a heavenly benefit and future kingdom benefit.

Paul's greatest desire was to be deemed faithful by Jesus, yearning to hear the commendation, "Well done, good and faithful servant." This drove him to endure pain, agony, suffering, ridicule, and hardships, considering them as light and fleeting compared to the surpassing value of knowing Jesus. He encourages us to keep our focus on what endures eternally. When we recognize that our current struggles lead to growth and eventual victory (2 Timothy 4:7–8), we can persevere through pain with the assurance of triumph in the end. This concept of prioritizing the eternal prize aligns with what Jesus refers to as "laying up treasures in heaven" (Matthew 6:20).

"Blessed are those who have been persecuted for the sake of righteousness, for theirs is the kingdom of heaven" (Matthew 5:10). Experiencing hurt for the sake of righteousness, being offended while defending the kingdom, enduring physical harm for the sake of caring for others or facing hatred for being a disciple of Jesus—these are but momentary and light afflictions in comparison to the eternal rewards that await.

> Remember Jesus Christ, risen from the dead, descendant of David, according to my gospel, for which I suffer hardship even to imprisonment as a criminal; but the word of God is not imprisoned. For this reason I endure all things for the sake of those who are chosen, so that they also may obtain the salvation which is in Christ Jesus *and* with *it* eternal glory. It is a trustworthy statement: For if we died with Him, we will also live with Him; If we endure, we will also reign with Him; If we deny Him, He also will deny us; If we are faithless, He remains faithful, for He cannot deny Himself (2 Timothy 2:8–13).

In 2 Timothy 2:8–13, Paul is writing to Timothy, encouraging him (not a new believer or unbeliever) to endure (2:1). He calls Timothy "my son." In verses 7, 9, and 10, the "I" is Paul referring to himself. The "we" is Paul and Timothy. Let's explore how believers can apply the principles of this passage to their lives as they strive to follow in Christ's footsteps.

In 2 Timothy 2:8–10, Paul acknowledges his sufferings, emphasizing that they are not in vain. Pain and persecution endured for the sake of a life lived for Jesus do not go unrewarded. Indeed, the manner in which you live today determines the reward you receive in glory. Despite facing persecution, Paul found himself living the blessed and content life that Jesus spoke of.

2 Timothy 2:11

Indeed, as Jesus teaches in Luke 9:23, when we deny ourselves, take up our cross daily (symbolizing a daily death to self), and follow Him, we find true life in Him. Essentially, it's a call to die to self in order to truly live.

2 Timothy 2:12

If we endure hardships, pains, suffering, deprivation, and persecutions, we are promised to reign with Him. This speaks to our inheritance—we will receive the privilege of joining believers who sit as rulers and judges (1 Corinthians 6:2), alongside those who have died for Christ (Revelation 20:1–6).

This inheritance is a unique blessing that few will attain, as it requires enduring faithfulness throughout life. It necessitates choosing to be a disciple of Jesus, wholeheartedly following His call to "follow Me" and living as His example. Just as Jesus faced opposition for the good works He demonstrated, we, too, may encounter attacks for the goodness others see in us. If we deny Jesus through our actions, surrendering to pressures or abandoning our faith, we forfeit the reward, the crown, and the privilege of reigning with Him.

I appreciate Paul's clarity in addressing potential confusion. He emphasizes that enduring hardships for the sake of eternal reward does not impact one's salvation; it pertains solely to the reward in the afterlife, not to the gift of eternal life itself.

2 Timothy 2:13

Even in moments of doubt, denial, or unfaithfulness, God remains steadfastly faithful. Like Peter, who denied Christ three times, God's faithfulness endures. Whether we struggle with doubts, uncertainties, or even unfaithfulness akin to a cheating spouse, God's faithfulness never wavers. He remains constant and true, always ready to extend grace and forgiveness to those who turn back to Him.

God's faithfulness endures even when we cause Him pain, for we are His beloved children, akin to the prodigal son in Luke 15:11–32. Imperfect though we may be, as disciples, we strive to live faithfully. As Jesus teaches in Matthew 5:10, we are blessed amidst our struggles today, knowing that our heavenly future is abundant and secure.

What a remarkable opportunity we have on this earth to contemplate, embody, and proclaim the gospel. Through our trust in

Jesus, we have been declared righteous, possessing a righteous standing before God. Though we may still falter and sin, God now views us as righteous. Thus, we are empowered to live as if sin has no hold on us, engaging in righteous deeds that bring glory to Him and advance His kingdom.

Living and acting out of guilt or for the sake of a reward lacks the depth of relationship and love that Jesus calls us to. As Jesus warns in Matthew 6, if our actions are motivated by obligation or a desire for public recognition, our reward is limited to earthly praise. Instead, we should strive to live lives that shine with love and bring glory to God. As Matthew 5:16 instructs, let our good works be a reflection of God's goodness, prompting others to glorify Him. Similarly, Colossians 3:23–24 encourages us to do everything for the Lord, knowing that our ultimate reward comes from Him.

Our lives should be lived to bring glory to God, to advance His kingdom, and to deepen our relationship with Him. We must remember that the true reward awaits us in the life to come, not in the fleeting pleasures of this world. Even in the face of opposition and persecution, we can find blessing in knowing that we are living righteously and that our ultimate reward comes from Jesus Himself.

CHAPTER 9

BECAUSE OF ME

"Blessed are you when people insult you and persecute you, and falsely say all kinds of evil against you because of Me. Rejoice and be glad, for your reward in heaven is great; for in the same way they persecuted the prophets who were before you."

—Matthew 5:11–12

Billy Graham's rise to prominence as an evangelist in the 1960s coincided with the widespread adoption of a term that came to define Christians both nationally and globally. This term "born-again" gained such popularity that by the mid-1970s, presidential candidate Jimmy Carter, when questioned about his faith, proudly identified himself as "born-again."

To be born again was to identify with the words of Jesus to the searching Pharisee, Nicodemus, in John 3:3, "Jesus answered and said to him, 'Truly, truly, I say to you, unless one is born again he cannot see the kingdom of God.'" To be "born-again" signified a public declaration of one's allegiance to Christ. However, with the adoption of this term came increased scrutiny and even hostility toward believers. As believers embraced the label "born-again," unbelievers began using derogatory terms like "Jesus freaks" to mock and ridicule them. Initially, believers found it offensive to have the name of Jesus associated with such a derogatory term as "freak." A freak was associated with the circus--bearded ladies, tattooed men, the world's smallest human, a man sleeping on a bed of nails--it was what you went to see to be stunned at how they looked, sounded, and acted.

As the term gained traction, believers began to embrace it as a badge of honor, signifying their willingness to be seen as peculiar, outcasts, or even a spectacle for the sake of Jesus. Their unconventional behavior, appearance, and actions marked them as different from the societal norms—a radical expression of their commitment to Christ. Instead of being seen as freaks of nature, they proudly identified as "Jesus freaks," boldly living out their faith and demonstrating the transformative power of Jesus in their lives. This was in line with Jesus's call for His followers to stand out and make a difference in society.

Blessed are those who are persecuted and hated. Matthew 5:11-12 is similar to Matthew 5:10, but the significant difference is that verse 10 is associated with the disciples' actions. Applying the verse to us today, it is about what *you* have done for Christ--the follower's actions of righteousness. In verse 11, Jesus said the disciples were blessed when people hated them, spoke badly about them, and made false claims against them because of *Him*.

THE REAL NAME IT CLAIM IT IS CHRIST

In this Beatitude, this mind of a disciple is tied to your claim of Jesus. You are blessed if people hate you because of Jesus. Because you say, "I am a Christian," and that claim leads to persecution because the words of your mouth are Jesus's, you are blessed.

Being reproached by society is a mark of blessing for a disciple. The Greek word *onididzoe* implies being disliked and corrected for one's behavior, particularly when that behavior reflects Christ. When others reject or oppose us because of our claims and actions of living in accordance with Christ's teachings, we can find happiness in knowing that we are aligning ourselves with Him.

Blessed are you when you are persecuted for the name of Jesus. Around the world every day, Christians are being killed and beaten for nothing more than admitting to others they believe in Jesus. Various governments have arrested missionaries. Kidnappings and bombings of buildings have happened all because the name of Jesus was said.

You're blessed if you are spoken falsely about. The word translated "spoken falsely" means to lie, purposefully misrepresent, or deceive. You are blessed when people twist your words all because you love Jesus.

And Jesus says you are blessed when evil is said about you because of Him.

> Brother will betray brother to death, and a father *his* child; and children will rise up against parents and cause them to be put to death. You will be hated by all because of My name, but it is the one who has endured to the end who will be saved. A disciple is not above his teacher, nor a slave above his master. It is enough for the disciple that he become like his teacher, and the slave like his master. If they have called the head of the house Beelzebul, how much more *will they malign* the members of his household (Matthew 10:21–22)!

> The one who listens to you listens to Me, and the one who rejects you rejects Me; and he who rejects Me rejects the One who sent Me (Luke 10:16).

Throughout history, God's messengers have been hated because they speak the truth for the sake of God and not themselves. Scripture speaks of the fate of the prophets:

> And what more shall I say? For time will fail me if I tell of Gideon, Barak, Samson, Jephthah, of David and Samuel and the prophets, who by faith conquered kingdoms, performed *acts of* righteousness, obtained promises, shut the mouths of lions, quenched the power of fire, escaped the edge of the sword, from weakness were made strong, became mighty in war, put foreign armies to flight. Women received *back* their dead by resurrection; and others were tortured, not accepting their release, so that they might obtain a better resurrection; and others experienced mockings and scourgings, yes, also chains and imprisonment. They were stoned, they were sawn in two, they were tempted, they were put to death with the sword; they went about in sheepskins, in goatskins, being destitute, afflicted, ill-treated (*men* of whom the world was not worthy), wandering in deserts and mountains and caves and holes in the ground (Hebrews 11:32–38).

And the follower of Christ can be one the world is not worthy of should they choose the life. Matthew 5:12 says to rejoice in all these things. The word *rejoice* carries the meaning of celebration, while "be glad" implies exultation and singing praise. Therefore, disciples should find joy in the fact that others have recognized Christ in them, even if it results in suffering or reproach.

1. Your relationship is such that you are not ashamed.
2. You are being counted alongside great people of faith, like the apostles and prophets.
3. Your reward is great.

There is blessing if one is willing to be content in suffering for the name and cause of Jesus.

THE REWARD THROUGH CALAMITY

> The Spirit Himself testifies with our spirit that we are children of God, and if children, heirs also, heirs of God and fellow heirs with Christ, if indeed we suffer with *Him* so that we may also be glorified with *Him.* For I consider that the sufferings of this present time are not worthy to be compared with the glory that is to be revealed to us. For the anxious longing of the creation waits eagerly for the revealing of the sons of God (Romans 8:16–19).

And just to clarify, these verses do not say going to heaven *is* your reward, like some people believe and teach. They teach that endurance is part of eternal salvation. The reward is not entrance into heaven; all believers enter eternity. The reward is given in heaven and relates to how one participates in the reign of the kingdom. The endurance of a follower is for eternal treasure where moth and rust do not destroy. You are not being rewarded heaven or admittance to heaven; that was gifted when you trusted Christ.

> Then I saw thrones, and they sat on them, and judgment was given to them. And I *saw* the souls of those who had been beheaded because of their testimony of Jesus and because of the word of God, and those who had not worshiped the beast or his image, and had not received the mark on their forehead and on their hand; and they came to life and reigned with Christ for a thousand years. The rest of the dead did not come to life until the thousand years were completed. This is the first resurrection. Blessed and holy is the one who has a part in the first resurrection; over these the second death has no power, but they will be priests of God and of Christ and will reign with Him for a thousand years (Revelation 20:4–6).

Our focus should not be on what we receive but on who we represent—Christ Himself. We must keep our eyes fixed on the goal of becoming more like Him. The greatest honor we can receive is to be recognized and celebrated as faithful followers of Christ.

CHAPTER 10

SALT

"You are the salt of the earth; but if the salt has become tasteless, how can it be made salty again? It is no longer good for anything, except to be thrown out and trampled under foot by men."

—Matthew 5:13

What does salt do to food? Salt preserves, purifies, and flavors. In a flavorless world where everyone blends in together, we are called the salt of the earth. But salt is useless if it sits on a shelf or in a saltshaker.

In Jesus's time, salt held immense economic and cultural value. People would traverse vast distances to obtain salt from mines and dried salt marshes, treating it as precious as gold. Soldiers were even paid in salt, giving rise to the phrase "worth his salt." The term *salad* originates from the Roman practice of using saltwater to clean vegetables. Additionally, salt was used symbolically in some cultures to seal peace treaties, signifying the enduring nature of the agreement. Therefore, when Jesus calls us to be the salt of the earth, He invites us to bring preservation, purification, and enduring flavor to the world around us, just as salt did in His time.

HOW CAN WE SALT THE EARTH?

Salting the earth begins with the flavor of our speech.

> Conduct yourselves with wisdom toward outsiders, making the most of the opportunity. Let your speech always be with grace, *as though* seasoned with salt, so that you will know how you should respond to each person (Colossians 4:5–6).

Eliminate vulgar language, gossip, and hurtful jokes from your speech, and let your words serve the purpose of salt—preserving, enhancing, flavoring, and purifying.

Verse 5 urges Christians to demonstrate God's wisdom in their daily interactions with society. "Conduct yourselves with wisdom toward outsiders, making the most of every opportunity."

Paul advises us to "walk in wisdom," meaning we should be mindful of how our actions and words may influence others' perceptions of Christianity. Rather than exacerbating prejudices or providing justification for their dislike, we should strive to do good for others and share our faith with them at the opportune moment.

The Greek verb *exagorazomenoi* in the phrase "make the most of every opportunity" means "to buy out, to purchase completely." As Christians, we are called to fully seize every opportunity that God provides us to share our faith in Jesus. We should invest in these opportunities with grace in our speech, allowing Jesus to overflow from our mouths because His message is too immense to contain. Let us preserve these opportunities with kindness, good speech, actions of love, and a lifestyle characterized by grace.

What are you willing to do so that the people you know will go to heaven? Will you invite them to church, share your testimony, give them a tract, offer a meal, or pray until they're saved? Your mission field is all around you, and you are called to salt it.

Verse 6 emphasizes the importance of how Christians speak. "Let your speech always be with grace, as though seasoned with salt, so that you will know how you should respond to each person." To be "full of grace" basically means to be gracious or pleasant in our speech. Before we can make disciples, we need to make friends and build rapport. So, sprinkle the salt of Christ in every moment.

PRESERVED THROUGH SALTING

Salting provides both flavor and preservation, both of which are valuable assets for Christians to commend their message to others. Part of the right flavoring involves tailoring your conversation to your audience. Being able to choose the best means of answering questions about your faith is essential to effective communication. Preserve everyone with the message of salvation by grace through faith and purify by encouraging and uplifting brothers and sisters with words and actions. Flavor this world with a life well-lived—a life of glorious service and unwavering commitment to Jesus.

Preserve, purify, and flavor your speech, actions, and lifestyle. That is what Jesus had in mind when He said you are the salt of the earth. You are worth saving, and you are the preservers, the flavor, the purity.

A professor of mine once shared a humorous yet cautionary tale from his wedding day. Some mischievous friends played a prank on him by placing fish in the hubcaps of his car. However, the scorching Dallas heat caused the fish to quickly putrefy, resulting in a horrendous smell that made his new wife sick. With no air conditioning in their old car, they had no choice but to endure the foul odor with the windows down to stay cool. Cleaning up the mess afterward was a daunting task, requiring considerable effort. This story illustrates that preservation requires deliberate effort, friendship, and careful choices of action and speech. In contrast, the fish in the hubcaps were not chosen to preserve but to spoil, stink, and ruin.

In Jesus's time, fishermen like Peter, James, John, and Andrew understood the importance of preserving their catch of fish. After hauling them in, their work wasn't finished. They would salt and sun-dry the fish, laying them out on nets to allow cool air to circulate around them. Rubbing them with salt helped to purify and preserve the fish meat, ensuring it would stay fresh year-round. When Jesus instructed His disciples to be salt, they understood the significance. He desired preservation, purity, and flavor—not putrid fish in a hubcap. Today, while we may not follow the same preservation methods due to modern conveniences like ice and refrigeration, the purpose remains the same: to bring preservation, purity, and flavor to the world around us.

LIVE YOUR PURPOSE

In ancient society, salt served various purposes beyond preserving fish and in trade. There was a widespread understanding of the agricultural benefits of salt as well. Jesus's analogy, particularly when considering the parallel teaching in Luke's gospel (Luke 14:35), encompasses this aspect. The underlying issue in the analogies of salt and light is not about salvation but about the usefulness of an object. Light serves to illuminate, brighten, and provide warmth. If it is hidden or fails to fulfill its purpose, it loses its significance. Similarly, salt purifies, flavors, tenderizes, and fertilizes. If salt ceases to perform any of these functions, it doesn't cease being salt, but it becomes useless. Therefore, Jesus's teachings emphasize the importance of believers fulfilling their intended purpose in the world.

Just as wiring a house for electricity is pointless if the switch is never turned on, so too is our effort wasted if we fail to obey God in our love and good deeds. This concept aligns with Jesus's words in Luke 17:7–10, where God speaks to faithful servants, disciples, or followers. He emphasizes that thanks are unnecessary because they are simply living out their purpose and design for creation—an important reminder that mature believers should relay to others. "So you too, when you do all the things which were commanded you, say, 'We are unworthy slaves; we have done *only* that which we ought to have done'" (Luke 17:10). A clockmaker has no need to thank a wristwatch for keeping time, as that is the watch's inherent design and purpose. Similarly, when believers faithfully fulfill their purpose and calling, there is no need for special recognition or thanks, as they are simply living out what they were created to do. As believers, our purpose is clearly stated in Matthew 5:16b: "that they may see your good works, and glorify your Father who is in heaven." Our actions should serve as a testimony to the goodness and glory of God, drawing others to Him through our conduct and character.

SALTY LIKE FERTILIZER

We have already spoken of the purpose of salt on food, but it held another use for the ancients. In an agricultural society situated in arid regions, salt played a crucial role in enhancing crop yields. When applied to soil, salt facilitated deep root growth, suppressed weed growth, and improved water retention—critical factors in regions where resources were scarce and crop cultivation was challenging. This application of salt was essential for sustaining livestock and ensuring successful crop production in such environments.

The importance of salt to soil is hinted at in Luke 14. Jesus begins this idea in verse 25 by emphasizing how growth and discipleship demand effort, sacrifice, and even turmoil. A disciple may face the loss of friends, family, and material possessions, and may need to forsake societal expectations and self-preservation in order to maintain their testimony for the sake of the gospel message. Jesus concludes this discussion of the challenging journey of learning and following Him, or becoming Christlike, by saying:

> Therefore, salt is good; but if even salt has become tasteless, with what will it be seasoned? It is useless either for the soil or the manure pile, *so* it is thrown out. The one who has ears to hear, let him hear (Luke 14:34–35).

Why would tasteless salt be used on dung or soil? Again, this is the fertilizing agent of salt. Salt collected in the Middle East resembles a closer elemental property to that of Epsom salt. Salts like Epsom salts were used as a property agent in fertilizer to help the soil retain potassium, nitrates, and other beneficial minerals that help glucose creation in photosynthesis. Because the soil in Israel is so poor due to harsh extremes in weather, adding salt allows for water retention and fertilizes the plants to stimulate vegetable growth while protecting from unwanted weeds.

Jesus frequently used agricultural metaphors and examples to convey spiritual truths. He likened people to wheat and chaff, described the world as a ripe harvest, used seeds as symbols of the gospel, referenced figs for signs, and compared salvation to a seed planted in various types of soil. These illustrations vividly depict the process of spiritual growth, the reception of the gospel message, and the importance of nurturing faith in fertile hearts. Let's consider the parable of the soils.

> When a large crowd was coming together, and those from the various cities were journeying to Him, He spoke by way of a parable: "The sower went out to sow his seed; and as he sowed, some fell beside the road, and it was trampled underfoot and the birds of the air ate it up. Other *seed* fell on rocky *soil,* and as soon as it grew up, it withered away, because it had no moisture. Other *seed* fell among the thorns; and the thorns grew up with it and choked it out. Other *seed* fell into the good soil, and grew up, and produced a crop a hundred times as great." As He said these things, He would call out, "He who has ears to hear, let him hear." His disciples *began* questioning Him as to what this parable meant. And He said, "To you it has been granted to know the mysteries of the kingdom of God, but to the rest *it is* in parables, so that SEEING THEY MAY NOT SEE, AND HEARING THEY MAY NOT UNDERSTAND. Now the parable is this: the seed is the word of God. Those beside the road are those who have heard; then the devil comes and takes away the word from their heart, so that they

will not believe and be saved. Those on the rocky *soil are* those who, when they hear, receive the word with joy; and these have no *firm* root; they believe for a while, and in time of temptation fall away. The *seed* which fell among the thorns, these are the ones who have heard, and as they go on their way they are choked with worries and riches and pleasures of *this* life, and bring no fruit to maturity. But the *seed* in the good soil, these are the ones who have heard the word in an honest and good heart, and hold it fast, and bear fruit with perseverance" (Luke 8:4–15).

Believers should cling to the word because it is the source of our spiritual growth and fruitfulness. While presenters, pastors, and teachers play a role in sharing and handling God's word, ultimately, we are responsible for receiving it, holding onto it, and bearing fruit from it in our lives. Each of us is accountable for how the word shapes and transforms us.

ARE YOU A FERTILE SOIL?

What type of soil are you, or what is the condition of your heart? In this passage, we encounter four types of soil, each representing different people or different states of the heart. Despite receiving the same word of God, the seed (word) falls on various types of soil (hearts), resulting in a variety of responses. Only one type of soil yields fruit, while the other three prove inhospitable to sustain growth. Jesus uses this analogy in the agrarian-based culture to illustrate four places where the seed lands: on a path, on rocky ground, among thorns, and on good soil.

HARD PATH

In Luke 8:12, we encounter the first group, represented by the hard path. These individuals hear the word but do not believe. In ancient times, the paths or roads were hardened strips of dirt, compacted and dry from generations of foot traffic and animal hooves. Seed falling on the roadside would simply sit atop this hard ground, vulnerable to being scooped up by birds, animals, or passersby. Similarly, those represented by the hard path do not respond to the word because the devil comes and snatches it away before it can take root in their hearts.

The hard heart remains unresponsive or unmoved by the word of God. It is the only soil (person) that does not receive the seed (gospel). While all other soils receive the seed and show varying degrees of growth, not all reach the point of producing fruit. As stated in Matthew 5, the ultimate purpose and design is fruit production, leading others to see our works and glorify our Father in heaven.

ROCKY SOIL

In Luke 8:13, we encounter the next soil, represented by rocky ground. In this soil, the heart is initially receptive to God's word. Individuals hear it, are moved by it, and experience a sprout of growth. However, the presence of rocks symbolizing worldly desires or distractions prevents the roots from penetrating deeply into their lives. When temptation arises, the shallow growth withers away, leaving only the worldly desires or distractions behind. Their lack of depth in faith becomes apparent because they never fully matured.

The rocky soil is similar to the hardening written about decades later in Hebrews 3:12–13,

> Take care, brethren, that there not be in any one of you an evil, unbelieving heart that falls away from the living God. But encourage one another day after day, as long as it is *still* called "Today," so that none of you will be hardened by the deceitfulness of sin.

Hardening signifies that the word cannot take root and grow deeply in your life. The Greek word for *harden, sklērynthē,* means to become inflexible or literally "to become dried out." When you continually indulge in sin, persist in sin, and seek satisfaction from sin, it spiritually dries you out, making your heart inflexible and resistant to the word of God.

When you seek satisfaction from any other source besides Jesus, you ultimately become spiritually dry. In John 4, Jesus refers to Himself as the living water. He desires those who hunger and thirst for Him to represent Him as disciples. Seeking fulfillment from anything other than Jesus leaves you feeling empty and spiritually dry.

WEEDS

The third type of soil, referred to as the weedy ground in Luke 8:14, represents those who hear the word but never reach maturity. These individuals are likened to the seed that falls among thorns. They hear the word, but as they continue on their journey, they become choked by worries, riches, and pleasures of this life. Consequently, they fail to bear fruit and mature spiritually. Jesus uses the term *choke* to illustrate how these individuals allow worries, doubts, and material possessions to suffocate the life-giving breath of the Spirit within them, hindering their spiritual growth.

In each of these examples, there is nothing wrong with the seed or the sower. The sower casts the seed liberally, expecting to receive a bountiful harvest (2 Corinthians 9:6), and does not discriminate about where the seed lands. The goal is to sow the seed wherever it has the potential to produce fruit. Whether it falls on the heart of a broken sinner or an upstanding citizen, the message is meant for all (1 Corinthians 3:6–9).

The thorny soil represents individuals who allow life's distractions to choke out their walk with God. These individuals may show interest in Jesus's message but fail to fully commit to it due to their preoccupation with material possessions—such as worries, riches, and pleasures. Although they hear the word, they do not deeply meditate on it or integrate it into their lives. Instead, they become entangled in the concerns of daily life and the pursuit of worldly success. Consequently, their misplaced priorities prevent the seed from taking root and bearing fruit in their lives. While they may grow superficially, they lack the spiritual nourishment necessary to mature in Christ. Instead of recognizing that true happiness comes from Christ alone, they mistakenly believe that achieving worldly success will satisfy them. Ultimately, their wrong priorities suffocate the seed of the word and hinder their spiritual growth.

GOOD AND FERTILE

Lastly, we encounter the good soil in Luke 8:15, "But the *seed* in the good soil, these are the ones who have heard the word in an honest and good heart, and hold it fast, and bear fruit with perseverance." Here we find the one type of soil or people with a fruitful outcome. The good soil represents those who not only hear the word but also hold fast to it. They receive the word with openness and sincerity, allowing it to take root deeply in their hearts. As a result, they remain steadfast in their faith and bear fruit in their lives.

Some seed falls on good soil, which is fertile, moist, and rich in nutrients necessary for growth. Unlike the other types of soil, good soil is not hardened or obstructed by foreign elements or life-sucking plants. It represents the fourth group of listeners who not only hear the word but also retain it and produce a crop. These individuals bear spiritual fruit, which serves as evidence of their spiritual life. Only the good soil is capable of bearing fruit according to Luke 8:8 and 15. The word of God transforms their hearts, which are described as noble and good. With an honest and receptive heart, they allow the word to take root and grow within them. They not only hear the word but also hold onto it and nurture it, enabling them to persevere through temptation.

As we scatter seed—the gospel message—we must act as good farmers, investing effort into fertilizing the soil through our walk, testimony, lifestyle, and speech, as highlighted in Matthew 5:13. Believers play a crucial role in fertilizing the ground of this world through their relationships, behavior, speech, and lived convictions. When others witness how we live out our faith, it helps the soil retain the living water—Christ—and adds the necessary spiritual nutrition for others to grow. Additionally, our example helps remove weeds in the lives of fellow believers, enabling them to thrive and bear fruit in their spiritual journey.

Again, one of the reasons why salt was added to dung was for fertilization of the soil. Fresh manure will rot rather than nourish the soil and can become detrimental to growth. So, a farmer would add salt to help break down and preserve the positive aspects of dung fertilizer. Sometimes unbelievers can't handle the full strength of the word but need it prepared to receive through one's life. Our efforts to prepare the world, relations, and individuals may be just what is needed to throw the gospel into a prepared life.[17]

USELESS SALT IS UNUSED SALT

In Matthew 5, the second part of verse 13 presents a puzzling statement: "but if the salt has become tasteless, how can it be made salty *again*? It is no longer good for anything, except to be thrown out and trampled under foot by men." This doesn't imply a loss of salvation; rather, Jesus isn't suggesting that the salt ceases to be salt or that its molecular structure changes. Even if salt loses its saltiness, it doesn't stop being salt. The key is that it's not fulfilling its intended purpose. In the agricultural context of Jesus's time, if salt got wet and began to dissolve or if its composition was more akin to gypsum than food salt, it could be used to strengthen roofs as a form of patio material. This doesn't render the salt ineffective, but it does mean it's not fulfilling its role as a preservative, flavor enhancer, cleaner, or fertilizer.

Jesus's question about how salt can become salty again prompts us to reflect on a truth we should all understand. It's not about re-trusting Christ to regain our "saltiness" because the salt remains salt; its fundamental nature doesn't change. When our saltshaker breaks or gets waterlogged, leading us to discard the salt, we don't deny that it was salt or claim it never existed. Instead, we lament the loss of its usefulness.

---

17. These thoughts on salt being agricultural and an additive to dung and soil are based on a reading of Thomas Constable, "Commentary on Matthew 5:13," *Expository Notes of Dr. Thomas Constable*, 2003, and Eugene Deatrick, "Salt, Soil, Savior," *JSTOR: The Biblical Archeologist*, May 1962, Vol. 25 No. 2, 41–48.

The essence of the second part of the verse is a call not to hoard what we've received in Christ. We're urged not to squander our "saltiness" but to utilize it for the glory of God. How do we avoid becoming tasteless? By returning to the source of our flavor and fertilizing qualities. We must draw nearer to Christ, who continually supplies us with light and serves as our eternal reservoir of salt. Preserve! Flavor! Purify! Salt has a duty, a purpose, and a mission. It must fulfill its design.

The term *tasteless* originates from the Greek term *moraine*, from which we derive our English word *moron*. However, in this context, it doesn't imply being dense or lacking sense; rather, it conveys being tainted or useless. When we fail to live according to our design, it's foolish because we won't experience fulfillment. You and I have a task and a purpose, and it's imperative that we fulfill it.

Jesus employs similar imagery in Matthew 5:14–16 when He discusses the function of a lamp: to provide light. If a lamp is extinguished, it doesn't cease to be a lamp; it simply requires more oil or a new wick. No one lights a lamp with the intention of hiding it in a dark place under a bushel. The purpose of lighting the lamp is to raise it up so that everyone can see. The same principle applies to salt: to be salty is to fulfill your intended purpose! Season your life, purify your lifestyle, and preserve with the message of grace. Salt without flavor is still salt, and a candle or lamp that isn't lit is still a light, but they are useless in function.

CHAPTER 11

LIGHT

"In Him was life, and the life was the Light of men. The Light shines in the darkness, and the darkness did not comprehend it. There was the true Light which, coming into the world, enlightens every man."

—John 1:4–5, 9

The allure of light is undeniable. I recently watched a program on Thomas Edison, who risked his reputation to develop a sustainable and safe light source. It was a journey marked by numerous failures and setbacks. Edison tirelessly experimented, often believing he had finally created a lasting lightbulb, only to see it burn out after mere minutes or hours.

Edison faced ridicule and criticism, labeled as a failure and even a quack by many. Yet, when the streets around his office were suddenly illuminated in the dead of night, the skeptics fell silent. Why? Because despite the mockery, people crave light. When you possess what others need, they may laugh at first, but once they see the brilliance, they will be drawn to it like moths to a flame.

Light possesses a remarkable ability to dispel fear. When the night light shines, the menacing monster lurking beneath the bed transforms into nothing more than a pile of laundry.

THE POWER OF LIGHT

When I was in high school, the youth and young adult's ministry went on a stress trip in the middle of the mountains in Tennessee. One day we had to hike twenty-eight miles from base camp to a subsite in order to do some mountain climbing in the morning. This required taking enough essentials for three days, including water, food, climbing gear, and tents/sleeping bags. When we finally arrived at the campsite, we were exhausted, but a group of us wanted to go to a water fall nearby, soak our bodies in the cold water, and enjoy the water falling on our sore backs. So, one of our guides took us on the journey to the falls. It was amazing. The only problem was it got dark fast, and none of us had brought a flashlight. To make things worse, the track back to camp had perilous drops off the side of cliffs. This is when you hope to have the one guy prepared for everything and anything with you. We had that guy. At the time, he was a Black Hawk pilot for the Army. He said, "I got this, guys" and he reached into his camo pants, pulling out a tiny glow stick. I chuckled, thinking in my head, "That will never work." But, when he cracked it and lifted it over his head, there was enough light for the six or so of us to huddle around him and follow the trail back to camp. Without that light, we could have slipped off the path and been terribly hurt. That little bit of light saved us. The size of the light was not the most important, but that it was raised for all to see. It only takes one person to bravely lift up the light and point the path to Jesus.

Jesus said, "I am the Light of the world; he who follows Me will not walk in the darkness, but will have the Light of life" (John 8:12). "While I am in the world, I am the Light of the world" (John 9:5). He revealed the way to a relationship with God.

Jesus, the Son of God, is indeed our light. Through Him, we receive the life-giving qualities needed to grow and flourish. Spending time with

Jesus illuminates our path, guiding us to live righteously, speak with kindness, and think with wisdom. His light fills us with courage and compassion, empowering us to share His love and grace with others.

YOU ARE THE LIGHT

This torch of light has been passed to us to illuminate the way for others. "You are the light of the world," Jesus proclaimed. But let me ask you, are you shining brightly, and is your light enduring?

> You are the light of the world. A city set on a hill cannot be hidden; nor does anyone light a lamp and put it under a basket, but on the lampstand, and it gives light to all who are in the house. Let your light shine before men in such a way that they may see your good works, and glorify your Father who is in heaven (Matthew 5:14–16).

God's divine purpose for humanity is to bring glory to Him. Matthew 5:14 illustrates that believers are like the light, positioned as a city on a hill, just like Jerusalem. Jerusalem, prominently situated, was visible from every surrounding valley. This city held significant biblical history, including the site where Abraham offered Isaac. God's promise to Abraham of a great nation was fulfilled on that hill--the very place where His Son would later be crucified.

We are called to be that city seen from any valley as a beacon of life and hope (Matthew 5:14). We are to be a people that no matter the pains and pitfalls, have eternal hope in Jesus. Jesus has not called His followers to hide, but to raise themselves up to be seen as an example.

We're not meant to merely speak well; we should set the tone for every conversation. It's not enough to just perform adequately; we should strive to be the best employee or student. Being a good boss isn't sufficient; we must lead by example. Jesus wants us to be visible, so others can look to us to understand what it means to live for Christ and follow Him in all our actions. Our light isn't meant to be concealed but displayed for all to see.

We're called to be like a lamp on a lampstand (Matthew 5:15–16). Such a lamp casts light into every corner of a room, overcoming darkness with its very presence. Similarly, God calls us to illuminate the darkness of this world, to infiltrate its shadowy places, not to conceal our light. Let's push back against the darkness. Instead of being closet Christians, let's be committed followers. Let's live consistently, avoiding contradictions, and not hide our light under a lampshade. Let's embrace our purpose and shine brightly.

One year, I led a group of teenagers to a remote part of Florida for a retreat. It was a stunning location right on the water, far from the hustle and bustle of city lights and noise. On clear nights, the sky was adorned with stars, and the moonlight offered ample illumination for navigation. However, on cloudy nights, the darkness was all-encompassing, making it impossible to see anything beyond immediate surroundings.

One evening, despite the cloud cover, a few boys decided to play basketball. In the middle of the field stood a concrete pad serving as a court, illuminated by a powerful floodlight. That floodlight bathed the entire court in light, cutting through the darkness like a beacon. When I stepped out of the dormitory, all I could see was the radiant glow of the court.

As I approached, I witnessed one of the boys lose control of the ball, causing it to roll out of the illuminated area and into the pitch-black expanse beyond. Stepping out of the light, the boy entered a realm of shadow, then darkness, until, at a mere two feet away, he disappeared entirely from view.

We are called to be like floodlights, designed to illuminate dark areas. When installed correctly, the floodlight itself remains unseen, with the focus solely on what it illuminates. Similarly, our actions and deeds should shine in a way that directs attention to God, not to ourselves. Let our lives point back to the One who sacrificed Himself to give us life, guiding others to glorify God through our words and deeds.

Why do we shine? The answer lies in verse 16. We shine for the glory of God. Our light is meant to illuminate the hope we have in Christ, our actions reflecting His love and grace. Through our lives, others should not praise us, but rather give glory to God the Father and Jesus Christ His Son.

The ultimate aim of every follower of Jesus is to bring glory to God, to radiate His presence so brightly that others see Jesus in us. Through our deeds, words, and conduct, we have the opportunity to magnify God's glory. Whose presence does your life illuminate as the focal point? Are people drawn to you as a source of light?

CHAPTER 12
FULFILL

"Do not think that I came to abolish the Law or the Prophets; I did not come to abolish but to fulfill. For truly I say to you, until heaven and earth pass away, not the smallest letter or stroke shall pass from the Law until all is accomplished."
—Matthew 5:17–18

Have you encountered someone proclaiming, "I am not under the law but under grace"? It's a common phrase that some interpret as a license to indulge in sin because Jesus's sacrifice has supposedly freed us from the consequences. They might argue, "Since Jesus died for our sins, we can live however we please." But this notion is problematic. It suggests that we can continue in sinful behavior without regard for its consequences. How does this attitude align with honoring God?

Paul said, "What shall we say then? Are we to continue in sin so that grace may increase? May it never be! How shall we who died to sin still live in it?" (Romans 6:1–2). Jesus did not come to end the law but to be the fulfillment on your behalf.

THE FULFILLMENT COMPLETE

There are three ways this fulfillment has taken place and will continue to take place in a believer's life.

- Fulfill means He came to be the lamb sacrifice. You are now saved--justification.
- Fulfill means He came to make a way for men to live clean and holy lives with God--sanctification.
- Fulfill means He made it possible for the future sense for you to live perfect in His millennial reign and in eternity free from the presence and temptation of sin--glorification.

THE LAW IS THE BOUNDARY LINE

The Law was never about saving but for living rightly. The Law was never about obedience to earn or merit heaven; that would contradict Scripture.

Scripture says:

> You foolish Galatians, who has bewitched you, before whose eyes Jesus Christ was publicly portrayed *as* crucified? This is the only thing I want to find out from you: did you receive the Spirit by the works of the Law, or by hearing with faith? Are you so foolish? Having begun by the Spirit, are you now being perfected by the flesh? Did you suffer so many things in vain—if indeed it was in vain? So then, does He who provides you with the Spirit and works miracles among you, do it by the works of the Law, or by hearing with faith? Even so Abraham BELIEVED GOD, AND IT WAS RECKONED TO HIM AS RIGHTEOUSNESS (Galatians 3:1–6).

Paul said that the Law did not earn anyone salvation by keeping it. No one was justified by the Law. In fact, when we go to court for speeding, it is the law that convicts. The law always condemns. The law condemns a murderer, a thief, and a lie under oath. The law is the guide to condemn lawbreakers! That is why Paul asked, Why are you trying to be obedient to the Law in order to be saved or justified? The Law did not save you; Jesus did. The Law reveals our shortcomings, which Jesus forgives.

Paul stated in Galatians 3:24 that the Law served as a tutor, highlighting his shortcomings. Likewise, in Romans 7:7, he explained that without the Law, he wouldn't have recognized sin. Just as our local and national laws delineate boundaries and their consequences, God's Law does the same. "For the wages of sin is death; but the free gift of God is eternal life in Jesus Christ our Lord" (Romans 6:23).

The Law stipulates that sin results in death. However, Jesus offers a free gift that grants life through faith. He proclaims freedom from sin, justifying believers. In the future, He enables them to live a life free from sin and to experience an existence without sin in His presence.

Abraham, predating the Law, temple worship, and the traditions of the rabbis and Pharisees, was considered righteous because of his faith.

> What then shall we say that Abraham, our forefather according to the flesh, has found? For if Abraham was justified by works, he has something to boast about; but not before God. For what does the Scripture say? "ABRAHAM BELIEVED GOD, AND IT WAS CREDITED TO HIM AS RIGHTEOUSNESS" (Romans 4:1–3).

In no way does this contradict James 2:21, where it states that Abraham was justified by works. James clarifies that the actions Abraham took were in faith to deepen his relationship with God, not to earn salvation. Faith in God saved him. He became a friend of God through his works. "Friend" denotes a relational aspect; all those witnessing Abraham's actions and hearing the testimony of Sarah, Isaac, and the slave would attest that Abraham loved God so much that he would hold nothing back to honor Him. Abraham's actions demonstrated his faith to others and solidified his friendship with the Most High.

> You foolish Galatians, who has bewitched you, before whose eyes Jesus Christ was publicly portrayed *as* crucified? This is the only thing I want to find out from you: did you receive the Spirit by works of the Law, or by hearing with faith? Are you so foolish? Having begun by the Spirit, are you now being perfected by the flesh? Did you suffer so many things in vain—if indeed it was in vain? So then, does He who provides you with the Spirit and works miracles among you, do it by works of the Law, or by hearing with faith? Just as Abraham BELIEVED GOD, AND IT WAS CREDITED TO HIM AS RIGHTEOUSNESS (Galatians 3:1–6).

Abraham's action was simple: he believed. In Galatians 3:1–6, the same word *believe* is used, which Jesus also calls individuals to do for everlasting life in John 3:16. The belief Abraham had, and the belief Jesus called Nicodemus to, is the same requirement for salvation today.

Jesus said in John 6:47, "Truly, truly, I say to you, he who believes has eternal life." Why? It is seen in the words Jesus said:

> Do not think that I came to abolish the Law or the Prophets; I did not come to abolish but to fulfill. For truly I say to you, until heaven and earth pass away, not the smallest letter or stroke shall pass from the Law until all is accomplished (Matthew 5:17–18).

Jesus said He came to fulfill the Law. The Law says when you cross this line, there is a punishment. The Law always has a consequence for missteps. But Jesus took our consequence for breaking God's Law. In other words, Jesus took our sin. "He made Him who knew no sin *to be* sin on our behalf so that we might become the righteousness of God in Him" (2 Corinthians 5:21). He became sin so you could be called righteous, holy, and blameless, and be seen in the court of God's law as not guilty. He did not come to abolish but fulfill the Law by taking our punishment.

TAKE THE YOKE OF LOVE

Jesus called His followers to live like free men. Don't go to a former life of condemnation. Peter put it well. Live as free men (1 Peter 2:16) and stay away from your former life (1 Peter 1:14). Peter more than likely was summarizing Jesus's words. We have received the writers' commentary and recollections of Jesus's teaching (John 14:26) and as we see written by the apostles (Galatians 5:14, 1 Peter 4:8, 1 John 4:20) and Jesus's instructions in the Gospels, He takes the right application of the Law (Matthew 22:34–40). The disciples were all applying their rabbi's interpretation; this rabbi was the Savior, and His interpretation was the true interpretation.

Jesus described the modern interpretation of Law as heavy burdens on the shoulders of men (Matthew 23:4). Yet He described His yoke of interpretation of "love God and people" in the most beautiful terms: "For My yoke is easy and My burden is light" (Matthew 11:30). His call was to release themselves of the other rabbis' unobtainable teachings (Matthew 11:28) and "Take My yoke upon you and learn from Me" (Matthew 11:29).

The yoke of Jesus, His interpretation of the Law, is love. In Mark 12:28–33, Jesus said that to love God and love others was greater than any sacrifice, oath, or ritual. Jesus's interpretation of the Law was love. The Pharisees interpreted the Law as rules and regulations that separated people from God; it singled out the elite. Jesus said, the Law is love; the Law is care.

> And a lawyer stood up and put Him to the test, saying, "Teacher, what shall I do to inherit eternal life?" And He said

to him, "What is written in the Law? How does it read to you?" And he answered, "YOU SHALL LOVE THE LORD YOUR GOD WITH ALL YOUR HEART, AND WITH ALL YOUR SOUL, AND WITH ALL YOUR STRENGTH, AND WITH ALL YOUR MIND; AND YOUR NEIGHBOR AS YOURSELF" (Luke 10:25–27).

The Law is fulfilled in Jesus's love, which put Him on the cross.

THE LAW OF LOVE

Luke 10:25 recounts a lawyer, also known as a scribe, asking, "What can I do to inherit the kingdom?" Observing the seventy returning and being promised eternal blessings, the scribe, belonging to a group known for interpreting and applying the law, seeks approval and blessings from Jesus, similar to what the disciples had received. This illustration by Bill Crowder exemplifies the scribe's place at that moment,

> Few people take time to study the US Internal Revenue Service income tax regulations—and for good reason. According to Forbes magazine, in 2013 tax codes surpassed the four million-word mark. In fact, the tax laws have become so complex that even the experts have a hard time processing all the regulations. It's burdensome in its complexity.
>
> The religious leaders in ancient Israel did the same thing in their relationship with God. They made it too complex with laws. The growing burden of religious regulations had increased to the point where even an expert in Moses' law struggled to understand its core.[18]

Jesus made it simple; the law is love. Anything beyond that, and you missed the mark. The law was to prepare people to stand right before God. The law was so people would know how to love God and people

---

18. https://ymi.today/2014/08/odb-power-of-simplicity/.

in everyday interaction, but sadly the "holy men" of the day made it a barrier between God and people.

> Owe nothing to anyone except to love one another; for he who loves his neighbor has fulfilled *the* law. For this, "YOU SHALL NOT COMMIT ADULTERY, YOU SHALL NOT MURDER, YOU SHALL NOT STEAL, YOU SHALL NOT COVET," and if there is any other commandment, it is summed up in this saying, "YOU SHALL LOVE YOUR NEIGHBOR AS YOURSELF." Love does no wrong to a neighbor; therefore love is the fulfillment of *the* law (Romans 13:8–10).

The yoke of putting yourself under God's control is love. Consider the Samaritan of Luke 10.

> But wishing to justify himself, he said to Jesus, "And who is my neighbor?" Jesus replied and said, "A man was going down from Jerusalem to Jericho, and fell among robbers, and they stripped him and beat him, and went away leaving him half dead. And by chance a priest was going down on that road, and when he saw him, he passed by on the other side. Likewise, a Levite also, when he came to the place and saw him, passed by on the other side. But a Samaritan, who was on a journey, came upon him; and when he saw him, he felt compassion, and came to him and bandaged up his wounds, pouring oil and wine on them; and he put him on his own beast, and brought him to an inn and took care of him. On the next day he took out two denarii and gave them to the innkeeper and said, 'Take care of him; and whatever more you spend, when I return I will repay you.' Which of these three do you think proved to be a neighbor to the man who fell into the robbers' hands?" And he said, "The one who showed mercy toward him." Then Jesus said to him, "Go and do the same" (Luke 10:29–37).

Knowing the man is a keeper of the Law, Jesus asks him in Luke 10:26, "What is written in the Law? How does it read to you?"

The term "read to you" does not mean read like we physically sit down and read a book or magazine. It is the combination of two words, *ana* meaning up or again and *ginosko* meaning to personally know. So, when Jesus says, *pōs anaginōskeis*, He is asking how do you interpret it, or how do you know it and apply it? The scribe answers that the interpretation of all God's Law is in two statements: love God and love your neighbor.

After the scribe answered Jesus correctly, Jesus tells him, "do this and live" meaning get active and busy at loving God and man, and you will have found the deeper meaning of life. When Jesus said you will live, He wasn't saying the scribe was dead, and He was not saying that was the way to heaven. The scribe had asked for an inheritance in heaven, not admittance (Luke 10:25). One's entrance comes at belief, and inheritance through discipleship and lifestyle.

The scribe's question revealed his reluctance to take action (Luke 10:29b). He asked Jesus, "Who is my neighbor?" A neighbor encompasses anyone in need, anyone unable to reciprocate assistance. Your neighbor is the one experiencing suffering, the one requiring compassion and care. Despite being related, Jews and Samaritans harbored animosity toward each other, rooted in religious differences, perhaps explaining why the scribe in Luke 10:37 avoids mentioning the Samaritan by name and instead refers to him as "the one." Jesus shows him that a neighbor is anyone near you in need. The Samaritan––even the one you hate the most––can be a good neighbor, a righteous neighbor, if he helps that need.

The Levite and the rabbi depicted in the illustration were so afraid of becoming ceremonially unclean that they lost sight of God's intended message in His Law: "love God and love others." They were so blinded by their adherence to tradition that they were willing to allow a man to die. Although the wounded man may have appeared lifeless, the rabbi chose to walk on the opposite side of the road to avoid any potential contamination. According to rabbinical law, encountering a corpse obligated him to provide burial care.[19] Therefore, to circumvent the responsibility of either assisting an injured person or burying a deceased one, he chose to avoid the situation entirely.

The first two men were happy staying comfortable; they were happy doing routine and ceremony rather than applying and practicing the Scripture they studied. To help meant inconvenience and getting uncomfortable to try to save a life. Sadly, Jesus was demonstrating that the *practice* of Scripture was not part of their *knowledge* of Scripture. As a result, both the priest and Levite in the illustration missed the chance to show love in action.

On the other hand, the Samaritan showed two key traits we all need (Luke 10:28, 33–34, and 37). Here we see two key traits of a person loving God: a change of heart followed by action. Compassion has a tendency to rearrange your priorities. In Luke 10:33, the Samaritan was filled with compassion, *esplanchnisthē,* experiencing an inner stirring. Later, in verse 37, he demonstrated this compassion through action *katedēsen* and *epicheōn*. The compassion he felt in his heart was followed by tangible acts of mercy and kindness.

Twice in this passage Jesus says, "do." The scribe answers Him, Love God, love man. Jesus says, "do." The scribe answers again, the one that felt compassion, Jesus responds, "do." The simple word *do*, *poiei*, means to make or act upon. With this word, Jesus gives the biggest lesson to us and to the heart of the scribe. Go act upon what you know.

Jesus came to fulfill love for us. Utilizing every resource, He sacrificed Himself on the cross, was buried, and rose again so that we could stand not condemned but freed, and so that we could walk in

---

19. "Guide to Jewish Funeral Practice," *The Rabbinical Assembly,* https://www.rabbinicalassembly.org/story/guide-jewish-funeral-practice.

love and relationship. Jesus came to fulfill, signifying our salvation from judgment, granting us the ability to freely love God and others, and ultimately to reign with Him, liberated from guilt and sin.

Jesus bore the pain and consequences of the Law so that you could live freely to love Him and others. As a follower of Christ, go and do likewise. Live under His yoke of love.

CHAPTER 13

GREAT IN THE KINGDOM

"Therefore, whoever nullifies one of the least of these commandments, and teaches others to do *the same, shall be called least in the kingdom of heaven; but whoever keeps and teaches them,* he shall be called great in the kingdom of heaven."
—Matthew 5:19

Jesus came to live the perfect life and die on the cross for our sins. "He made Him who knew no sin *to be* sin on our behalf so that we might become the righteousness of God in Him" (2 Corinthians 5:21).

He became sin so you could be called righteous, holy, blameless, and be seen in the court of law as not guilty. He did not come to abolish but fulfill the righteous standard it demands. He came and did what was required by law (because you could not) and made it so you would not have to.

Jesus freed you from the law of sin and death, the law that separated you from God and said you could never obtain salvation. And in Matthew 5:19, Jesus says to be great in the kingdom, you should love greatly.

HOW DO I LOVE GREATLY?

Love is not merely a sentiment expressed in words; it is revealed through actions. Whether it's reaching out to a friend struggling with depression, visiting someone in the hospital, or providing assistance to those in need, love is demonstrated through tangible deeds. As 1 John 3:17-18 reminds us, "But whoever has the world's goods, and sees his brother in need and closes his heart against him, how does the love of God abide in him? Little children, let us not love with word or with tongue, but in deed and truth" (1 John 3:17-18).

To serve is to embody love, and greatness is found in acts of service, reflecting the character of God Himself. This theme is echoed not only in Matthew 5:19 but also in the profound example set by Jesus in John 13 when He washed the feet of His disciples. This act of humble service was a powerful demonstration of love in action, teaching us the importance of serving one another. However, the significance of this act becomes even clearer when we consider the context in which it occurred during the Passover meal, as described in the Gospel of Luke. In this context, Jesus exemplified that true greatness is found in selflessly stooping low to serve others.

> And there arose also a dispute among them as to which one of them was regarded to be greatest. And He said to them, "The kings of the Gentiles lord it over them; and those who have authority over them are called 'Benefactors.' But it is not this way with you, but the one who is the greatest among you must become like the youngest, and the leader like the servant. For who is greater, the one who reclines at the table or the one who serves? Is it not the one who reclines at the table? But I am among you as the one who serves" (Luke 22:24-27).

The disciples' dispute over greatness in the messianic kingdom revealed their preoccupation with positions of authority and power.

They were eager to know who among them would hold prominent roles when Jesus established His reign. However, Jesus responded to their ambitions in a profound and unexpected way. Instead of rebuking them for their ambition or dismissing their concerns, He chose to teach them a powerful lesson through action.

Jesus, demonstrating humility and servanthood, rose from the table, removed His outer garments, and wrapped a towel around His waist. He then proceeded to wash the disciples' feet, a task typically reserved for servants or the lowest of social classes. This act of humility and service was intended to challenge the disciples' understanding of greatness and leadership. It was a stark contrast to the world's definition of greatness, which often emphasizes authority, status, and recognition.

Jesus's actions conveyed a profound message: true greatness is found in selfless service and humility. By washing the disciples' feet, Jesus exemplified the sacrificial love and servant-heartedness that should characterize His followers. He redirected their focus from seeking positions of prominence to serving one another with humility and love. This act served as a powerful lesson on the nature of leadership in the kingdom of God.

Serving is leadership. Serving is an expression of love. Serving is following Jesus. Serving affords greatness in God's kingdom.

It is not a coincidence that this example by Jesus follows the disciples' argument in Luke 22 about who would hold the greatest position in the kingdom. It is Jesus's way of putting them in their place, "Oh, you want to know greatness? It's judged on how greatly you serve others." Jesus, being Master of them all, served them, and He is the King of the kingdom. He ends with such strong words:

> Now that I, your Lord and Teacher, have washed your feet, you also should wash one another's feet. I have set you an example that you should do as I have done for you. I tell you the truth, no servant is greater than his master, nor is a messenger greater than the one who sent him (John 13:14–16).

The undertone is set as to how Christ wants His followers to live. Christ's example serves as a standard of humble service and, therefore, as a call of Jesus's disciples to action. We have not come to sit; as believers, we have come to serve as followers.

> For you were called to freedom, brethren; only do not turn your freedom into an opportunity for the flesh, but through love serve one another. For the whole Law is fulfilled in one word, in the statement, "YOU SHALL LOVE YOUR NEIGHBOR AS YOURSELF" (Galatians 5:13–14).

When Jesus accomplished the hard work of the cross, He liberated us from the bondage of slavery and the burden of the law. However, our freedom in Christ shouldn't breed laziness or entitlement. Since Jesus came to serve and bore our sins, dying and rising again—a feat beyond our capability—we are called to follow His example.

While He undertook the challenging task of redemption, we are called to the easier task of expressing love through action and truth. By humbly serving one another, we emulate Jesus's greatness and set the stage for future greatness in His kingdom.

LOVE IS A VERB

In coming to fulfill the Law, Jesus says I want you to keep these commandments, but not in the way of ceremony and circumstance. Do these things not to be seen or heard, but so people can see your love lived through the law of love. Remember, Jesus is still speaking to His disciples, and a crowd is also listening. Jesus taught Matthew chapters 5, 6, and 7 in a matter of a few hours. Jesus said this way of applying the law in love and compassion would distinguish His followers from the world. He fulfilled the law because they could not, so now they can live the application of Scripture which is love. So your devotion to Him will be seen in your love for people.

> A new commandment I give to you, that you love one another, even as I have loved you, that you also love one another. By this all men will know that you are My disciples, if you have love for one another (John 13:34–35).

People will know you are following Jesus by your love. Notice Jesus did not say they will know you believe; He did not say they will know you are saved. Instead, Jesus said people would know you are learners of His by your love.

Look closely at John 13:34--a new commandment. Jesus says a new action I tell you to do--love. I like that He does not leave a blank for us to fill in for who to aim the love at. He says to love *one another*. The focus is off of yourself, and it is on the *one anothers* in your life. And it takes away the feeling, or choice of a decision of who we should have actions of love toward. He says an all-inclusive *one another*.

The word *love* is a verb; it is an action we must do. Being a verb makes it a decision; it is a choice we must make. "I will love you even when you are unlovely, even when you don't deserve it, and my actions, speech, and lifestyle will reflect this commitment. Why? Because I follow the Master of love. I am a disciple of Jesus. Having tasted and experienced His perfect love, I am compelled to live it out."

This is what the verse is getting to about being a great disciple. This is how we show discipleship. This is how the world, and those we are showing love to, can see that we follow Jesus. "By this all men will know that you are My disciples, if you have love for one another" (John 13:35).

The choice to love demonstrates that the choice to follow Jesus has been made. This is how we accomplish the goal of glorifying Jesus, by fulfilling His mission of love.

If you desire greatness in the kingdom, Jesus teaches that serving others with actions of love is the path to achieve it. He emphasizes that the way one demonstrates love in the present directly impacts their future greatness. Therefore, to attain greatness, one must fulfill the law of love, which entails serving others selflessly.

CHAPTER 14
RIGHTEOUSNESS

"For I say to you that unless your righteousness surpasses that of the scribes and Pharisees, you will not enter the kingdom of heaven."

—Matthew 5:20

When you live righteously, you are living for the kingdom. Righteousness, *diakaiosune*, is integrity, virtue, purity of life, rightness, correctness of thinking, feeling, and acting as God sees right.[20]

King David was spoken of as a man after God's own heart, but his actions were less than perfect. So how could God see him the way He did? The same way He can look at us in love, through the love we have for Him. David loved Yahweh above all with a pure heart.

---

20. Thayer and Smith, "Greek Lexicon entry for Dikaiosune," *The NAS New Testament Greek Lexicon*, 1999.

THE WRONG RIGHTEOUSNESS

In talking to His disciples in the Sermon on the Mount, Jesus is speaking to men familiar with acts of righteousness. The disciples and the crowd had seen the "holy men" of their day pound their chests, and adorned with head coverings, tassels, and prayer chords. They might look the part externally but would abuse the poor, mistreat their parents, and take advantage of orphans and widows. Jesus emphasized this point. Righteousness is not merely about outward actions that are seen, but it involves the intentions of the heart behind those actions, which should not be done for the sake of being seen by others. "Beware of practicing your righteousness before men to be noticed by them; otherwise you have no reward with your Father who is in heaven" (Matthew 6:1). In Matthew 5:20 Jesus says, "For I say to you that unless your righteousness surpasses *that* of the scribes and Pharisees, you will not enter the kingdom of heaven." The Pharisees' righteousness was what Matthew 6:1 explains as giving money to be applauded for their charity and not out of care to support the needy (Matthew 6:2). Their prayer was not to God but to be heard by men (Matthew 6:5). The fast done to be seen was not for seeking holiness but seeking attention (Matthew 6:16). Their righteousness was a good outward show, but inside it was empty. People looked at their shouts of song and prayer, their big money giving, and their hungry faces, but this empty display was not for God's glory; it was for approval of men. This is why Jesus continually says they are hypocrites receiving their prize in full.

Jesus wanted His disciples, and by extension, His followers, to possess His righteousness on the inside and let it radiate outward into their lifestyle. Loving Jesus should stem from the inside and manifest outwardly. So, why did Jesus emphasize that the righteousness of His followers must surpass that of the scribes and Pharisees?

In Jesus's time, the Pharisees (Hebrew, *parush*, "set apart") were seen as the holy and righteous.

> Woe to you, scribes and Pharisees, hypocrites! For you are like whitewashed tombs which on the outside appear beautiful, but inside they are full of dead men's bones and all uncleanness. So you, too, outwardly appear righteous to men, but inwardly you are full of hypocrisy and lawlessness. Woe to you, scribes and Pharisees, hypocrites! For you build the tombs of the prophets and adorn the monuments of the righteous, and say, "If we had been living in the days of our fathers, we would not have been partners with them in shedding the blood of the prophets." So you testify against yourselves, that you are sons of those who murdered the prophets. Fill up, then, the measure of the guilt of your fathers. You serpents, you brood of vipers, how will you escape the sentence of hell? (Matthew 23:27–33).

He called them hypocrites, snakes, evil, empty of compassion and love. And He ends by saying, how will you be saved from hell when your righteousness is a show?

Paul, who was a Pharisee, was blameless to the Law,

> for we are the *true* circumcision, who worship in the Spirit of God and glory in Christ Jesus and put no confidence in the flesh, although I myself might have confidence even in the flesh. If anyone else has a mind to put confidence in the flesh, I far more: circumcised the eighth day, of the nation of Israel, of the tribe of Benjamin, a Hebrew of Hebrews; as to the Law, a Pharisee; as to zeal, a persecutor of the church; as to the righteousness which is in the Law, found blameless. But whatever things were gain to me, those things I have counted as loss for the sake of Christ (Philippians 3:3–7).

But when Paul found Christ, he saw that whatever he could accomplish as a law-abiding Pharisee was rubbish. He said I was righteous according to the Law, but not righteous to God. Listen to what Paul says about being righteous to God:

> ...as it is written, "THERE IS NONE RIGHTEOUS, NOT EVEN ONE; THERE IS NONE WHO UNDERSTANDS, THERE IS NONE WHO SEEKS FOR GOD; ALL HAVE TURNED ASIDE, TOGETHER THEY HAVE BECOME USELESS; THERE IS NONE WHO DOES GOOD, THERE IS NOT EVEN ONE" (Romans 3:10–12).

No one has the covering of righteousness, not even a blameless Pharisee. The prophet Isaiah said:

> For all of us have become like one who is unclean, And all our righteous deeds are like a filthy garment; And all of us wither like a leaf, And our iniquities, like the wind, take us away (Isaiah 64:6).

Isaiah takes it further than Paul by saying that any righteousness we may claim is filthy rags--used feminine rags. The Pharisees missed that righteousness is not an act but a love lifestyle.

> Therefore let us not judge one another anymore, but rather determine this—not to put an obstacle or a stumbling block in a brother's way. I know and am convinced in the Lord Jesus that nothing is unclean in itself; but to him who thinks anything to be unclean, to him it is unclean. For if because of food your brother is hurt, you are no longer walking according to love. Do not destroy with your food him for whom Christ died. Therefore do not let what is for you a good thing be spoken of as evil; for the kingdom of God is not eating and drinking, but righteousness and peace and joy in the Holy Spirit. For he who in this *way* serves Christ is acceptable to God and approved by men (Romans 14:13–18).

Did you catch that? Paul says the kingdom of God is not found in eating, drinking, and rituals, meaning the laws. Instead, the kingdom is found in a righteous lifestyle of serving in love.

Love is a lifestyle, not a duty. Love isn't reserved for anniversaries and Valentine's Day. If it is, then you have a Pharisaical view of love. They reserved love for God to holy days and the sabbath. They were acting the part of love, but love was far from their hearts.

THE RIGHT RIGHTEOUSNESS

Focusing back to Matthew 5:20, we need to encounter what Jesus meant by surpassing the Pharisees righteousness. Unless your righteousness goes past the fakeness, you will not have a grand entrance into your kingdom life. The Pharisees seemed holy and righteous, but sadly, they were doomed without Christ. Jesus said they were whitewashed tombs (Matthew 23:27). This meant they looked pretty on the outside, nice and clean, maybe flowers outside and good smells, but dead on the inside--a rotting corpse, dead man's bones. A religious life separated from Jesus is a dead life. Why? Because apart from Jesus, your actions mean nothing. Our words, thoughts, and actions are nothing without Jesus.

Let's go back to Paul's words in Philippians 3.

> More than that, I count all things to be loss in view of the surpassing value of knowing Christ Jesus my Lord, for whom I have suffered the loss of all things, and count them but rubbish so that I may gain Christ, and may be found in Him, not having a righteousness of my own derived from *the* Law, but that which is through faith in Christ, the righteousness which *comes* from God on the basis of faith, (Philippians 3:8-9).

Jesus makes us righteous, and living a life of love for Him and others is His standard of righteous living.

When you live out love, when your heart is filled with love for God and love for your fellow man, you are living the righteousness in Him and have surpassed the scribe and Pharisee.

THOSE MADE RIGHTEOUS SHOULD LIVE RIGHTEOUS

But what did Jesus mean when He said, "you will not enter the kingdom of heaven (Matthew 5:20)"? Does that mean works are necessary for eternal life? No! Remember, Jesus is addressing His followers. So the main address and focus are directed to people who have already believed in Him.

Remember, Jesus says eternal life is through believing (John 3:1, 6:4) and Paul reiterates the way to get into the kingdom of heaven is belief. "For He rescued us from the domain of darkness, and transferred us to the kingdom of His beloved Son, in whom we have redemption, the forgiveness of sins" (Colossians 1:13–14).

So, what is Jesus implying with the phrase "enter the kingdom"? He is teaching them His standard for living. "But seek first His kingdom and His righteousness, and all these things will be added to you" (Matthew 6:33). Jesus's standard is to seek Him, His kingdom, and His righteousness.

When Jesus speaks of entry in Matthew 5, He reminds His audience that they need to seek true righteousness, which only comes by faith in Him, rather than relying on external deeds of the Law, which was the false righteousness prescribed by the Pharisees and scribes. Admittance to the kingdom comes through belief (John 6:47), and the welcome is determined by the fellowship we cultivate throughout life, which becomes a type of reward in itself.

> Therefore, brethren, be all the more diligent to make certain about His calling and choosing you; for as long as you practice these things, you will never stumble; for in this way the entrance into the eternal kingdom of our Lord and Savior Jesus Christ will be abundantly supplied to you (2 Peter 1:10–11).

RIGHTEOUSNESS

Peter suggests that when we fulfill our purpose as righteous ambassadors, we will receive a grand entrance upon our arrival into the kingdom. Salvation in Christ grants us entry into the eternal presence of Jesus, and the manner in which we live our lives will determine the type of reception we will receive upon arrival (Matthew 25:14–30). For believers in Christ, living righteously in the present will pave the way for a triumphant entry into the Millennial Kingdom of God.

A VICTORY PARADE FOR A RIGHT LIFE

When someone achieves success in their endeavors, it's often celebrated with recognition and commemoration. A prime example is the soldiers returning victorious after World War II. In cities like New York, they were honored with victory parades, showcasing their achievements and expressing gratitude for their service.

When the Miami Heat won their back-to-back championships in 2012 and 2013, Miami held a championship parade down Biscayne Blvd., but in 2014 when they lost in the finals, there was no parade in Miami. This pattern reflects a common sentiment: celebrations typically follow victories. Just as we celebrate the triumphs of others, our Savior also rejoices in our successes and accomplishments.

The concept of a celebratory entrance is evident in various parts of Scripture. Jesus himself was celebrated as He entered Jerusalem, an event often referred to as His triumphal entry. In Matthew 5, Jesus emphasizes that each of us, as His followers, has the potential for a triumphant entrance into the kingdom. This triumph is achieved by faithfully fulfilling His call to love God and love others with our lives.

Throughout the Old and New Testaments, the concept of entering often carries connotations of a celebrated or grand entrance. Jesus desires that we experience such a grand entrance into His kingdom, where our lives are celebrated for their significant contribution to the expansion and enrichment of His kingdom.

To put it simply, living righteously means following Jesus's example of love rather than adhering to religious rituals. Thus, by loving deeply, we pave the way for a grand entrance into the kingdom.

He was calling all who would follow Him to live a persevering life now in order to have a triumphant and glorious entrance with Him. As it's written, "His master said to him, 'Well done, good and faithful servant. You have been faithful with a few things; I will put you in charge of many things. Come and share your master's happiness!'" (Matthew 25:21). Friend, live in such a way that when you enter heaven as a citizen of the kingdom, you enter as one who is celebrated with the joy of your Master.

CHAPTER 15

MAKE FRIENDS

"You have heard that the ancients were told, 'YOU SHALL NOT COMMIT MURDER' and 'Whoever commits murder shall be liable to the court.' But I say to you that everyone who is angry with his brother shall be guilty before the court; and whoever says to his brother, 'You good-for-nothing,' shall be guilty before the supreme court; and whoever says, 'You fool,' shall be guilty enough to go into the fiery hell. Therefore if you are presenting your offering at the altar, and there remember that your brother has something against you, leave your offering there before the altar and go; first be reconciled to your brother, and then come and present your offering. Make friends quickly with your opponent at law while you are with him on the way, so that your opponent may not hand you over to the judge, and the judge to the officer, and you be thrown into prison. Truly I say to you, you will not come out of there until you have paid up the last cent."

—Matthew 5:21–26

It doesn't take much effort to engage in an argument, does it? Especially in the social media realm, one can easily find themselves adopting the persona of a social media "tough guy" with quick and snarky comebacks. Not to mention, winning an argument or an imaginary confrontation in your thoughts, that's a piece of cake, right? You know what I mean, that mental scenario where you envision confronting your boss, but it remains purely a mental exercise because it never materializes in reality.

But really, isn't that an indicator that we have a sinful nature that needs to be kept in check? Before hitting send, writing that angry rant, or responding to a social media post, we should pause to check the status of our heart.

THE POWER OF THE MIND

"The good man out of the good treasure of his heart brings forth what is good; and the evil *man* out of the evil *treasure* brings forth what is evil; for his mouth speaks from that which fills his heart" (Luke 6:45). "Out of the overflow of the heart"—the heart status is what you think, speak, write, and act upon. When Jesus spoke this portion of the Sermon on the Mount, He wasn't saying inward heart change is not "I will not physically kill you." That is only one aspect. The inward heart and a proper life before God is when the heart commits to refrain from physical, mental, and verbal harm towards others. It's a pledge not to injure others with actions, words, or thoughts: "I will not cut you with a knife, beat you with my tongue, or shoot you with my mind."

There is a song that says:

> It seems I'm always close minded with an open mouth
> And the worst of me just seems to come right out
> But I've never broken bones with a stone or a stick
> But I'll conjure up a phrase that can cut to the quick

And sometimes I say things that I wish that I could take back
The smartest thing to say is to tell myself

To keep quiet, quiet, don't let it all come undone
'Cause if I dare open my mouth, it'll just be to bite my tongue
I gotta keep quiet, quiet and listen to your voice
Because the power of your words can repair all that I've destroyed[21]

LAW OF THE MIND

Change of speech resulting from a change of mind is what the Lord desires. He wants people to recognize that it's an internal struggle not only to refrain from physically harming others but also to avoid assassinating people's character with our words. This is because the character of a disciple goes beyond the human law of "do not murder" to God's law of the heart and mind.

The apostle Paul said he felt he was blameless to the Law because it was a physical checklist. But that was until he realized it was not just physical dos and don'ts. He relayed that coveting turned the Law into the mental state of an individual (Romans 7:7–11). He understood from the Law's injunction against coveting that it wasn't merely a list of dos and don'ts for one's physical actions; it served as a moral and mental guide. Pleasing God wasn't just about outward actions; it involved the mental state and thought processes of an individual. Friend, let's follow the example of Jesus and strive to be like Him. He said: "Take My yoke upon you and learn from Me, for I am gentle and humble in heart, and YOU WILL FIND REST FOR YOUR SOULS" (Matthew 11:29). Let's learn from Jesus what it truly means not to murder; let's learn from His teachings and example how to apply this command to avoid causing harm in any form.

---

21. Relient K, "Bite My Tongue" by Matthew Thiessen, on *Five Score and Seven Years Ago* (Capital Gotee Records, March 6, 2007).

The statement, "the ancients say" is in reference to the Law of Moses that says *do not murder*! And the Talmud and Rabbinic teaching says, if you kill someone you will go to court (Matthew 5:21).

A FOLLOWER CONTROLS THEIR MIND

But Jesus takes this further than the outside—do not kill. He takes it past controlling one's physical rage. In Matthew 5:22, Jesus uses the word *angry* (*orgidzomenos*) which means to stand in opposition to someone. This is a different anger than Ephesians 4 where it says, "don't let the sun go down on your anger" (Ephesians 4:26). The anger spoken of in Ephesians 4 is *parorgismo*, which means to be irritated. In Matthew 5:22, Jesus is instructing us not to harbor hatred towards our brothers in Christ. A straightforward interpretation of this would be: do not oppose certain individuals simply because you don't like them.

This call to character comes with an effect of causality. If you oppose someone out of spite and without a just cause, in God's court you *stand guilty*. Why? Hebrews 4:12 says He is able to judge the thoughts and intentions of the heart.

A DISCIPLE CONTROLS THEIR MOUTH

Jesus goes on to say in the second half of Matthew 5:22, "whoever says to his brother, 'you good-for-nothing,' shall be guilty before the supreme court; and whoever says, 'you fool,' shall be guilty *enough to go* into the fiery hell."

Jesus is saying get control of your mind and your tongue. We all know that words have the power to hurt, but words also have the power to kill someone's character. Do not attack or assassinate others with your tongue. Only the King stands in authority to judge His subjects (Matthew 25:26), so do not judge your family in Christ with your words. Although Scripture does say believers will assist at the Judgment Seat, believers will judge–they do not stand as judge; they will judge fallen angels and unbelievers (1 Corinthians 6:2–3). It does not say we will judge our brothers and sisters in Christ.

AN OUT-OF-CONTROL PERSON

Can a believer hate a brother in Christ? Can a believer speak evil about the family of God? Some say no, but Peter says "yes."

> Make sure that none of you suffers as a murderer, or thief, or evildoer, or a troublesome meddler; but if *anyone suffers* as a Christian, he is not to be ashamed, but is to glorify God in this name. For *it is* time for judgment to begin with the household of God; and if *it begins* with us first, what *will be* the outcome for those who do not obey the gospel of God? AND IF IT IS WITH DIFFICULTY THAT THE RIGHTEOUS IS SAVED, WHAT WILL BECOME OF THE GODLESS MAN AND THE SINNER? (1 Peter 4:15–18).

Peter advises us to refrain from these actions, but he doesn't explicitly say it's impossible for believers to commit them. Can a believer or follower of Yahweh commit murder and still go to heaven? Let's ponder: Is Moses in heaven? (Read Exodus 2:11–14.)

One might argue that Moses's act of defending a Hebrew against the Egyptian might not be classified as murder. While this is debatable, let's examine King David, often described as a man after God's own heart. Despite his notorious actions detailed in 2 Samuel 11, it's widely believed that he is in heaven. David, at one point, was both a murderer and an adulterer. Therefore, David's example suggests that even someone with such past deeds can enter heaven.

Peter implies that Christians facing earthly consequences, particularly for serious offenses like murder, theft, and slander, is beneficial. If God holds believers accountable for their actions as His children, then the judgment for those who are not His children will likely be more severe. However, it's crucial to clarify that the punishment God's children receive is not necessarily as intense as Hell. While believers can face consequences and discipline from God, the ultimate punishment of Hell is reserved for those who reject God's grace and salvation entirely.

THE FIERY HELL

How should we interpret Matthew 5:22b? "And whoever says, 'You fool,' shall be guilty enough to go into the fiery hell." Are we talking about the eternal Hell or Gehenna?

At first glance, some may believe it suggests that believers could face severe punishment, even eternal Hell, for speaking badly about someone or, as a future chapter will explore, for lustful thoughts, etc. This extreme notion of being cast into Hell for such actions may seem like an exaggerated punishment. However, delving deeper into the historical context of Jesus's words illuminates the original textual meaning before any translational changes occurred.

According to A. T. Robertson, the term "fiery hell" in this verse refers to Gehenna, a valley outside Jerusalem used as a garbage dump, where fires were continually burning to consume refuse; he distinguishes this from Hades and the Lake of Fire, which is considered the place of eternal judgement.[22] Jesus often used Gehenna as a metaphor to illustrate the consequences of sin and unrighteousness.

HATE = MURDER

We've acknowledged that believers are capable of committing murder, a distressing reality that I hope, echoing Paul's words, never becomes a reality among us (Ephesians 5:3). However, let's delve deeper into this notion: can a believer harbor hatred? The answer is yes, though it's not something they should.

Jesus says in 5:22 this type of talk is useless and stands condemned to be thrown into Gehenna. James similarly tells believers, "And the tongue is a fire, the *very* world of iniquity; the tongue is set among our members as that which defiles the entire body, and sets on fire the course of *our* life, and is set on fire by hell (James 3:6)." Confusion has surrounded this passage because many translations translated the word

---

22. Archibald Thomas Robertson, *Word Pictures in the New Testament Vol. I*, (Nashville, TN: Broadman Press, 1930), 44.

as Hell, but when speaking of the physical location of Hell as an eternal torment for the unbelieving and demonic forces Gehenna is not Jesus's choice. Scripture usually calls that Hades—*ado* or *ades* (Matthew 11:23; 16:18; and most noteworthy the account of Lazarus and the rich man in Luke 16:23). The other word used of the place of eternal suffering is Hell—*Tartarōsas* (2 Peter 2:4). But here in this passage, the word translated Hell that Jesus uses is the word Gehenna, which is a real physical place, the southwest valley of Jerusalem.[23] Indeed, Gehenna held a significant meaning for the Jewish people. It was situated between two mountains, forming a valley known as Hinnom. The city disposed of its waste, trash, unclean objects, dead animals, and even excrement there, setting it ablaze to mitigate the foul odor. This practice provides a vivid backdrop to Jesus's teachings, adding depth to His warnings about the consequences of certain behaviors.[24] In the Old Testament times, Hinnom was where people took unclean things to purify in the fires if they were not destroyed in the burning or throw them out if they were of non-use.[25]

> "[Gehenna] became the common lay-stall garbage dump of the city, where the dead bodies of criminals, and the carcasses of animals, and every other kind of filth was cast."[26]

The Hinnom Valley or Gehenna was where the Jews betrayed Yahweh and worshipped the god Molech that demanded infant sacrifice.

> He also defiled Topheth, which is in the Valley of the Son of Hinnom, so that no one would make his son or his daughter pass through the fire for Molech. (2 Kings 23:10)

---

23. Joseph Thayer, *Thayer's Greek-English Lexicon of the New Testament*. (Peabody, MA.: Hendrickson, 2007), 111.
24. https://thebiblesays.com/commentary/dig-deeper/gehenna-hell-hades/
25. Jody Dillow, *Final Destiny: The Future Reign of the Servant Kings* (Woodlands, Tx: Grace Theology Press, 2016), 875-909.
26. https://www.newworldencyclopedia.org/entry/gehenna

Because of the association to pagan worship of Demon gods, the Jews saw Gehenna as an accursed ground.

GEHENNA WAS A REAL PLACE

Gehenna indeed served as a physical location where the city's waste and useless items were discarded, not to be confused with the eternal place of torment known as Hell. It was essentially the sewer of ancient times.

When Jesus addressed His followers, His disciples, He cautioned them that speaking gossip or wicked words against others was akin to contributing to a dumpster fire, adding useless excrement to the heap. In Matthew 12:36, Jesus emphasizes that believers will give an account for every idle word, including what could be considered "sewer talk." This passage encourages believers to purify themselves and advance the kingdom by ridding themselves of hate, eliminating hateful speech and lust from their lives.

Fire is often associated with purification, as seen in Malachi 4, which speaks of the future cleansing of the earth, a theme echoed in 2 Peter 3:7 and 10. According to Hebrews 12:29, the earth and all its inhabitants will be judged and cleansed by fire in preparation for the establishment of a new heaven and earth, as described in Revelation 21:1. Similarly, believers undergo a refining process through the fires of building faith and purifying actions in anticipation of receiving rewards (1 Peter 4:12-17; 1 Corinthians 3:12-15).

A parallel passage to this concept is found in Mark 9:38-50, where Jesus discusses the rewards of discipleship tested by the fires of Gehenna, determining whether one's actions are useful or useless. This imagery underscores the importance of examining our words and deeds.

In response, Jesus describes a scene where people are gathered, salted, and fired, where the worm does not die, and the fire does not end. This imagery can be understood in various ways. It may reflect the purification process of a body for burial, where bodies were placed in the caves of the Hinnom Valley until only bones remained. Alternatively, it could allude to the preparation of pottery, where clay was salted to remove moisture and fired to ensure it could hold oils, waters, and wines without cracking. Regardless of the interpretation, the underlying message remains consistent: this is not a condemnation to Hell, but rather a solemn acknowledgment of the sorrow caused by sinful thoughts and the necessity of preventing sinful actions and purifying your life to remain in fellowship.

As Robert Doran states,

> "Most scholars have suggested that just as salt preserves meat, fish, etc., so fire preserves. The fire seen as purging, not consuming, is found frequently. The most straightforward argument was put forward by Julius Wellhausen:
>
> But here the fire is not Hellfire, but a purging fire (*Fegefeuer*) that everyone has to undergo, that consumes only the worst in him/her, but on the other hand precisely preserves the good, the essential, and so has the action of salt.

Doran continues to state the case for Gehenna being a place of cleansing and not of eternal condemnation by stating the similarities Lightfoot noted in Isaiah 66:24 as a reference to Mark 9:48. He continues:

> Πᾶς, *all*, is not to be understood of every man, but of every one of them "whose worm dieth not," &c. ... Carcasses crawl with worms; and instead of salt which secures against worms, they shall be cast into the fire, and shall be seasoned with flames, and yet the worms shall not die. But he that is a true sacrifice to God shall be seasoned with the salt of grace to the incorruption of glory.
>
> Derrett further suggested that salt and fire/heat were used in antiquity to cauterize wounds such as the amputations proposed in Mark 9:43–47."[27]

---

27. Robert Doran, *Salting with Fire*, Novum Testamentum 62 (2020) 363, 364.

NOT HELL BUT A PLACE FOR USELESS THINGS

From these teachings, it's clear that the disciples, and indeed all believers, aren't under the threat of eternal damnation from sin. Why would Jesus call them to a form of penitence, atonement, or payment for something He fully intends to address and atone for Himself? No, this is a summon to resist temptations and wrestle with sin before it takes root and inflicts further harm. It's about purifying oneself in the metaphorical fires of Gehenna, or as 1 John 1:9 instructs, seeking forgiveness for the sins we recognize, knowing that He is faithful to cleanse and restore our relationship. Jesus emphasizes the importance of maintaining close accounts in our relationships.

When someone harbors hatred towards their brother or speaks evil against them, Jesus suggests that they're squandering their life; they should instead discard such negativity and purify themselves. It's far preferable to experience a moment of painful remorse for speaking ill than to endure the profound loss of friendship, damage to one's relationship with the Lord, community, and the future repercussions. It's easier to repent and rid oneself of a harmful thought now than to face the remorse, pain, judgment, and consequences of sin later. The call is clear: choose love over hate.

Jesus taught that if hate resides in your heart or if evil manifests in your speech, it's imperative to halt whatever you're doing. Whether it's serving the Lord, participating in communion, engaging in worship, or studying the Bible, if you recall a wrongdoing against your brother, pause and make amends.

> Therefore, if you are presenting your offering at the altar, and there you remember that your brother has something against you, leave your offering there before the altar and go; first be reconciled to your brother, and then come and present your offering (Matthew 5:23-24).

Jesus extends the principle even further. He says if someone dislikes you, go make friends, make peace with them. God wants our inward man to be one of love and peace with others—a heart that thinks of how we can impact someone's life for Christ and not how to crush someone with our thoughts, speech, and actions. A follower should be focused on how to help rather than how to hurt. The better view of the Gehenna passages of the New Testament should be a disciple cleansing sin for relationship restoration, and in other uses as a Pharisee or false teacher as being useless (i.e., Matthew 23:15, 33; Mark 9:43) and not the fiery pits of Hell.

YOU ARE JUDGED

There are five times in Matthew 5:21–26 that Jesus mentions judgment, court, or a type of punishment for harboring hate in the heart. The only time in Scripture that we see a believer stand in a type of judgment to give account is at the Judgment/Bema Seat of Jesus, also known as the Reward Seat, and it also mentions fire like Gehenna.

> Now if any man builds on the foundation with gold, silver, precious stones, wood, hay, straw, each man's work will become evident; for the day will show it because it is *to be* revealed with fire, and the fire itself will test the quality of each man's work. If any man's work which he has built on it remains, he will receive a reward. If any man's work is burned up, he will suffer loss; but he himself will be saved, yet so as through fire (1 Corinthians 3:12–15).

In this passage, it's indicated that worthless actions carried out during our lifetime will be consumed by fire, while the good deeds will be rewarded. This aligns with the concept presented in Matthew 5. Therefore, it stands to reason that worthless words will also be subject to judgment and burn up at the Bema Seat.

The word *test* (*dokimazo*) in 1 Corinthians 3 means to assess for approval or authenticity. I recall a high school experience when I bought a pair of Oakley sunglasses from the back of someone's car for twenty dollars. At the time, they retailed for around one hundred dollars, so I thought it was a great deal. However, upon closer inspection, I realized the "O" logo wasn't authentic. I ended up with a pair of what we called "foakleys"—fake Oakleys. They failed the test. As believers, our salvation is secure; however, our actions will be evaluated to determine their reward.

Paul states the quality of a man's work is revealed by fire. Quality (*hopoios*) is a correlative and qualitative pronoun that means a sort or kind. The Lord will test the quality of each believer's work to see the intentions. Did you work for the Lord or selfish ambition? Matthew 5:16 says, "so men see and glorify our Father in heaven." Were our works done for earthly merit, for our own satisfaction and pride, or for His kingdom and glory?

Something special about the word *test* (*dokimazo*) in 1 Corinthians 3 means to assess for approval or authenticity and the term was largely used for money. You see, back in ancient times, they didn't use paper money; they used silver, gold, and other metals. The merchants would shave metal off the coins and remelt the excess gold or silver to deceive people, essentially robbing them of the genuine value. The situation became so severe that Athens enacted eighty different laws against this practice. However, some honest sellers chose not to engage in this deception and instead used scales to demonstrate the authenticity of their currency, while also testing that of others. God is asking us to be faithful to His word. Let's keep it pure and never diminish its integrity.

> Therefore do not go on passing judgment before the time, *but wait* until the Lord comes who will both bring to light the things hidden in the darkness and disclose the motives of *men's* hearts; and then each man's praise will come to him from God (1 Corinthians 4:5).

Judgment is coming, but it is not for us to give.

> For we must all appear before the judgment seat of Christ, so that each one may be recompensed for his deeds in the body, according to what he has done, whether good or bad (2 Corinthians 5:10).
>
> Behold, I am coming quickly, and My reward *is* with Me, to render to every man according to what he has done (Revelation 22:12).

We are not rewarded with eternal life because eternal life is a gift given freely, without cost. There are no late fees, shipping and handling charges, and no contract or extended warranty required. If it had a cost to us or could be lost, the words used to describe salvation throughout Scripture like "gift" and "eternal" would be deceptive.

There is an aspect of a believer's life that is costly and requires effort. Certain aspects of the Christian walk can be lost or taken away. Your reward is based on the life you choose, a life of a disciple serving, representing, and noticing the hurt, oppressed, and outcast. A rewarding life is one that decides to take action, and though it may entail hardship and struggles, they ultimately lead to reward.

On the flip side, there is a life of self-serving gratification, indifferent to the hurt and needs of others. Across his three epistles, John emphasizes how our unity, love, and interactions with one another shape our relationship with God. Simply put, when we demonstrate love towards others, it is God's love flowing through us—a manifestation of fellowship.

> Watch yourselves, that you do not lose what we have accomplished, but that you may receive a full reward. Anyone who goes too far and does not abide in the teaching of Christ, does not have God; the one who abides in the teaching, he has both the Father and the Son. If anyone comes to you and does not bring this teaching, do not receive him into *your* house, and do not give him a greeting; for the one who gives him a greeting participates in his evil deeds (2 John 1:8).

John is saying, do not lose your reward in heaven. Do not lose the celebrated arrival for fleeting pleasure.

The writer of Hebrews says: "And without faith it is impossible to please *Him,* for he who comes to God must believe that He is and *that* He is a rewarder of those who seek Him" (Hebrews 11:6).

KEEP YOUR MIND & ACTIONS CONTROLLED TO KEEP YOUR REWARD

Jesus wants us to live at peace and in love for one another. He wants us to live as disciples under the command of love looking forward to His arrival and reward. He wants us to live in such a way as we read in the last chapter, that we have a glorious entrance into the kingdom, and He wants us to live inwardly righteous in step with Him letting our love show outwardly. Think and pray before you act, speak, write, or hit send. Make friends with your enemies and live with love in your heart for the family of God.

CHAPTER 16
EYE MAKES YOU STUMBLE

"If your right eye makes you stumble, tear it out and throw it from you; for it is better for you to lose one of the parts of your body, than for your whole body to be thrown into hell."
—Matthew 5:29

When I was in high school, my weightlifting coach told us a story of the day he arrived in Vietnam. He said he (in his early twenties) had recently finished special training and had reported to a superior officer for some further field training. The superior officer began telling him and his fellow soldiers all about the tunneling that the Viet Cong had become known for and how they tethered themselves to trees for surprise attacks. The officer showed them things they could and could not eat. He taught them which snakes to avoid. Just as he was handling one of the snakes, it bit his finger! The man immediately took out his knife and chopped off the finger. He applied a tourniquet and said better to lose a finger than his life and walked away to the medical tent. My weightlifting coach said all of them realized at that moment the seriousness of their fight.

We are in a serious war. Except ours is one being waged for souls, and it is not about losing a finger.

> You have heard that it was said, "YOU SHALL NOT COMMIT ADULTERY'; but I say to you that everyone who looks at a woman with lust for her has already committed adultery with her in his heart. If your right eye makes you stumble, tear it out and throw it from you; for it is better for you to lose one of the parts of your body, than for your whole body to be thrown into hell. If your right hand makes you stumble, cut it off and throw it from you; for it is better for you to lose one of the parts of your body, than for your whole body to go into hell. It was said, "WHOEVER SENDS HIS WIFE AWAY, LET HIM GIVE HER A CERTIFICATE OF DIVORCE"; but I say to you that everyone who divorces his wife, except for *the* reason of unchastity, makes her commit adultery; and whoever marries a divorced woman commits adultery (Matthew 5:27–32).

BURNING

Once again, we are confronted with Gehenna, but let's draw our understanding from the previous chapter, not of eternal Hell, but as a place for useless and rotten things to be cleansed by fire. Some believe that the ancient Hebrews and Semitic people would go to the Hinnom Valley when mourning sin. Psalm 84:6 uses illustrative language to show that God has seen a repentant heart and stopped the fires in the valley. In the valley of Baca, there is soothing rain. Job, unsure why he was afflicted, dressed in sackcloth, went out of the city and sat on the ash heap. God told Jeremiah to prophesy of repentance from the gate of broken pots in the valley of Ben-Hinnom, or Gehenna, in Jeremiah 19. With that in mind, cleansing your eyes before falling makes much more sense than going to hell for looking at something wrong. Jesus says it's better to lose sight than to compromise purity. He transitions from the eye to the hand, advising to cleanse your hand before it causes your entire body to fall.

I once listened to a preacher discuss this passage, but unfortunately, he took it out of context by declaring it was about maintaining salvation through works. Instead, the passages teaching underscores the seriousness of sin and the radical steps needed to combat it. Misconstruing it to suggest salvation through works distorts its true message and could indeed lead to widespread misunderstanding and extreme actions.

But this passage is not about salvation; it pertains to reward, growth, and discipleship. With discipleship and growth in mind, the meaning shifts, conveying that it is better to endure deprivation on earth than to forfeit rewards you have earned in heaven.

BETTER TO GO WITHOUT THAN LOSE OUT AT THE END

Jesus and Paul have similar ideas when it comes to earning a crown of righteousness.

> Do you not know that those who run in a race all run, but *only* one receives the prize? Run in such a way that you may win. Everyone who competes in the games exercises self-control in all things. They then *do it* to receive a perishable wreath, but we an imperishable. Therefore I run in such a way, as not without aim; I box in such a way, as not beating the air; but I discipline my body and make it my slave, so that, after I have preached to others, I myself will not be disqualified (1 Corinthians 9:24–27).

Better is the end than the beginning of a race, because only then do we know who won. It is not the person with the best start and form off the block that wins the race. Let us consider why athletes get removed the competition.
- Cheating
- Being out of bounds

- Using performance enhancers
- Giving up
- Muscle problems

Athletes train both mentally and physically to overcome weaknesses and surpass the competition, and gain a reward. Their goal isn't merely to finish but to win. As 2 Timothy 2:5 states, "Also, if anyone competes as an athlete, he does not win the prize unless he competes according to the rules."

When Paul speaks of "rules" (*nomimōs*), he refers to the oath taken to train and compete. It was a promise sworn to abide by the regulations of training and competition.

Why do so many Christians that are trying to build something in God's name lose their testimony? For the same reasons an athlete fails; they are not staying within the guidelines. There is a reason why Paul paints this strong analogy between Christian life and athletics. "For this reason I endure all things for the sake of those who are chosen" (2 Timothy 2:10).

Paul emphasizes the concept of endurance, similar to the athletic term *upomenō*, which refers to showing perseverance and stamina. Just as athletes build endurance through rigorous training, believers cultivate endurance through consistent dedication to spiritual discipline. Winning in life, like in sports, requires sustained effort and commitment. Just as athletes devote themselves to training their bodies, believers train their minds through immersion in God's word and worship, preparing themselves for life's challenges.

THE ETERNAL REWARDS

Paul says in 1 Corinthians 9:25 that we work for the imperishable. As Jesus says in Matthew 6:20, our reward is in heaven.

Paul shows the contrast in the world. The world is perishing. It is fading and forgotten. Perishable (*phtharton*) means to decay or fall apart. This decaying is the reward from the world. It is the prize of living life for self; self pays you in fading and forgotten currency that moth and rust destroy (Matthew 6:19).

God gives an imperishable (*aphtharton*) reward, meaning a superior, lasting wreath. This prize is alpha. It cannot be lost, taken, decay, or fade. When your life is lived for the Lord, it is never forgotten. When you act for the Lord, it is never without reason. When you speak on behalf of the Lord, every word carries weight and significance, for He observes, remembers, and ultimately rewards.

CHRISTIAN A.D.D.

Many Christians today seem to lack the right focus in life. They live as if this present life is all there is, but Paul warns against such a perspective. He likens it to shadow boxing: it may appear impressive momentarily, but ultimately, it lacks substance. Running aimlessly may lead you somewhere eventually, but it will take longer and come at a greater cost. Living solely for oneself or for the pursuits of this world is like engaging in endless, directionless races.

In 1 Corinthians 9:24, Paul urges us to "run to win." This means seizing victory, maintaining focus, and not losing sight of our goal. We must remain balanced and avoid disqualification in our life's testimony. Paul later speaks of the crown he diligently pursued, disciplined himself for, and fought to attain.

> For I am already being poured out as a drink offering, and the time of my departure has come. I have fought the good fight, I have finished the course, I have kept the faith; in the future there is laid up for me the crown of righteousness, which the Lord, the righteous Judge, will award to me on that day; and not only to me, but also to all who have loved His appearing (2 Timothy 4:6–8).

Paul said he trained so he would not get disqualified from his life of serving for Jesus.

Paul is saying he would rather lose worldly pleasure than lose his testimony because of a fleshly vice, and Jesus is saying it is better to go without on earth to receive heavenly gain.

You can see why Paul says the Christian life is a fight. The word *fight* is from the Greek word *agōna*. We get our English word *agony* from it. It means to get into a deep muscle wrenching struggle. We are to strive to keep the faith--to do what is right.

People often wrestle with pursuits that ultimately hold little significance. They toil for long hours at work to acquire a larger home and a more luxurious car, but in doing so, they sacrifice precious time with their family. They strive to present themselves in a certain way to impress others, yet in the process, they forfeit their identity in Christ.

YOU CANNOT RUN FOR THE WORLD WHILE CHASING CHRIST

Similarly, in Matthew 5, Jesus is saying it is better to go without staring, lusting, touching, and cheating than to lose out in the kingdom. Jesus is not suggesting self-mutilation in order to stay pure. He is not saying someone that lusts will go to hell. The word is Gehenna, which was the place outside the city for burning refuse. It was also a place where Jews went when they were showing remorse for sin or perceived sin. Jesus is saying it is better to pluck out your eye that wanders than suffer pains in Gehenna.

Jesus is saying that it is better for you to reject the pleasure of the eyes, the pleasure of sexual sin, than to have all you strive for in the kingdom lost. Oh, but friend, there is hope yet because we have already been forgiven. Our advocate, Jesus, cleanses us, our eyes, ears, hands, and mind. He helps us as we embark on our agony to stay pure, in the fight to keep our testimony, and in the struggle to keep clean.

> If we say that we have fellowship with Him and *yet* walk in the darkness, we lie and do not practice the truth; but if we walk in the Light as He Himself is in the Light, we have fellowship with one another, and the blood of Jesus His Son

cleanses us from all sin. If we say that we have no sin, we are deceiving ourselves and the truth is not in us. If we confess our sins, He is faithful and righteous to forgive us our sins and to cleanse us from all unrighteousness. If we say that we have not sinned, we make Him a liar and His word is not in us (1 John 1:8–10).

John, the disciple of Jesus, tells us fellowship with the Lord is restored when we acknowledge our sin, when we are aligning ourselves with God's desire for purity in our lives and seek reconciliation. God, who is pure light, cannot coexist with darkness stemming from wicked deeds and intentions. Therefore, to mend our relationship with Him, we must humbly seek forgiveness for our transgressions.

If you say you have no sin, you lie. Remember Jesus's definition of sin in Matthew 5. It is not just acting out on lust. It is not just touching or doing. It is thinking and looking. So do not say just because your actions haven't mirrored the mind that you are pure, because your mind is not pure.

But if you cleanse your mind and your eyes (as Jesus says "thrown in Gehenna"), if you remember your sin and ask for cleansing and forgiveness, Jesus *will* forgive. It is better to remove the sin than stay in what separates from fellowship with Jesus.

John defines the process of cleansing. If my eye causes me to sin, talk to the Lord about it, ask for cleansing in the struggle to stay the course, and receive the crown of righteousness, purity, and right standing.

CHAPTER 17

YOUR STATEMENT

"Again, you have heard that the ancients were told, 'YOU SHALL NOT MAKE FALSE VOWS, BUT SHALL FULFILL YOUR VOWS TO THE LORD.' But I say to you, make no oath at all, either by heaven, for it is the throne of God, or by the earth, for it is the footstool of His feet, or by Jerusalem, for it is THE CITY OF THE GREAT KING. Nor shall you make an oath by your head, for you cannot make one hair white or black. But let your statement be, 'Yes, yes' or 'No, no'; anything beyond these is of evil."
—Matthew 5:33-37

Do you remember the childhood trick of "getting out of things" by crossing your fingers? You'd make a promise, but then slyly cross your eyes, fingers, or toes to nullify it. Yet, despite this clever tactic, the end result was often frustration and a loss of trust from those around you.

Similarly, people eventually had to stop relying on handshakes to seal agreements because, sadly, a handshake wasn't legally binding like paperwork in a court of law. However, for a believer striving to emulate Christ, He calls us to be people of our word.

> Again, you have heard that the ancients were told, "YOU SHALL NOT MAKE FALSE VOWS, BUT SHALL FULFILL YOUR VOWS TO THE LORD." But I say to you, make no oath at all, either by heaven, for it is the throne of God, or by the earth, for it is the footstool of His feet, or by Jerusalem, for it is THE CITY OF THE GREAT KING. Nor shall you make an oath by your head, for you cannot make one hair white or black (Matthew 5:33–37).

In this passage, much like in Matthew 5:21–26 ("you shall not commit murder"), Jesus highlights what the Law states. He enumerates what people might have heard interpreted by the rabbis, and He concludes with the truth of what God desires. He penetrates to the heart of the matter. Jesus (Matthew 5:33) states that according to the Law, one should not swear before God or use His name in an oath (Leviticus 19:12, Numbers 30:2, Deuteronomy 23:21–23).

That is the Law concerning interactions with others, but Jesus aims to address the heart, striking at the very place where people knew their holy men had fallen short. In Matthew 15:1–11, Jesus exposes how the religious leaders of the time were causing harm with their external practices, religious rituals, and outward displays of mental and physical purity. However, inwardly, they were corrupt and devoid of God's law to love Him and others.

He says in Matthew 5:34–36: "But I say to you, make no oath at all, either by heaven, for it is the throne of God, or by the earth, for it is the footstool of His feet, or by Jerusalem, for it is THE CITY OF THE GREAT KING. Nor shall you make an oath by your head, for you cannot make one hair white or black." Why did He say that? Because the Pharisees had a particular way of making oaths that they knew they could break.

DOES NOT COUNT

In the times of Jesus, the Talmud, Mishnah, and writing in the Sanhedrin said that when you made a binding oath, it was sworn "by the life of your head." It could be sworn by the life of your children's living head or father's living head as well. The idea was to have the phrase 'living head' in the oath for it to be binding. But the Pharisees would mingle words to get away with lies, and the group approved it because the individual should have caught the trick. The Pharisees would swear by their head and not by their *living* head and because the words were not exact, it was not seen as binding.

> A defendant, having been sentenced to deny by oath the claims of the plaintiff, obtains a concession from the latter, who declares, "Vow thou by the life of thy head". But now the plaintiff wants to withdraw the concession and insist on the original oath. This is granted by R. Meir, but not by his contemporaries. This Halakha clearly shows that the legal oath was different from such expressions as "by thy head" which were used in ordinary speech for the sake of asseveration. The former was regarded as superior in binding force to the latter-at least so in popular opinion. But it also shows that the rabbis regarded such a vow, if intended as such, to be legally binding in monetary affairs, and that no trifling was allowed with such formulae of oath.[28]

The omission of one word can indeed change the meaning of something. Not too long ago, I took my son to the Colombian bakery down the street to get some freshly made *pan de bono* and empanadas

---

28. Jacob Mann, "Oaths and Vows in the Synoptic Gospels," *The American Journal of Theology*, 21, no. 2 (April 1917), 263.

for lunch. Before we left, my son asked if we could have a favorite treat from there called a *pan de bono de guava*. It's a cheese bread filled with jammed guava paste, so delicious but very sugary. My wife responded with a resounding "no" because the kids each had a slight cough, and she didn't want that to escalate. So, no sugar in the house.

When we got to the bakery, my son decided to ask again if he could get one of those treats. I said, "No, mom said no sugar at home; you guys are sick." He looked at me with a grin and said, "She said not in the house; she said nothing about eating sugar in the car!" One word can indeed change the meaning and outcome of things.

A FOLLOWER OF CHRIST SHOULD STICK TO THEIR WORD

In Matthew 23, Jesus lets us see the tricks of the scribes and Pharisees.

> Woe to you, blind guides, who say, "Whoever swears by the temple, *that* is nothing; but whoever swears by the gold of the temple is obligated." You fools and blind men! Which is more important, the gold or the temple that sanctified the gold? And, "Whoever swears by the altar, *that* is nothing, but whoever swears by the offering on it, he is obligated." You blind men, which is more important, the offering, or the altar that sanctifies the offering? Therefore, whoever swears by the altar, swears *both* by the altar and by everything on it. And whoever swears by the temple, swears *both* by the temple and by Him who dwells within it. And whoever swears by heaven, swears *both* by the throne of God and by Him who sits upon it (Matthew 23:16–22).

Once again, Jesus reveals how they were deceiving others with their words. Saying, "I swear by the temple" was considered acceptable to break, but if one swore by the temple gold, it was deemed obligatory. Similarly, swearing by the altar was permissible to break, but if one swore by the sacrifice on the altar, it was binding. They were manipulating their words to deceive people and were thus appearing as hypocrites before God.

But Jesus did not want His followers to use word games in life. He wanted His people to be known as honest and people of their word. So, Jesus is saying in this statement that the people of God should be known for their word not trickiness.

Christ-followers should be known for "yes" or "no", not "well my eyes were crossed, and my tongue was tied so it does not count".

James says the same thing in James 5 but explains why: "But above all, my brethren, do not swear, either by heaven or by earth or with any other oath; but your yes is to be yes, and your no, no, so that you may not fall under judgment" (James 5:12).

The phrase "fall under judgment" in most Greek manuscripts (i.e., the Majority Text and 1550 Textus Receptus) is *eis hupocretes*, meaning "fall into hypocrisy." This suggests a believer deviating from this will be seen as a hypocrite or a fake. When someone does not stand true to their word, they are a hypocrite; they say one thing and do another. "But who honors those who fear the LORD; He swears to his own hurt and does not change" (Psalm 15:4b).

A person who honors the Lord, when they make a promise, follows through, even if they regret it or it becomes difficult to fulfill later. This demonstrates letting your word stand for itself, living as a person with integrity. "Do not let kindness and truth leave you; Bind them around your neck, Write them on the tablet of your heart. So you will find favor and good repute in the sight of God and man" (Proverbs 3:3–4). To be a person of reputation and integrity, bind truth around you.

LIES COME FROM THE LIAR

If you are being deceitful, you are not in alignment with the Lord's will. Look at Matthew 5:37: "But let your statement be, 'Yes, yes' *or* 'No, no'; anything beyond these is of evil."

From the original Greek, the evil, or the evil one, is a term used many times in the New Testament for Satan. Jesus says,

> You are of *your* father the devil, and you want to do the desires of your father. He was a murderer from the beginning, and does not stand in the truth because there is no truth in him. Whenever he speaks a lie, he speaks from his own *nature,* for he is a liar and the father of lies. But because I speak the truth, you do not believe Me (John 8:44–45).

The word lie is *pseudomai.* We get the word *pseudonym* from it. A pseudonym is a fictitious name. *Pseudomai* means to give false information or disguise the truth.

In Genesis 3 in the garden, Satan disguised the truth from Eve; he gave enough truth to confuse her and trick her into believing what he wanted her to believe. Jesus says (Matthew 5:37) if you mince words to confuse people, that is like using the tricks of Satan.

The practice of using oaths to confuse people and break them, as well as employing sayings that conceal the truth, is not from God. This is hypocritical living, and as Matthew 6 informs us, hypocrites seek earthly rewards. They rely on what the world can offer rather than turning to the Lord for sustenance.

But before we chew up and spit out people that swear and don't follow through, consider Peter that looked like a hypocrite in the eyes of the crowd and the eyes of the other disciples.

> Then Jesus said to them, "You will all fall away because of Me this night, for it is written, 'I WILL STRIKE DOWN THE SHEPHERD, AND THE SHEEP OF THE FLOCK SHALL BE SCATTERED.' But after I have been raised, I will go ahead of you to Galilee." But Peter said to Him, "*Even* though all may fall away because of You, I will never fall away."

YOUR STATEMENT

Jesus said to him, "Truly I say to you that this *very* night, before a rooster crows, you will deny Me three times." Peter said to Him, "Even if I have to die with You, I will not deny You." All the disciples said the same thing too (Matthew 26:31–35).

We read about that same night as Peter followed by the wayside in the darkness, after swearing to his own life, that he would rather die than reject Jesus:

And again he denied *it* with an oath, "I do not know the man." A little later the bystanders came up and said to Peter, "Surely you too are *one* of them; for even the way you talk gives you away." Then he began to curse and swear, "I do not know the man!" And immediately a rooster crowed. And Peter remembered the word which Jesus had said, "Before a rooster crows, you will deny Me three times." And he went out and wept bitterly (Matthew 26:72–75).

Friend, while we may never swear against Jesus or claim we never knew Him, our actions, speech, and lifestyle can sometimes make us appear hypocritical. However, just like Peter, Jesus sees beyond outward appearances and looks into our hearts. It's never too late to begin anew in Christ. In Jesus's eyes, He sees our hearts, just as He saw Peter's, and that's how He looks at each one of us.

Guard your tongue. Be mindful of your words. Let your "yes" be "yes" and your "no" be "no". Let your actions and life reflect Jesus. Jesus desires that honor emanates from the heart of His followers.

CHAPTER 18

GO THE EXTRA MILE

"Whoever forces you to go one mile, go with him two."
—Matthew 5:41

We all appreciate excellent customer service, don't we? It's wonderful when service comes with a smile and the person is gracious. And let's be honest, we love it when they go the extra mile. Like the other day, I visited the bakery, and because the *pan de yuccas* were small, the lady threw in two more for good measure. It really made my day. When we receive more than we expect, it brings us joy. We're inclined to leave a glowing Google or Facebook review, praising them for exceeding customer satisfaction. "They went above and beyond with their service."

But why does that matter to us? While we expect to receive what we pay for or what is required, it's truly a blessing to receive more than expected. In reality, this aligns with a biblical principle.

> You have heard that it was said, "AN EYE FOR AN EYE, AND A TOOTH FOR A TOOTH." But I say to you, do not resist an evil person; but whoever slaps you on your right cheek, turn

the other to him also. If anyone wants to sue you and take your shirt, let him have your coat also. Whoever forces you to go one mile, go with him two. Give to him who asks of you, and do not turn away from him who wants to borrow from you (Matthew 5:38–42).

Jesus is affirming the principle of just retribution in the Law (Matthew 5:39). He is quoting from Leviticus 24:17–20. It's essentially the principle of fairness: "I owed you three apples, so I gave you three apples; you killed my donkey, you owe me a donkey."

> If a man takes the life of any human being, he shall surely be put to death. The one who takes the life of an animal shall make it good, life for life. If a man injures his neighbor, just as he has done, so it shall be done to him: fracture for fracture, eye for eye, tooth for tooth; just as he has injured a man, so it shall be inflicted on him. Thus the one who kills an animal shall make it good, but the one who kills a man shall be put to death. There shall be one standard for you; it shall be for the stranger as well as the native, for I am the LORD your God. Then Moses spoke to the sons of Israel, and they brought the one who had cursed outside the camp and stoned him with stones. Thus the sons of Israel did, just as the LORD had commanded Moses (Leviticus 24:17–23).

This passage draws attention to the principle of fairness. If I accidentally kill your ox, I owe you an ox—fair compensation for the loss. It also stresses treating foreigners with the same fairness as required for a neighbor. God was essentially saying that His people shouldn't have to resort to lawsuits to ensure fairness. Whether you are a Jew or Greek, living in the land or elsewhere, you should receive what is due to you. This law was crucial because in other lands, foreigners were often mistreated, seen as second class, and taken advantage of. However, in the Land of Promise, in the land claimed by Yahweh, this injustice should not be tolerated.

ONE RULE FOR YOU AND ONE FOR ME

Jesus extends the principle of fairness and justice beyond mere material compensation, as seen in the "eye for an eye" principle, to a higher standard of love and selflessness. He goes beyond the concept of equal retribution for Jews and Gentiles. Jesus teaches us to go the extra mile, to give beyond what is required, and to respond to aggression with forgiveness and grace. The term "extra mile" originates from the Greek word *angareia*, which refers to forced service.

What Jesus was addressing pertained to the governance of the Romans. Under Roman rule, anyone born in Rome or considered property of Rome was granted Roman citizenship. However, Jerusalem stood apart from this system. The Jewish people rejected Roman citizenship, affirming Israel as their land, God as their king, and Jerusalem as their capital. Consequently, Jerusalem operated as an annex of Rome, allowing Herod to rule to maintain peace. However, the residents of Jerusalem were still subject to Roman authority. Rome even installed a puppet king in Herod, whom the Jews didn't fully accept due to his lack of familial ties to David. This arrangement also meant that the Romans did not have to treat the Jews as equals. This is precisely why, in Acts 16:22–24, when the Roman authorities beat Silas and Paul, they became fearful upon discovering that they were Roman citizens. According to Roman law, a Roman citizen could not be subjected to criminal punishment without undergoing a trial by Roman officials. It was the responsibility of the centurion to ensure that the soldiers adhered to specific regulations regarding the treatment of nationals and non-nationals. There were defined rules for citizens and non-citizens.[29]

---

29. Wyatt Sawyer, "Two Mile Teenagers," Harding University (1964), https://scholarworks.harding.edu/wyatt-sawyer-sermons/574/.

When Paul asserted to the magistrates upon being released that he refused to leave because he was a Roman citizen and his rights had been violated, they were terrified (Acts 16:35–40) because they would be subject to punishment for not following Roman law.

Foreigners had very few rights under Roman law. Consequently, unaware of their citizenship, they had promptly stripped off Paul and Silas's clothing and publicly flogged them as a form of public humiliation.

Under the Roman system of unequal treatment, the Jews in Judea were often exploited. They faced double taxation and lacked representation in laws, regulations, and courts. Roman soldiers took advantage of the Jews' vulnerable position; non-citizen Jews were compelled to carry their heavy packs, weighing up to sixty pounds, without the ability to protest. They were required to comply as foreigners.

This context sheds light on the scene in Matthew 27:27–32, where Jesus, unable to carry His cross any longer, was assisted by Simon. Simon was compelled by law to comply with the Roman soldiers' demand. Though the specifics are not precisely documented, most historians suggest that this law of forced aid to soldiers was limited to one mile.

GO ABOVE AND BEYOND

Jesus is conveying that the Law in Leviticus instructs to provide what is just and fair. While Roman law mandates carrying whatever a Roman soldier commands for one mile, living as salt and light entails surpassing both Jewish law and Roman occupation law. To demonstrate that disciples are not solely governed by legal obligations but also by love, Jesus instructs them to go the extra mile. He says, "Whoever forces you to go one mile, go with him two. Give to him who asks of you, and do not turn away from him who wants to borrow from you." This exemplifies a spirit of generosity and selflessness that transcends mere legal requirements.

Jesus is instructing the disciples on living as followers of Christ: fulfill the requirements of the law but recognize that going beyond is a blessing. While everyone should adhere to what the law mandates, going further out of care enhances one's testimony. Thus, fulfilling an obligation and then exceeding it can serve as an opportunity to demonstrate the love of Christ.

Do you know what happens when we embrace this approach? Going the extra mile often elicits the question "why?" Why go above and beyond? Why offer more than expected? Why show kindness and joy despite hostility? Just as in Jesus's time, going beyond provides an opportunity to exemplify the law of love in action.

> Owe nothing to anyone except to love one another; for he who loves his neighbor has fulfilled *the* law. For this, "YOU SHALL NOT COMMIT ADULTERY, YOU SHALL NOT MURDER, YOU SHALL NOT STEAL, YOU SHALL NOT COVET," and if there is any other commandment, it is summed up in this saying, "YOU SHALL LOVE YOUR NEIGHBOR AS YOURSELF." Love does no wrong to a neighbor; therefore love is the fulfillment of *the* law *(Romans 13:8-10).*

It is in the extra steps we take—turning the cheek when already hurt, giving the undershirt when the coat is taken—it is in going the extra mile that we demonstrate Jesus is the difference in our lives. Let love be our only debt.

> Beloved, I urge you as aliens and strangers to abstain from fleshly lusts which wage war against the soul. Keep your behavior excellent among the Gentiles, so that in the thing in which they slander you as evildoers, they may because of your good deeds, as they observe *them,* glorify God in the day of visitation *(1 Peter 2:11-12).*

The essence is to allow others to witness Christ through you. The actions that may seem incomprehensible to them, such as going the extra mile, can ultimately lead them to the Lord.

We can affirm this truth, understanding that even if others exploit our generosity, even if our kindness is unappreciated, even if our efforts are ignored, we do it not for their sake but for the Lord's.

> Whatever you do, do your work heartily, as for the Lord rather than for men, knowing that from the Lord you will receive the reward of the inheritance. It is the Lord Christ whom you serve *(Colossians 3:23-34).*

The beauty of being a follower, the solace found in discipleship, lies in doing everything for Him—for His kingdom and righteousness (Matthew 6:33). Regardless of the outcome, whether our actions are embraced or spurned, He acknowledges and values our efforts.

In John 13, Jesus stated that others would recognize our discipleship through our love. Love motivates us to go the extra mile. Where in your life do you need to practice this kind of love-driven action?

CHAPTER 19
BE PERFECT

"Therefore you are to be perfect, as your heavenly Father is perfect."

—Matthew 5:48

Could you pray for the well-being of someone who harbors hatred towards you? Would you rejoice in the success of someone who holds animosity towards you? Would you be willing to sacrifice something precious to you for your enemy? These are challenging questions to ponder, but they are the path where Jesus leads His followers in His teachings on the mount, and it mirrors His own example.

> Beloved, let us love one another, for love is from God; and everyone who loves is born of God and knows God. The one who does not love does not know God, for God is love. By this the love of God was manifested in us, that God has sent His only begotten Son into the world so that we might live through Him. In this is love, not that we loved God, but that He loved us and sent His Son *to be* the propitiation for

> our sins. Beloved, if God so loved us, we also ought to love one another. No one has seen God at any time; if we love one another, God abides in us, and His love is perfected in us. By this we know that we abide in Him and He in us, because He has given us of His Spirit. We have seen and testify that the Father has sent the Son *to be* the Savior of the world (1 John 4:7–14).

This was the sacrifice of God made for those who hated Him, rejected Him, despised Him, and were His enemies. "In yet while we were still sinners, Christ died for us" (Romans 5:8). The love of God motivated Him to send Jesus to do good for us, even when we were hostile towards Him and living in sin.

Becoming Christlike entails reflecting His image, being a learner and follower of His teachings. We should strive to act upon His lessons if we claim to follow Him. In John 13:15, Jesus said, "I have set you an example that you should do as I have done for you." Imitating His example is following Him.

LOVE ABOVE

To let love conquer, let love forgive, and let love prevail above hurt and pain was at the heart of Jesus's message to His disciples.

> You have heard that it was said, "YOU SHALL LOVE YOUR NEIGHBOR and hate your enemy." But I say to you, love your enemies and pray for those who persecute you, so that you may be sons of your Father who is in heaven; for He causes His sun to rise on *the* evil and *the* good, and sends rain on *the* righteous and *the* unrighteous. For if you love those who love you, what reward do you have? Do not even the tax collectors do the same? If you greet only your brothers, what more are you doing *than others?* Do not even the Gentiles do the same? Therefore you are to be perfect, as your heavenly Father is perfect (Matthew 5:43–48).

BE PERFECT

In saying these words, Jesus is quoting the Law from Scriptures.

> You shall not hate your fellow countryman in your heart; you may surely reprove your neighbor, but shall not incur sin because of him. You shall not take vengeance, nor bear any grudge against the sons of your people, but you shall love your neighbor as yourself; I am the LORD (Leviticus 19:17–18).

The second half of Matthew 5:43 was not a quote from the Old Testament, or the teaching of the rabbis or Pharisees; it was a popular belief spread by the Zealots and Sicarii.

The Zealots had a saying during the time of Christ:

> Love your neighbor, but hate your enemy. That is to say, "Love your fellow-Jew (i.e., your neighbor), but hate the Romans." The Dead Sea community in Qumran went even further. They taught their followers to "love all the sons of light ... and hate all the sons of darkness," understanding the sons of light as members of their own sect and sons of darkness to be other Jews outside of their sect (Dead Sea Scrolls).[30]

During Jesus's life and thereafter, two militant groups of Jews often revolted violently against Rome. One group was called the Zealots. Simon, a disciple of Jesus and part of the twelve (Luke 6:15) seems to be named as part of this group. They were called Zealots because they believed in a free Jerusalem that could only be ruled by the rightful king, the Messiah. They also believed in creating chaos to try to make the Romans want to leave.

The other group was called the Sicarii, and they were known for being violent. Their name, Sicarii, comes from a dagger they carried, a

---

30. First Fruits of Zion staff, "Love Your Neighbor but Hate Your Enemy," *Kehila News* (March 2016), https://news.kehila.org/love-your-neighbor-but-hate-your-enemy/.

sica, that was a short, curved sword. They murdered Roman guards any chance they had because they believed it was their right to remove occupation from Israel. It is believed that Judas may have been part of this group, as his title, Judas son of Iscariot, could refer to the fact that he followed the teachings of the Sicarii.[31] Some scholars see Judas Iscariot as a title and not a sir-name, that son of Iscariot was actually saying he belonged to the sons of Sicarii. The only notable mention of the Sicarii in the Bible is in Acts 21:38, where Paul was mistaken for being part of the group.

Sadly, the religious leaders at the time of Jesus condoned the actions of the Zealots and Sicarii. There were no attempts by the rabbis or priests to usher in peace with Rome by telling the Zealots to stop rebelling, and they did not tell the Sicarii to stop murdering. The historian Josephus, a self-proclaimed Zealot, said that the actions of the two groups met the approval of the religious leaders.

The rabbis taught "love your neighbor", and for most people in Jerusalem, that meant the person nearest to them. This question of neighbor explains the parable in Luke 10:25–37 (the parable of the Good Samaritan). When the scribe asks, "And who is my neighbor?" Jesus extends it past Jewish people, or people of like culture, or people of the same religion. To Jesus, a neighbor is anyone in need, even the Romans. Why? Because God loved them and, Jesus came to die to save them, too.

LOVE HAS NO PREJUDICE

Jesus didn't sacrifice Himself solely for those striving for holiness or those actively seeking Him. His purpose was far broader. As John 3:16 declares, He gave His life for the entire world.

> For while we were still helpless, at the right time Christ died for the ungodly. For one will hardly die for a righteous man; though perhaps for the good man someone would dare even

---

31. James Martin, "Why Did Judas Do It?" *America The Jesuit Review* (April 20, 2011), https://www.americamagazine.org/content/all-things/why-did-judas-do-it.

to die. But God demonstrates His own love toward us, in that while we were yet sinners, Christ died for us. Much more then, having now been justified by His blood, we shall be saved from the wrath *of God* through Him. For if while we were enemies we were reconciled to God through the death of His Son, much more, having been reconciled, we shall be saved by His life (Romans 5:6–10).

Despite humanity's rebellion and enmity toward God, Jesus willingly laid down His life as a payment for sin, offering salvation and reconciliation to all people, regardless of their background or status. This truth highlights the universality of Jesus's sacrifice, extending redemption to Jews and Gentiles, to those who were deeply religious and to those who were hostile to God's ways. It reveals the inclusive nature of God's love, reaching out to every individual, inviting them into a restored relationship with Him through faith in Jesus Christ.

When we internalize this truth and allow it to shape our actions, we are indeed demonstrating the perfect love of Christ. Praying for those who harbor animosity towards us, rejoicing in their blessings, and even extending forgiveness and acceptance to them—these are all tangible expressions of Christ's love working through us. It's a profound way to reflect His character and share His love with others, even those who may oppose or mistreat us.

BE PERFECT—BE LOVE

We need to let Christ's love perfect us, so we in turn can share His perfect love with all people.

> Once you were alienated from God and were hostile in your minds because of your evil deeds. But now He has reconciled you by Christ's physical body through death to present you holy, unblemished, and blameless in His presence (Colossians 1:21–22).

Being a loving person doesn't necessitate following Jesus, but following Jesus necessitates that you be a loving person. According to Jesus, discipleship is defined by individuals who, in the face of hate, choose love; in the presence of wickedness, offer prayers; and in moments of vengeance, share the message of grace. Loving those who harbor hatred towards you, praying for those who persecute or attack you, with your foremost concern being the salvation of the lost, embodies the essence of walking as a follower of Jesus.

Jesus said love (the same type of love that saved the world--John 3:16) would be what defines His followers (John 13:35), and it would be what binds His church (Colossians 3:14).

Perfection is a love that looks past wrongs, looks past harms, looks past evils, looks past the guilt and pain inflicted from another, and cares enough to save, heal, and forgive. Jesus calls you to share with others the gift of salvation, forgiveness, and healing.

> There is no fear in love; but perfect love casts out fear, because fear involves punishment, and the one who fears is not perfected in love. We love, because He first loved us. If someone says, "I love God," and hates his brother, he is a liar; for the one who does not love his brother whom he has seen, cannot love God whom he has not seen. And this commandment we have from Him, that the one who loves God should love his brother also (1 John 4:18-21).

Perfect love transcends circumstances and extends beyond human limitations. It's a love that persists despite flaws, failures, and offenses. This is precisely the love that motivated Jesus to endure the cross for the sake of humanity's redemption. In Matthew 5, Jesus calls His followers to embody this same perfect love—a love that forgives, extends grace, and seeks reconciliation even in the face of adversity or opposition. It's a love that mirrors the unconditional love of God and transforms hearts and lives.

CHAPTER 20

GIVE

"So when you give to the poor, do not sound a trumpet before you, as the hypocrites do in the synagogues and in the streets, so that they may be honored by men. Truly I say to you, they have their reward in full."

—Matthew 6:2

In Matthew 6, Jesus offers His guidance to both His disciples and the surrounding crowd, imparting the foundational principles of discipleship relevant to their everyday lives, which encompass their thoughts, actions, and devotion. Across this chapter, Jesus delineates between actions driven by a desire for attention, self-preservation, or vanity, and those rooted in authentic growth, conviction, meaningful discourse, and the expectation of heavenly rewards.

"Beware of practicing your righteousness before men to be noticed by them; otherwise you have no reward with your Father who is in heaven" (Matthew 6:1). Do not do things to be noticed by man. Instead, let the overflow of God's love in your life motivate your actions. Reflect on your deeds with a mindset like this: "Lord, your love is moving me to take these steps that your grace is drawing me to, and your mercy is overwhelming me to do." This is the essence of a relationship with Christ: driven by His love, grace, and mercy. It blossoms through the growth that stems from trusting and fully surrendering to Him.

THE MIND OF GIVING

In Matthew 6, Jesus raises the issue of motivation. What fundamentally motivates your giving, praying, fasting, valuing possessions, and worrying? Ultimately, what guides all our actions? In each teaching on these topics, Jesus links us back to the main idea in verse one using the word ὅταν, which means "therefore" or "consequently" in English. Each point emphasizes His call to abandon hypocrisy. Summarized, it reads: "Therefore, when you pray, give, fast, or worry, what motivates these actions?"

> I have been crucified with Christ; and it is no longer I who live, but Christ lives in me; and the life which I now live in the flesh I live by faith in the Son of God, who loved me and gave Himself up for me (Galatians 2:20).

Do everything with the aim of growing in Jesus. Let every action be directed towards transforming your life in Him. The greatest reward is found in growth and deepening relationship with Him, even though Jesus also promises eternal rewards.

> Beware of practicing your righteousness before men to be noticed by them; otherwise you have no reward with your Father who is in heaven. So when you give to the poor, do not sound a trumpet before you, as the hypocrites do in the synagogues and in the streets, so that they may be honored by men. Truly I say to you, they have their reward in full. But when you give to the poor, do not let your left hand know what your right hand is doing, so that your giving will be in secret; and your Father who sees what is done in secret will reward you (Matthew 6:1–4).

When you give, you are not to do it with the thought that you are adding to your salvation or buying a piece of your grace. Approaching giving with the wrong intentions is hypocritical.

There is a funny little story of a grumpy old believer, Mr. Johnson. He seldom engaged in church or community activities, rarely offered assistance to the homeless or the church, and remained unmoved even during emotional TV ads with Sarah McLachlan's heartfelt music playing in the background. Whenever the volunteer sheet circulated for events, he'd boldly write his name with a note saying, "don't bother to ask."

On the contrary, his wife, Mrs. Johnson, was generous to whoever asked. She volunteered for everything and shared the message of Jesus with anyone she could. When Mr. Johnson passed away, he found himself being shown around heaven. God instructed the ushering angel to take him to Johnson Lane. Excited at the thought of having an entire road named after him, Mr. Johnson eagerly approached the huge, beautiful mansion at the end of the lane. However, he was surprised to see a sign on the door that read "Mrs. Johnson." Even more bewildering was the fact that the door was marked "reserved." As he glanced at the neighboring squatty shack, he noticed his name written in bold letters. Frustrated, he turned to the angel and demanded an explanation. With a shrug, the angel replied, "We did the best we could with what you sent ahead of you."

While the theology and doctrine of that story may be questionable, it does shed light on the mental state of many today. People often give God their second best, offering only scraps of their time, talent, and finances. They may be content with making small sacrifices but shy away from larger ones. Yet, in exchange for these minimal offerings, they expect significant recognition and celebration. In stark contrast, Jesus gave everything for us. He held nothing back to demonstrate His love. Speaking of our approach to giving, Jesus said:

> "He who is faithful in a very little thing is faithful also in much; and he who is unrighteous in a very little thing is unrighteous also in much. Therefore if you have not

been faithful in the *use of* unrighteous wealth, who will entrust the true *riches* to you? And if you have not been faithful in *the use of* that which is another's, who will give you that which is your own? No servant can serve two masters; for either he will hate the one and love the other, or else he will be devoted to one and despise the other. You cannot serve God and wealth." Now the Pharisees, who were lovers of money, were listening to all these things and were scoffing at Him. And He said to them, "You are those who justify yourselves in the sight of men, but God knows your hearts; for that which is highly esteemed among men is detestable in the sight of God. The Law and the Prophets *were proclaimed* until John; since that time the gospel of the kingdom of God has been preached, and everyone is forcing his way into it" (Luke 16:10–16).

The way we behave, whether in significant or trivial matters, whether in public or in private, demonstrates our trustworthiness and competence in the kingdom that Jesus will establish when He returns. Hypocrites showcase faithfulness only in the presence of an audience, whereas a true follower remains faithful even when unseen. While the Law governs outward actions, the gospel profoundly impacts the heart. Those who act out of duty often seek acknowledgment for their deeds, whereas individuals motivated by love will serve regardless of recognition.

Jesus desires that your heart be fully engaged in your actions. In Matthew 6:1, He warns, "Beware of practicing your righteousness before men to be noticed by them; otherwise, you have no reward with your Father who is in heaven." Your actions should not seek human applause but rather aim to glorify the Lord. Colossians 3:23 instructs us to do everything "heartily as unto the Lord," recognizing that our reward does not come from people. It's not about receiving praise, popularity, or earthly rewards. Instead, our reward is a valuable inheritance from the Lord (Colossians 3:24).

THE WRONG APPROACH

Hebrews 4:12 reminds us that the Lord can discern the thoughts and intentions of the heart. If God operates in the unseen realm, then our approach to actions must align accordingly. Therefore, we should avoid the hypocrisy of the Pharisees who perform deeds solely to gain human approval.

I heard a story about a couple, John and Diana. After years of dating, John had finally planned to propose to Diana. Everything was set: flowers adorned the table, candles flickered, and soft music played in the background. In what should have been the perfect moment, John said, "Well, Diana, we've been together for years, and I don't really think we're good for each other, and I'm not in love with you, but after all this time, I guess we should get married anyway." Diana must have been swept off her feet, right? This action was unacceptable because of the attitude, heart, and mindset behind it.

It was a stance of "I am doing this because I have to" rather than "because I love you." Jesus pointed out that the hallmark of hypocrisy is the attitude of obligation rather than genuine love. And because there's no love motivating their actions, hypocrites seek recognition. Those who prioritize relationships often seek to do more without expecting acknowledgment, while those who care less about relationships are inclined to seek credit for their efforts.

People who seek credit often do so loudly, seeking notoriety and visibility. They perform their actions to be seen by others. Matthew 6:2 warns against this behavior, stating, "do not sound a trumpet before you, as the hypocrites do." This doesn't mean they literally played a trumpet like "When the Saints Go Marching In." Matthew 6:3 provides insight into the meaning of this statement, "they have their reward." In other words, their actions were noticed, and they received recognition.

At that time, the treasury boxes at the temple were often crafted from fine metal or intricately carved wood. These boxes typically featured cut horns of a sheep or goat on the top, allowing people to drop coins into the horn, which then fell into the box below.

Individuals seeking recognition for their lavish donations would often deliberately jingle their coins together as they retrieved them from their money pouch. They would then drop each coin, one by one, into the horn, creating loud noises that would attract attention. In their minds, this display aimed to impress both onlookers and, they believed, the Lord Himself.

The phrase "sounding a horn" referred to the clattering of the coins as they were poured into the horn of the offering box, made of gold, silver, and bronze. However, despite the grandiosity of this act, it lacked the genuine spirit of generosity. Though their giving may have been large and loud in appearance, it remained empty in terms of true heartfelt generosity.

THE RIGHT APPROACH

So, how is our heart to approach giving?

> So I thought it necessary to urge the brethren that they would go on ahead to you and arrange beforehand your previously promised bountiful gift, so that the same would be ready as a bountiful gift and not affected by covetousness. Now this I say, he who sows sparingly will also reap sparingly, and he who sows bountifully will also reap bountifully. Each one must do just as he has purposed in his heart, not grudgingly or under compulsion, for God loves a cheerful giver. And God is able to make all grace abound to you, so that always having all sufficiency in everything, you may have an abundance for every good

deed; as it is written, "HE SCATTERED ABROAD, HE GAVE TO THE POOR, HIS RIGHTEOUSNESS ENDURES FOREVER." Now He who supplies seed to the sower and bread for food will supply and multiply your seed for sowing and increase the harvest of your righteousness; you will be enriched in everything for all liberality, which through us is producing thanksgiving to God (2 Corinthians 9:5–11).

According to this passage, when we give, our hearts should overflow with joy. We ought to be thrilled at the opportunity to join the family of God in giving. We should eagerly anticipate the joy of giving because, as Paul explains in 2 Corinthians 8, it is a manifestation of grace. When we give, we participate in extending grace to meet someone's needs. And when we give generously, the seeds of grace are scattered abundantly.

Giving with excited anticipation not only brings praises and thanksgiving to God but also fills the giver with cheerfulness. In essence, when we give joyfully, God receives all the glory.

When we observe the giving of hypocrites, it often stems from their desire for vain glory, duty, or to be seen. However, Paul teaches that genuine giving is not driven by compulsion or a sense of obligation. Instead, it is prompted by the heart, fueled by love, and free from worry, doubt, fear, or greed. It's a mindset where one acknowledges that everything belongs to the Lord, and giving becomes an act of praise.

The term "cheerful giver" originates from the Greek word *hilaros* from which we derive our English word *hilarious*. This indicates that giving brings pure joy and delight, akin to experiencing hilarity, when parting with money.

In the church age, we are not bound by tithing, which is a fixed amount mandated by the Law and considered a duty. Instead, we have the privilege of giving offerings out of grace and gratitude to our Lord for the blessings in our lives. These offerings are expressions of appreciation, given in anticipation of what He can do in our times of need and what He will provide in times of plenty. So, how do we approach giving? How do we offer our finances as an offering? When it comes to giving, our approach should be one of sincerity, gratitude, and trust in the Lord's provision. Let's examine how Paul instructed the early church in how to structure collections.

> Now concerning the collection for the saints, as I directed the churches of Galatia, so do you also. On the first day of every week each one of you is to put aside and save, as he may prosper, so that no collections be made when I come (1 Corinthians 16:1–2).

In this passage, Paul provides guidance on cultivating a habit of grace giving. What was the collections of the saints for and why did Paul think it was important?

He instructs the Corinthian church to adopt the same method he taught the Galatian church for collecting offerings. Paul advises them to gather their gifts at the beginning of each week when they come together as a congregation, and to use it within their meeting place and abroad to further the gospel, help widows, orphans and others in need. Notice that he gives no percentage or amount. This is because, as he will write in a later passage, giving is out of the leading of the Holy Spirit.

In the passage, he emphasizes that when he visits, he does not want a collection to be made. Paul purposefully supported himself as a tentmaker (Acts 18:1-4). Although historically, traveling rabbis would have their expenses paid by the temple and people of the town. They would supply them housing, food, and any other financial needs for those listening to their teaching. And the tradition of the church was similar, where teachers were taken care of by the attendees so they could focus on ministering (Luke 9:1-6, 10:7; 1 Corinthians 9:9-15; 1 Timothy 5:18, 19). Yet Paul intentionally would forgo accepting money from the people he was teaching in the town.

The word *saves* (*thesaurizo*) used here in 1 Corinthians is the same word found in Matthew 6:19–20, where Jesus instructs us not to store up treasures on earth but to store up treasures in heaven. This connection underscores the importance of prioritizing eternal treasures over temporal wealth.

> Do not store up for yourselves treasures on earth, where moth and rust destroy, and where thieves break in and steal. But store up for yourselves treasures in heaven, where neither moth nor rust destroys, and where thieves do not break in or steal…

The word *thesaurizo* is translated as *treasure* in Matthew 6. So, in essence, Paul is telling the Corinthians that their giving to the Lord is treasures of heaven.

> "For where your treasure is, there your heart will be also" (Matthew 6:20-21).

It is a treasure to share in the grace of God. And in this context, the grace being shared is manifested through financial giving. Jesus said that a disciple's heart is characterized by giving that stems from a grateful heart, acknowledging the abundance of grace received from Him.

> And He sat down opposite the treasury, and began observing how the people were putting money into the treasury; and many rich people were putting in large sums. A poor widow came and put in two small copper coins, which amount to a cent. Calling His disciples to Him, He said to them, "Truly I say to you, this poor widow put in more than all the contributors to the treasury; for they all put in out of their surplus, but she, out of her poverty, put in all she owned, all she had to live on (Mark 12:41-44).

The Bible says Jesus sat down near the entrance to the court where the men worshipped, and He observed the people walking in and dropping their coins into the horn of the treasury box. People were coming with large amounts and jingling in every coin, getting their notoriety. But, off in the distance, stood a widow holding all her earthly possessions in the palm of her hand. In her hand are two small copper coins, or a *mite* as some translations put it. *Coins* (from the Greek *lepta*, or *lepton*) means two very thin coins. They were probably cut to melt some of the copper in a trade in the market. By the description of the coins, you have a sense she is struggling to make it day by day. These thin coins equaled maybe half a cent and yet Jesus describes it as "all she had."

Consider the widow: She quietly approaches the treasury box, unnoticed by the crowd, and drops in two small coins. As the coins roll through the horn, they make scarcely a sound due to their thinness. She receives no applause or recognition from those nearby.

It is the heart, not the amount. It is the heart, not the size. It is the heart that Jesus desires to transform, shape, and witness displayed.

Jesus concludes His teaching on giving in Matthew 6:3-4 by emphasizing the importance of giving privately. He advises, "Do not let your left hand know what your right hand is doing, so that your giving will be in secret; and your Father who sees what is done in secret will reward you." Some alternate Greek texts, like the Stephanus Textus Receptus 1550, Scrivener's Textus Receptus 1894, and Byzantine Majority Text 2005, have the added statement that when we give to the Lord without the note of notoriety that He 'rewards openly.' It is the idea that because our goal was to please Him, He will reward us openly at His *Bema Seat*.

GIVING FOR CHRIST

Giving is not about adhering to a set percentage, but rather about approaching it with a prayerful inquiry: "Lord, how much?" It's not limited to a monthly or biweekly routine, but rather a question we pose to the Holy Spirit: "When?" And it goes beyond the recipient, because when our hearts and minds are aligned with Him, we are giving unto the Lord Himself.

As Revelation 22:12-13 reminds us, "Behold, I am coming quickly, and My reward is with Me, to render to every man according to what he has done. I am the Alpha and the Omega, the first and the last, the beginning and the end." When we withhold any area of our lives from God, we fall short of truly following Him.

Water boils at one hundred degrees Celsius. Just one degree less, and it won't reach the boiling point. Similarly, Jesus desires us to be fervent in our love for Him, but it requires wholehearted commitment—100%. If we hold back in any area, we cannot fully experience that fervent love for Him. Some may be withholding in prayer, fasting, life priorities, or worry. Others may hold back in their giving. But we must surrender every aspect of our lives to Jesus. Ask Him to guide your relationships, job, family, marriage, and finances.

> Do not be deceived, God is not mocked; for whatever a man sows, this he will also reap. For the one who sows to his own flesh will from the flesh reap corruption, but the one who sows to the Spirit will from the Spirit reap eternal life. Let us not lose heart in doing good, for in due time we will reap if we do not grow weary (Galatians 6:7-9).

We invest in the treasures that capture our heart's desires, attract our gaze, and occupy our thoughts. Eventually, the contents of that treasure box will be revealed. But what will it hold? Earthly prizes or spiritual abundance? Will it overflow with the treasure of grace?

Here are some key principles to consider:

- **Pray:** Begin by seeking guidance from God through prayer. Ask Him to reveal how much to give and where to allocate your finances.
- **Give Cheerfully:** As mentioned earlier, give with joy and enthusiasm, knowing that your gift is making a difference in furthering God's kingdom.

- **Give Generously:** Be willing to give sacrificially, not just out of your excess, but out of a genuine desire to honor God and bless others.
- **Give Regularly:** Make giving a consistent practice in your life, rather than just an occasional gesture. Set aside a portion of your income for giving and stick to it faithfully.
- **Give Proportionally:** Consider giving a percentage of your income rather than a fixed amount. This could be a tithe (10%) or any other percentage that you prayerfully determine.
- **Give Purposefully:** Identify ministries, charities, or individuals in need that align with your values and priorities. Direct your offerings to support causes that you are passionate about.
- **Give with Trust:** Trust that God will multiply your offerings and use them for His purposes. Have faith that He will provide for your needs as you give obediently.

By approaching giving in this manner, you can experience the joy and fulfillment that comes from partnering with God in His work and blessing others with your finances.

CHAPTER 21
WHEN YOU PRAY

"When you pray, you are not to be like the hypocrites; for they love to stand and pray in the synagogues and on the street corners so that they may be seen by men. Truly I say to you, they have their reward in full."

—Matthew 6:5

Communication stands out as a prevalent issue in relationships today. In the workplace, inadequate communication between a boss and an employee can sow seeds of discord, hindering productivity. Similarly, within marriages, a lack of effective communication between spouses can erode trust and compromise the love and respect essential for a thriving partnership. Recognizing this, it's evident that fostering open and honest communication is crucial for growth. From a spiritual perspective, Jesus emphasized the importance of nurturing faith through action, with prayer serving as a vital means of communication with the divine. Through prayer, we engage in verbal dialogue with our Heavenly Father, fostering a deeper connection and understanding.

Many people grapple with the same questions: Where do I begin? How do I approach it? These uncertainties are not uncommon. In Luke 11:1, we find a relatable scenario: "It happened that while Jesus was praying in a certain place, after He had finished, one of His disciples said to Him, 'Lord, teach us to pray just as John also taught his disciples.'" This passage highlights the disciples' recognition of the significance of prayer and their desire to learn from Jesus Himself. It's a reminder that seeking guidance and instruction in prayer is a natural and essential part of spiritual growth.

In Matthew 6, Jesus not only taught about prayer but also exemplified it in His own life for His followers to observe and follow. Throughout His ministry, Jesus's life was steeped in prayerful communion with the Father. Before performing miracles, Jesus sought solitude in prayer. For instance, after feeding the five thousand in Matthew 14, Jesus withdrew to pray alone. And notably, prior to the most challenging moments of His life, such as in the garden of Gethsemane (Matthew 26), Jesus dedicated extended periods to fervent prayer. These instances served as powerful demonstrations to His disciples, underscoring the vital importance of constant communication with God.

JESUS SHOWED THEM THE IMPORTANCE OF PRAYER

The disciples were firsthand witnesses to Jesus's habit of retreating into solitude for extended periods of prayer. Even after expending Himself in acts of compassion, healing, teaching, and feeding multitudes, Jesus prioritized moments of replenishment through prayer. He didn't just perform miracles; He prayed before each one. Through His actions, Jesus imparted a crucial lesson to His disciples and to us. If the Messiah, the embodiment of God, the Creator, and the Lord, found sustenance and guidance in prayer, how much more do we, as His followers, need prayer in our lives?

The disciples grasped the significance of this practice when they observed Jesus withdrawing to pray. Their ceremonial prayers seemed hollow compared to the profound intimacy Jesus exhibited with the

Father. They were witnessing a revolutionary approach to prayer, one characterized by depth and authenticity. This prompted them to approach Jesus, asking Him to teach them to pray, realizing that what they had been doing lacked the vibrancy and depth they observed in Jesus's prayer life.

In their religion, the priests prayed for forgiveness and help over sacrifices using incense and candles. Their prayers were routine, practiced, scheduled, and ritualistic for the most part. Some prayers were written down and memorized, or they would pray Psalms. But Jesus talked to God personally about what He was thinking, doing, or about to do, and He spoke to God about problems. Jesus's prayers were different, and how He told them to pray was new. Jesus taught them to call God "Father," to ask for forgiveness, to offer praise, and speak their mind. This style of prayer was new and had never been done. Jesus was teaching them how to have a conversation with God; He was teaching them to communicate.

> When you pray, you are not to be like the hypocrites; for they love to stand and pray in the synagogues and on the street corners so that they may be seen by men. Truly I say to you, they have their reward in full. But you, when you pray, go into your inner room, close your door and pray to your Father who is in secret, and your Father who sees what is done in secret will reward you. And when you are praying, do not use meaningless repetition as the Gentiles do, for they suppose that they will be heard for their many words. So do not be like them; for your Father knows what you need before you ask Him (Matthew 6:5–8).

Jesus begins His teachings on prayer by cautioning the disciples against adopting a hypocritical approach. For hypocrites, prayer becomes a mere ritual, devoid of genuine connection. The Pharisees exemplified this, interrupting their daily activities to perform ostentatious prayers.

Their prayers often consisted of recited Psalms or rabbinic texts, accompanied by dramatic gestures of piety, such as falling on their faces. Yet, their outward devotion masked inner hypocrisy. It was not uncommon to witness these same individuals engaging in deceitful practices shortly after their public displays of piety. For instance, they might exploit unsuspecting merchants shortly after their public prayers on street corners. Prayer for some had become more about outward appearances than genuine connection. Shouting or performing rituals isn't necessary when communicating with a God who is ever-present.

True prayer isn't about spectacle or recitation; it's about engaging with a personal God who desires to hear the authentic voice, thoughts, and emotions of His children. The hypocrite may seek recognition or status through their prayers, but for a genuine believer, the aim is a deep, intimate relationship with the Divine.

PRAYER IS SPIRITUAL COMMUNICATION

Jesus emphasizes that prayer is more than just a religious duty; it's a heartfelt plea for divine assistance, a personal cry to our Heavenly Father for help. Consider the familiar saying, "When all else fails, ask for help!"

A couple of years ago, we embarked on a canoeing and camping trip with a group of kids to Peace River. These excursions are always a blend of adventure and personal growth for both the kids and the staff involved. On this particular trip, we had a few younger guys eager to prove themselves to the older high school participants. As the staff circulated to assist in setting up tents, these confident youngsters insisted, "We've got this!"

Opting to handle things independently, they ventured off to assemble their five-man tent. That night, however, nature had other plans. Ferocious winds reaching fifty miles per hour accompanied by relentless rain battered our campsite. Amidst the howling wind and drumming rain, voices soon rose in frustration and dismay. "There's water in my sleeping bag!" "This tent is a swimming pool!" "I'm drenched; this roof isn't holding up!"

The next morning, weary and soaked boys approached the staff, humbled by their overnight ordeal, and requested assistance. We made our way to their tent and found it situated at the base of a slope, where rainwater had pooled around it. To our surprise, instead of using the tent poles provided, they had improvised by tethering the roof to nearby tree branches.

It was a lesson learned the hard way, but it reveals the importance of humility and seeking guidance when needed. As we worked together to relocate and properly set up their tent, it became a vivid reminder that in the face of challenges, it's okay to ask for help, especially when the safety and comfort of everyone involved are at stake.

"When all else fails, ask for help!" This simple adage resonates profoundly in the aftermath of the camping mishap. Had these boys heeded the guidance of their leaders, they could have averted the chaos that ensued. Instead, they endured soggy clothing and missed out on the initial day's festivities, their sleep disturbed by discomfort.

In our spiritual journeys, we often find ourselves following a similar pattern. We forge ahead independently, only to realize too late the consequences of our ill-advised decisions. It's a familiar cycle: we make mistakes, and then, faced with the repercussions, we turn to God for assistance.

Yet, there's a better way. Rather than forging ahead blindly, we should seek help and guidance from the outset. Just as the boys could have benefited from the leaders' expertise before setting up their tent, we can avoid many pitfalls by pausing to seek instruction from our spiritual guide. It's a lesson in humility and wisdom, acknowledging our limitations and relying on the wisdom of those who have gone before us.

In our household, we've established a practice we call "talk time." It's a designated period during which each of our kids can request uninterrupted attention. When it's their turn, they have our undivided focus as my wife and I lend them our ears and time. During this special moment, they're free to express their thoughts, fears, problems, dreams, and joys without any fear of interruption or judgment. We're there to embrace them, listen intently, and engage in heartfelt conversation, providing a safe and supportive space for them to open up and share whatever's on their minds or in their hearts.

This echoes the guidance found in the Bible regarding prayer and our relationship with our Heavenly Father. In Matthew 6:6, it's advised, "But you, when you pray, go into your inner room, close your door, and pray to your Father who is in secret, and your Father who sees what is done in secret will reward you." Just as in our family's "talk time," this verse emphasizes the importance of finding a quiet, secluded space for intimate communication with God. It's in these moments of private, heartfelt connection that we can freely express ourselves to our Heavenly Father, knowing that He sees and hears us, and will respond in ways that are meaningful and rewarding.

HOW PRAYER SHOULD NOT BE

When teaching prayer, Jesus again uses the Pharisees as an example. "They prayed frequently but always in a public place – in the synagogue or on the street corner. They sought to impress people with their piety. Christ said they had already received their reward – they got what they were praying for, the plaudits of people (Matthew 6:5)."[32] Jesus communicates the "do nots" in verses 7–8.

> And when you are praying, do not use meaningless repetition as the Gentiles do, for they suppose that they will be heard for their many words. So do not be like them; for your Father knows what you need before you ask Him (Matthew 6:7–8).

Don't approach God with a rehearsed script. He isn't interested in hearing the same prayer repeated mechanically. What He truly desires is to hear from you, His child. He wants to listen to your unique voice,

---

32. J. Dwight Pentecost, *The Words and Works of Jesus Christ*, (Grand Rapids, MI: Zondervan, 1981), 182 -183.

your authentic words, and the thoughts of your mind. When you pray, you're engaging in direct communication with your Heavenly Father. So, don't hesitate to pour out your doubts, worries, struggles, praises, and thanksgiving. God desires nothing less than open and honest communication from you.

In the Bible class I teach, we have a fun tradition called "spoon feed." When a student responds to my question with what they think I want to hear—a textbook answer instead of an authentic, heartfelt response from their own thoughts—the whole class shouts out, "spoon feed," and I playfully mime spoon-feeding them. After all, if I wanted a textbook answer, I'd simply consult the textbook. And if I sought a regurgitation of memorized information, I'd ask their other teachers. What I truly value is their genuine, thoughtful engagement with the material. Each answer they provide is a window into their unique perspective and understanding, and I encourage them to think critically and speak honestly.

This mirrors how God desires us to approach prayer—with a piece of our authentic selves offered up to Him. He isn't looking for rote recitations like "now I lay me down to sleep" or quoting the Lord's Prayer verbatim. Instead, He longs for genuine, unfiltered dialogue from you. He wants to hear your unique voice, your personal thoughts, and feelings.

I recall vividly the first time I engaged in an open conversation with God. It happened when I was around twelve years old. Until then, my prayers had followed a familiar pattern: brief, scripted phrases like "Lord, thank you for this food, Amen" or "God, bless me as I sleep and give me a good day tomorrow." I even tried the occasional desperate plea for divine intervention during tests, asking for correct answers to magically appear in my mind. Yet, unsurprisingly, that particular prayer never seemed to get a response. But this prayer was different.

I remember it like it was yesterday. I was just a little boy, overwhelmed with emotion. My brother and I were enjoying a casual morning together when our dad entered the room with a grave expression. He informed us that he had to fly out to Detroit immediately because our grandparents were in crisis. Grandpa, whom I adored and considered my closest companion, was gravely ill in the hospital. What shook me to the core was learning that the asthma he had battled for a decade was actually cancer, a misdiagnosis that had allowed the disease to spread unchecked throughout his body.

The news devastated me. Grandpa wasn't just a relative; he was my confidant, my hero. I couldn't bear the thought of losing him. As my dad left to be by Grandpa's side, my brother suggested we pray. I agreed, but in truth, I had no idea where to begin. So, I simply lay on the ground, tears streaming down my face, and poured out my heart to God. In a desperate plea, I begged, "God, please save my grandpa. Take the cancer away. Make him better!" It was a prayer unlike any I had uttered before—a raw, unfiltered plea straight from the depths of my soul. In that moment, I allowed God to hear me, to witness my vulnerability and my deepest desires. It was the first time I truly let Him hear from me.

Two weeks later, my beloved grandpa passed away, leaving me with a whirlwind of emotions. In the midst of my grief, I couldn't help but feel a surge of anger towards God. I questioned why my fervent prayers hadn't been answered, why He hadn't intervened to save my grandpa from the grip of cancer. It took time and life experience for me to come to terms with his passing and to recognize that God had indeed listened to the desperate pleas of a scared twelve-year-old boy. He had answered my prayer in His own way by relieving my grandpa of his pain and suffering, granting him a new, cancer-free body in his eternal home in Heaven.

Reflecting on that journey, I've come to understand that God doesn't always answer our prayers in the way we expect or desire. He works in mysterious ways, and His plans are beyond our comprehension. Yet, He hears every word, every cry of our hearts. He wants us to come to Him with honesty and authenticity, to speak to Him in our own voice, even when the words fail us. Even when all we can do is utter the name of Jesus amidst tears and pain, He invites us to pray.

So, when was the last time you spoke to God? When was the last time you cried out to Him? Remember, He doesn't seek rehearsed or superficial prayers. He longs to hear your voice, your heart, your deepest thoughts. Even in moments of overwhelming sorrow or silence, never hesitate to pray, for He is always listening, always ready to comfort and guide us through every trial and triumph of life.

HOW TO PRAY

"Pray, then, in this way: 'Our Father who is in heaven, Hallowed be Your name'" (Matthew 6:9). These opening words of the Lord's Prayer encapsulate the essence of heartfelt communication with God. They invite us to address Him in the most intimate and reverent manner, crying out to Him as a beloved child would call out to their loving Father.

In the original Greek language, the phrase *Pater hemon o* translates to "The Father of us," emphasizing the familial bond and personal relationship we share with God. It reminds us that He is not just a distant deity but our compassionate and caring Heavenly Father who is ever-present and attentive to our needs.

These are Paul's thoughts when he writes: "Because you are sons, God has sent forth the Spirit of His Son into our hearts, crying, 'Abba! Father!'" (Galatians 4:6). The word *crying* is from the Greek *krazo*, meaning to make an unintelligible noise, like a bird's caw or the croaking of a frog. It's a cry of ahh! It's crying on the shoulder of your Father, who is holding you to His chest in comfort.

Because you are His child, you have the privilege of crying out to the Father in your moments of pain, just as a child runs to his parent for comfort after falling off a bike, saying, "Dad, help me." In prayer, we can address God with the intimate terms of Abba, Daddy, or Father, expressing our deep need for His presence and assistance. And just as a loving parent attentively responds to their child's cries, God gives us His undivided attention.

But the beauty of our relationship with God doesn't end there. Scripture reveals a profound truth: even in our weakness, the Spirit intercedes for us (Romans 8:26). As His beloved children, we are never left alone. We have been blessed with the Helper, the *Parakletos,* the Holy Spirit, who comes alongside us in our times of need. He not only comforts us but also advocates for us before the Father, interpreting and conveying our pains, fears, and circumstances in a way that transcends human understanding. With the Holy Spirit as our ally, we can approach the Father with confidence, knowing that our cries are heard and understood, and that we are never abandoned or forgotten.

Isn't it a beautiful concept? In addressing God as "Our Father," Jesus taps into a fundamental longing ingrained in every human heart—the desire for paternal connection and care. Deep within us, there's an innate craving for the protective, nurturing, and loving presence of a parent. By inviting believers to address God as "Father," Jesus is extending an invitation into a profound relationship with Yahweh, the Creator of the universe.

What's striking is that Jesus doesn't begin with imagery of a distant king and his subjects or a creator demanding obedience from his creation. Instead, He chooses to frame our relationship with God in the tender and intimate terms of a parent and child. This approach softens our hearts and opens our minds to the idea of sharing our deepest thoughts, fears, and desires with our Heavenly Father. It reassures us that God isn't a distant ruler to be feared or a harsh master to be obeyed, but a loving Father who longs for relationship and communion with His children.

In the former Soviet Union, including countries like Latvia, Belarus, Russia, and Ukraine, researchers encountered a puzzling phenomenon: seemingly healthy babies with stunted growth, disproportionately large heads, and underdeveloped bodies. These children exhibited poor motor skills and struggled to develop socially and mentally. Initially, the cause of these symptoms eluded researchers. However, upon closer observation of the children's lives, a troubling pattern emerged.

These infants had been orphaned from birth and were raised in overcrowded orphanages. Their only human interaction consisted of routine tasks like diaper changes, occasional washing, and being handed a bottle. The absence of parental touch and engagement had profound consequences on their physical and mental development, leading to stunted growth and a range of health issues. For instance, infants were often left in highchairs by windows, given bottles, and left to entertain themselves for hours on end.

Ultimately, doctors coined the term "failure to thrive" to describe this condition, highlighting the critical importance of parental involvement in a child's growth and development. Without nurturing care and affection, these infants struggled to thrive physically and emotionally.

This example spotlights a broader truth: just as parental involvement is crucial for a child's healthy growth and development, our relationship with our heavenly Father is essential for our spiritual well-being. Without regular contact with Christ through prayer and engagement with His Word, we risk spiritual stagnation and underdevelopment, remaining as spiritual infants rather than mature believers. Just as the infants in the orphanages needed parental touch and involvement to thrive, we need the nurturing presence of our Heavenly Father to grow and flourish in our spiritual lives.

YOUR FATHER IS GOD!

You know, there comes a pivotal moment in every child's life when they realize that their mom and dad aren't quite the superheroes they once believed them to be. It's a sobering realization. Most children inherently hold their parents in the highest regard, expecting nothing but greatness from them. But as they grow older, they inevitably witness their parents' flaws and imperfections, and the illusion of Superman and Wonder Woman begins to crumble.

However, the beauty of our relationship with our heavenly Father is that there's never any disappointment or disillusionment. When we declare, "Hallowed be Your name," we're acknowledging the holiness and greatness of God's name. Unlike earthly parents who may fall short of our expectations, God's name is eternally holy and honorable. The passive nature of this statement reminds us that it's not our efforts that make His name holy; rather, it is God Himself who brings honor, sanctification, and holiness to His own name. He is the ultimate source of perfection and greatness, and there's never any letdown in His awesomeness.

Scripture depicts angels encircling God's throne, continuously declaring, "Holy, Holy, Holy," and we, as His children, have the privilege of approaching Him. The holiness of God's name remains constant, regardless of whether His children are living in holiness or not. God's holiness transcends human acknowledgment or denial. That's why Jesus asserted in Luke 19:40, "if these [people] become silent, the stones will cry out." Why? Because our Father is holy, and His holiness demands recognition and praise, even from the most unlikely sources.

What does "hallowed be Thy name" mean? To understand the full significance of this phrase, we should start with the premise that God's holiness is an attribute of His divine nature, not an action or a developed character. God's name is most holy and honorable. The original language says, "make Your name holy." Passive language is used because God, not us, is the one that brings honor, sanctification, and holiness to His name. So we pray to God, "Lord, make Your name holy and keep it holy here on earth, as Your nature keeps it holy in heaven." God's name remains sacred and holy, irrespective of whether His children acknowledge it as such or not. Even in the face of denial or disregard, the sanctity of His name endures.

> In the year of King Uzziah's death I saw the Lord sitting on a throne, lofty and exalted, with the train of His robe filling the temple. Seraphim stood above Him, each having six wings: with two he covered his face, and with two he covered his feet, and with two he flew. And one called out to another and said, "Holy, Holy, Holy, is the LORD of hosts, The whole earth is full of His glory." And the foundations of the thresholds trembled at the voice of him who called out, while the temple was filling with smoke.

Then I said, "Woe is me, for I am ruined! Because I am a man of unclean lips, And I live among a people of unclean lips; For my eyes have seen the King, the LORD of hosts." Then one of the seraphim flew to me with a burning coal in his hand, which he had taken from the altar with tongs. He touched my mouth with it and said, "Behold, this has touched your lips; and your iniquity is taken away and your sin is forgiven." Then I heard the voice of the Lord, saying, "Whom shall I send, and who will go for Us?" Then I said, "Here am I. Send me!" (Isaiah 6:1–8).

In Jewish tradition, the name of God, Yahweh, was regarded with such reverence and sanctity that it was considered too sacred to be spoken aloud. This name was held in the highest esteem, deemed the holiest of all names of God. Such was the reverence for Yahweh that sinful lips were deemed unworthy to pronounce it. When reading the Torah, if Yahweh was written you were to change what you read aloud to *Elohim* or *Adoni* in order to honor the most sacred name of God. Yet, despite His holiness and majesty, this God—the King of glory, surrounded by angels singing His praises—desires a personal relationship with you. He longs to be not just a distant deity, but your Father, as Jesus Himself teaches in the prayer.

Pause for a moment to truly comprehend this extraordinary concept: The very Creator of the universe desires for you to address Him as Father.

> O LORD, our Lord,
> How majestic is Your name in all the earth,
> Who have displayed Your splendor above the heavens!
> From the mouth of infants and nursing babes You have established strength
> Because of Your adversaries,
> To make the enemy and the revengeful cease.

> When I consider Your heavens, the work of Your fingers,
> The moon and the stars, which You have ordained;
> What is man that You take thought of him,
> And the son of man that You care for him?
> Yet You have made him a little lower than God,
> And You crown him with glory and majesty!
> You make him to rule over the works of Your hands;
> You have put all things under his feet,
> All sheep and oxen,
> And also the beasts of the field,
> The birds of the heavens and the fish of the sea,
> Whatever passes through the paths of the seas.
> O LORD, our Lord,
> How majestic is Your name in all the earth!
> (Psalm 8).

It's truly remarkable to consider that the Creator of the world, the One who spoke everything into existence, desires for you to address Him as Daddy. And it's not merely about acknowledging His paternal role; He invites us to engage with Him in conversation, to cry out to Him at any moment.

THE ALMIGHTY GOD CALLS YOU CHILD

> For it was fitting for Him, for whom are all things, and through whom are all things, in bringing many sons to glory, to perfect the author of their salvation through sufferings. For both He who sanctifies and those who are sanctified are all from one Father; for which reason He is not ashamed to call them brethren… (Hebrews 2:10–11).

We need to realize we have a relationship as children to God as our Father.

> So I say to you, ask, and it will be given to you; seek, and you will find; knock, and it will be opened to you. For everyone who asks, receives; and he who seeks, finds; and to him who knocks, it will be opened. Now suppose one of you fathers is asked by his son for a fish; he will not give him a snake instead of a fish, will he? Or if he is asked for an egg, he will not give him a scorpion, will he? If you then, being evil, know how to give good gifts to your children, how much more will your heavenly Father give the Holy Spirit to those who ask Him (Luke 11:9–13)?

Ask from your Father; cry out to Him, for He loves and cares deeply for you. In times of need, He will provide what you require; your Helper is ever-present, guiding and supporting you.

When Jesus instructed us to pray, "Hallowed be Your name," He was urging us to seek guidance in upholding the honor of God's name as His children. We should pray, "Father, Your name is exalted; help me honor our family name. Enable me to make my Heavenly Father proud." Let us honor the One we rely on and call out to—the One who loves us unconditionally.

CHAPTER 22
YOUR WILL BE DONE

"Your kingdom come. Your will be done, On earth as it is in heaven."

—Matthew 6:10

"Your will be done" is a challenging statement to embrace, isn't it? Yet, it's crucial for us to reflect and ask ourselves: Do I genuinely desire the Lord's will for my life? Embracing His will entails significant relational growth as we actively seek to bless others and honor His name. While it may involve hardships, it also brings blessings.

Jesus instructs us to pray for His plan to unfold smoothly in our lives, without unnecessary detours. What are you pursuing? "Cease striving and know that I am God," as Psalm 46:10 tells us. In Hebrew, "cease striving," *raphah,* means to relax. God reassures David, and us, in times of battle, stress, relationships, and peace: "Relax. Trust in Me." He continues, "I am to be actively exalted among the nations, I am to be actively exalted in the earth."

Yet, we often become consumed with chasing after money, prestige, acclaim, and knowledge, neglecting to actively pursue God. We're so preoccupied with obtaining, striving, and achieving that we fail to focus on the Lord. We become too busy with everything else, neglecting the One who created all things, sustains all things, and guides all things. But that's not the right approach. Our lives should be centered on Him.

> Give ear to my words, O LORD, Consider my groaning. Heed the sound of my cry for help, my King and my God, For to You I pray. In the morning, O LORD, You will hear my voice; In the morning I will order my prayer to You and eagerly watch (Psalm 5:1–3).

As I begin my day, I will engage with You—I will speak, cry, laugh, and spend time in conversation with You. Throughout the day, I will witness Your provision, find comfort in Your presence, delve into Your Word, and marvel at the beauty of Your creation. My heart is eager to hear from You.

When I rise in the morning and step out of bed, You will be on my mind. This is how we set the tone for a fulfilling day. There's no better way to start the day than by conversing with the One who has intricately planned every aspect of my day, my life, and my eternity. As Proverbs 16:9 reminds us, "The mind of man plans his way, But the LORD directs his steps."

The Lord's plan unfolds according to His perfect timing, and its fulfillment is inevitable. He is fully aware of our failures and successes, and nothing takes Him by surprise. In His divine blueprint, He has already accounted for all the possible paths we might take.

Therefore, walk hand in hand in prayer with the One who can help you build a sure foundation.

His plan always unfolds, despite our resistance, but He urges us to align with His will. His will is revealed in His word, guiding us along the path He intends for our lives.

LORD WILLING

Have you ever used the phrases "Lord willing" or "God willing"? What do people typically mean when they say that? And what about you? When you use those phrases, are you actively seeking to align your life with the Lord's will in every situation? The reality is, many people may not truly desire God's will in their lives. If they did, their actions and decisions would reflect it—they would be actively living it out. Instead, often what people truly want is their own will to be fulfilled.

However, the Bible instructs us to pray for God's will to be done, implying that we are seeking His help to implement it in our lives.

I WANT YOUR KINGDOM REIGN NOW

This is the prayer and longing of every believer. Scripture even depicts the earth itself eagerly yearning and groaning for its arrival.

> For the anxious longing of the creation waits eagerly for the revealing of the sons of God. For the creation was subjected to futility, not willingly, but because of Him who subjected it, in hope that the creation itself also will be set free from its slavery to corruption into the freedom of the glory of the children of God. For we know that the whole creation groans and suffers the pains of childbirth together until now. And not only this, but also we ourselves, having the first fruits of the Spirit, even we ourselves groan within ourselves, waiting eagerly for our adoption as sons, the redemption of our body (Romans 8:19–23).

Until the day we either breathe our last breath or are called up in the rapture, we have a responsibility: to live out God's will for our lives here on earth. The latter part of the verse is particularly convicting, as it pertains to our actions, choices, and how we live our lives. The beginning of the prayer lets us know God's role to us as Father and how His holiness is sustained in His ever-perfect, never-changing nature.

"Pray, then, in this way: 'Our Father who is in heaven, Hallowed be Your Name'" (Matthew 6:9).

But this next part is: "Your kingdom come, Your will be done, On earth, as it is in heaven." As we endeavor to live for Him, we eagerly anticipate the arrival of His kingdom on earth, where His will shall be fulfilled here as it is in heaven.

NOT WHAT I WANT, WHAT YOU WANT

To pray this prayer with genuine significance and impact, it's essential to understand the meaning of the word *will*. In Greek, *thelema* denotes a request, desire, or wish—something one earnestly wants. In essence, what Matthew 6:10 is conveying is: "God, what you want to be done, let it happen in my life."

Jesus reveals God's will, enacts God's will, enables us to live by it, draws us into it, and invites all to be a part by His grace and the power of the Holy Spirit. "For whoever does the will of God, he is My brother and sister and mother" (Mark 3:35).

Living out God's will as an ambassador of His kingdom is not without its challenges, especially as we strive to reflect the joy of living for Him. Therefore, let us pray for guidance, peace, and the fulfillment of His will, eagerly anticipating the coming of His kingdom.

As we faithfully follow God's will in our lives, His chosen path becomes clearer and more bearable. This doesn't necessarily make the journey easier or less painful, but it brings a sense of purpose and coherence as we step forward. Are you resisting God's will and plan for your life? Release your own desires and bring glory to the Father.

"Life is but a Weaving" (the Tapestry Poem)

My life is but a weaving
Between my God and me.
I cannot choose the colors
He weaveth steadily.

Oft' times He weaveth sorrow;
And I in foolish pride
Forget He sees the upper
And I the underside.

Not 'til the loom is silent
And the shuttles cease to fly
Will God unroll the canvas
And reveal the reason why.

The dark threads are as needful
In the weaver's skillful hand
As the threads of gold and silver
In the pattern He has planned

He knows, He loves, He cares;
Nothing this truth can dim.
He gives the very best to those
Who leave the choice to Him.[33]

As Corrie ten Boom's reflections and poem suggest, our life resembles a tapestry being woven. Here on earth, amidst pains, joys, sorrows, and happiness, we may perceive a tangled mess and question God's plan and direction for our lives. However, it is only when we reach the other side—in heaven, with perfect knowledge—that we will behold the glory and beauty that our experiences have brought forth.

---

33. Corrie ten Boom, *Tramp for the Lord* (Fort Washington, PA: CLC Pub., 2010), 12.

CHAPTER 23

EARTH & HEAVEN

"How can I live out God's will? What does God intend for my life?" These questions are common inquiries among believers. While I cannot outline God's specific plan for your life, He has revealed His will in His Word for those who seek it. "Your kingdom come. Your will be done, on earth as it is in heaven" (Matthew 6:10).

Jesus instructs us to pray for and strive to live in obedience to God's will. Yet, regrettably, many believers prioritize earthly kingdoms, seeking human approval, social status, and worldly pleasures.

However, we must recognize a fundamental truth: our earthly desires, if rooted in selfishness, will not endure into eternity. Fame and fortune are fleeting. Moreover, regardless of who holds political office, whether donkey or elephant, Jesus reigns on the heavenly throne and demands our loyalty on earth. Our allegiance is to His kingdom, and thus, we are called to seek it and pray for its manifestation.

The phrase "your kingdom come" is often recited without deep contemplation of its significance. So, what exactly is the "kingdom of Christ"?

> ...then comes the end, when He hands over the kingdom to the God and Father, when He has abolished all rule and all authority and power. For He must reign until He has put all His enemies under His feet. The last enemy that will be abolished is death. For HE HAS PUT ALL THINGS IN SUBJECTION UNDER HIS FEET. But when He says, "All things are put in subjection," it is evident that He is excepted who put all things in subjection to Him. When all things are subjected to Him, then the Son Himself also will be subjected to the One who subjected all things to Him, so that God may be all in all (1 Corinthians 15:24–28).

The kingdom of Christ is the kingdom of heaven or the kingdom of God, will come to earth in fulfillment of God's covenants, and will also include the church reigning with Him.

> Then I saw the thrones, and those seated on them had been given authority to judge. And I saw the souls of those who had been beheaded for their testimony of Jesus and for the word of God, and those who had not worshiped the beast or its image, and had not received its mark on their foreheads or hands. And they came to life and reigned with Christ for a thousand years. The rest of the dead did not come back to life until the thousand years were complete. This is the first resurrection. Blessed and holy are those who share in the first resurrection! The second death has no power over them, but they will be priests of God and of Christ, and will reign with Him for a thousand years (Revelation 20:4–6).

The King will sit on His throne without the need for a vote. His reign is earned through His sacrificial blood, and this is the kingdom we should earnestly pray for. When we pray for the kingdom, we are entreating for the one who conquered sin and death to reign on the throne of David in Jerusalem. Ultimately, He will lift the curse from the land.

Our prayer for the kingdom aligns with God's original intention, which was marred by Adam's sin. It is a plea for humanity's rule over an uncursed earth to be restored. We beseech a merciful God to fulfill the prophecy of Isaiah 11, where the lineage of David, the root of Jesse, will rule with righteousness (Isaiah 11:1–5). In this kingdom, the lion and the calf will graze together, and the wolf and lamb will peacefully coexist (Isaiah 11:6–7) as there will be no predator or prey. Even infants will play near venomous snakes without fear of harm (Isaiah 11:8). This prophecy encapsulates what our hearts should fervently plead for when we cry out in prayer.

WHAT A DAY OF REJOICING THAT WILL BE

The prophecy extends further in Isaiah 2:4, painting a vivid picture of the future kingdom. The land will be incredibly fertile, free from weeds, thorns, dryness, or sand. So abundant will be the fertility of the earth that people will be drawn to cultivate it, transforming their weapons into farming implements. Throughout the millennia, there will be no presence of demons, the devil, or wars—only enduring peace under the perfect rule of the King, the Savior, the Messiah.

This vision of peace and prosperity is what every believer should earnestly pray for, long for, and eagerly anticipate. It is the longing of the earth itself, as Scripture attests:

> For the anxious longing of the creation waits eagerly for the revealing of the sons of God. For the creation was subjected to futility, not willingly, but because of Him who subjected it, in hope that the creation itself also will be set free from its slavery to corruption into the freedom of the glory of the children of God. For we know that the whole creation groans and suffers the pains of childbirth together until now. And not only this, but also we ourselves, having the first fruits of the Spirit, even we ourselves groan within ourselves, waiting eagerly for our adoption as sons, the redemption of our body (Romans 8:19–23).

Lord, we implore You to liberate us from corruption and sin, to eradicate the evil that surrounds us—the pain, disease, and cancer. When Jesus reigns, the world will witness the fulfillment of God's original plan for the garden. Yet, until that glorious day, we have a responsibility, and that is part of our prayer too: "Your kingdom come."

Lord, we yearn for that time, and we earnestly desire to be part of it. Scripture says the saints will rule in His return (2 Timothy 2:12, Revelation 20:4-6, Revelation 5:10, Daniel 7:26-27, 1 Corinthians 6:1-3, Galatians 3:29, and Romans 8:17).

THE REWARD FOR THE DILIGENT DISCIPLE

Scripture unequivocally teaches that eternal life with God is a gift, freely given and unearned. It came at no cost to us, but at a great price to Jesus. However, rewards are something different: they are earned through our efforts for the kingdom of Jesus, which are duly noted now that we are under the righteousness of Christ. While it may not be a popular topic, it's crucial to pay attention to the concept of rewards as Scripture instructs us to do. "And without faith it is impossible to please Him, for he who comes to God must believe that He is and that He is a rewarder of those who seek Him" (Hebrews 11:6).

So, be a busy servant (Matthew 25) seeking the "well done, my good and faithful servant." And what does busy look like? Applying the second part of Matthew 6:10 concludes that if I am not currently in the kingdom, then I should still live as a kingdom ambassador because we are citizens of the kingdom that will one day come (Colossians 1:13). Are you embracing your role as a kingdom ambassador? A helpful measure is to evaluate ourselves against the Beatitudes—not as a means of earning salvation, but as a gauge of our Christlike character and influence.

CHAPTER 24

PRAY FOR YOUR DAILY BREAD

"Give us this day our daily bread."

—Matthew 6:11

Are you relying on the Lord to be your provider and sustainer? In essence, are you seeking Him to supply your needs in life? Jesus instructs that a portion of our prayer time, our dialogue with our Heavenly Father, should include a request for His provision. He directs His followers to pray for God's provision to sustain them.

> When you pray, you are not to be like the hypocrites; for they love to stand and pray in the synagogues and on the street corners so that they may be seen by men. Truly I say to you, they have their reward in full. But you, when you pray, go into your inner room, close your door and pray to your Father who is in secret, and your Father who sees what is done in secret will reward you. And when you are praying, do not use meaningless repetition as the Gentiles do, for they suppose that they will be heard for their many words. So do not be like them; for your Father knows what

you need before you ask Him. Pray, then, in this way: "Our Father who is in heaven, hallowed be Your name. Your kingdom come. Your will be done, on earth as it is in heaven. Give us this day our daily bread" (Matthew 6:5–15).

I appreciate how Jesus transitions us into kingdom-focused thinking in verse 10 of the prayer. "Lord, help me dwell on Your kingdom, Your will, and Your ways." Then, He seamlessly connects this to earthly provisions in verse 11; it's as if our prayers should be, "Lord, help me prioritize You, while also providing for my needs." Jesus exemplified this concept to His followers and the crowds.

Then Jesus went up on the mountain, and there He sat down with His disciples. Now the Passover, the feast of the Jews, was near. Therefore Jesus, lifting up His eyes and seeing that a large crowd was coming to Him, said to Philip, "Where are we to buy bread, so that these may eat?" This He was saying to test him, for He Himself knew what He was intending to do. Philip answered Him, "Two hundred denarii worth of bread is not sufficient for them, for everyone to receive a little." One of His disciples, Andrew, Simon Peter's brother, said to Him, "There is a lad here who has five barley loaves and two fish, but what are these for so many people?" Jesus said, "Have the people sit down." Now there was much grass in the place. So the men sat down, in number about five thousand. Jesus then took the loaves, and having given thanks, He distributed to those who were seated; likewise also of the fish as much as they wanted. When they were filled, He said to His disciples, "Gather up the leftover fragments so that nothing will be lost." So they gathered them up, and filled twelve baskets with fragments from the five barley loaves which were left over by those who had eaten. Therefore when the people saw the sign which He had performed, they said, "This is truly the Prophet who is to come into the world" (John 6:3–14).

WHAT A MIRACLE

In this passage, we observe several intriguing points. Firstly, there were around five thousand men counted on the hillside, each representing a household. This suggests an estimated gathering of about fifteen thousand people when considering women, children, and others who weren't counted. The actual number could have been higher, considering various factors such as unmarried individuals and slaves. The disciples would understandably feel overwhelmed by such a large crowd.

Secondly, a significant aspect is the offering of a little boy's food. Though his name is not mentioned, he becomes a willing vessel for the Lord's work. Even though Mark 6 doesn't specify the boy, it underscores that the vessel used by God is secondary to the work being accomplished. This illustrates the concept of relying on the Father as our provider, feeling assured that He will meet our daily needs.

YOU ARE MY ALL IN ALL

But what does it mean to have the Father be our provision? The implication is man has more than just physical needs. "And Jesus answered him, It is written, 'MAN SHALL NOT LIVE ON BREAD ALONE'" (Luke 4:4).

A full belly is not all you need to survive in a world that constantly challenges your identity, principles, and beliefs. As believers committed to following Christ, we require spiritual nourishment.

> Jesus answered them and said, "Truly, truly, I say to you, you seek Me, not because you saw signs, but because you ate of the loaves and were filled. Do not work for the food which perishes, but for the food which endures to eternal life, which the Son of Man will give to you, for on Him the Father, God, has set His seal" (John 6:26–27).

With satisfied bellies, you follow Jesus. Yet, what Jesus offers is sustenance for the eternal—nourishment for your soul. He desires to meet mankind's everlasting needs, to be the source of our spiritual fulfillment day by day. "Give us this day our daily bread" (Matthew 6:11).

The term *daily, epiousios,* is a word used exclusive of Yahweh, as only He can supply our daily bread. It is mentioned only twice in the entire Bible, here and when Luke gives an account of the same teaching in Luke 11:3. This is a fascinating linguistic phenomenon known as a *hapax legomenon,* a term that appears only within a particular context or body of literature. In this case, it signifies that there's no other recorded instance of its use in history or written language.

Remarkably, this term has been found in only one other place within the entire Greek language among various stories, histories, and epics. The Apocrypha uses it to illustrate the Lord's provision in 2 Maccabees in the Septuagint, describing how God miraculously supplied the needs of the Jewish people who were surrounded by the Seleucid Empire with dwindling supplies. In this narrative, God multiplied their food and oil, a pivotal event that later gave rise to the celebration known as Hanukkah.

Christ's instruction to pray for bread extends beyond mere sustenance for physical existence; it encompasses what God graciously provides to His children. In Latin, it was translated as "super sufficient." Essentially, Jesus is saying, "God, grant me your superabundant bread. Provide not only for my physical needs but also for my spiritual nourishment." This term, uniquely used by Christ, signifies something exclusive that only He offers. Thus, we must daily seek Him to receive this provision for both our physical and spiritual lives.

> For the bread of God is that which comes down out of heaven, and gives life to the world. Then they said to Him, "Lord, always give us this bread." Jesus said to them, "I am the bread of life; he who comes to Me will not hunger, and he who believes in Me will never thirst" (John 6:33–35).

Jesus is saying, "stay with Me, grow with Me, and you will not want for your soul. You will be filled, and you will drink and not want, and no longer hunger."

WHEN JESUS IS OUR ALL, WE NEED NOTHING ELSE

Jesus is all we need.

> Truly, truly, I say to you, he who believes has eternal life. I am the bread of life. Your fathers ate the manna in the wilderness, and they died. This is the bread which comes down out of heaven, so that one may eat of it and not die. I am the living bread that came down out of heaven; if anyone eats of this bread, he will live forever; and the bread also which I will give for the life of the world is My flesh (John 6:47–51).

Jesus is all we need because we need freedom from sin, and to be reunited with our God. When Jesus says "Truly, truly, I say to you, he who believes has eternal life" (John 6:47), He is letting us know our soul can be satisfied when we depend on Him to be our provision.

When Jesus proclaimed that He is all we need, it stirred controversy among His listeners, just as it might challenge us today. In John 6:53, we see the Jews grappling with this idea, questioning how Jesus could provide them with His flesh to eat. Their reaction reflects our own skepticism: How can He supply our physical needs such as food, money, relationships, healing, and other necessities?

Yet, Jesus's response reassures us not to fret about tomorrow. He assures us that He has everything under control. Just as He provides physical nourishment for our bodies, He also offers sustenance for our souls. So, rather than worrying about the future, we are encouraged to trust in His provision and partake of what He offers to satisfy our deepest needs.

> So Jesus said to them, "Truly, truly, I say to you, unless you eat the flesh of the Son of Man and drink His blood, you have no life in yourselves. He who eats My flesh and drinks

> My blood has eternal life, and I will raise him up on the last day. For My flesh is true food, and My blood is true drink. He who eats My flesh and drinks My blood abides in Me, and I in him. As the living Father sent Me, and I live because of the Father, so he who eats Me, he also will live because of Me. This is the bread which came down out of heaven; not as the fathers ate and died; he who eats this bread will live forever" (John 6:53–58).

The statement Jesus made unsettled many, because it challenged their desire for worldly comfort and physical satisfaction. People are often content with indulging in the pleasures of the world and being physically satisfied while remaining spiritually blind. Jesus's assertion disrupted this mindset by highlighting the importance of spiritual nourishment over worldly pleasures.

> Therefore many of His disciples, when they heard this said, "This is a difficult statement; who can listen to it?" But Jesus, conscious that His disciples grumbled at this, said to them, "Does this cause you to stumble? What then if you see the Son of Man ascending to where He was before? It is the Spirit who gives life; the flesh profits nothing; the words that I have spoken to you are spirit and are life" (John 6:60–63).

Jesus desires more than just a superficial encounter with us; He wants us to fully consume Him, to take Him in completely. Comparing this to the samples offered in stores, we see how those tiny tastes can leave us craving more, leading us to indulge in unhealthy choices. Similarly, merely tasting Jesus's provision may leave us seeking satisfaction elsewhere, fixating on worldly pleasures. Instead, Jesus wants to be our constant sustenance, satisfying our every need so that we don't have to rely on temporary fixes or earthly desires.

Jesus wants to be what fills us and keeps us going. He wants us to completely take Him in and be satisfied. He wants us to take in all the grace, mercy, and love, be filled, and not have to look around for unhealthy pleasures.

"But store up for yourselves treasures in heaven, where neither moth nor rust destroys and where thieves do not break in or steal" (Matthew 6:20). In other words, do not satisfy yourself with worldly pleasure when your soul is hungry and thirsty for the fullness of God's provision.

Take a moment for self-reflection. Are you truly embracing Christ and allowing Him to be the source of fulfillment in your life? Are you entrusting Him to provide for your needs and sustain you? Are you fully dedicated to nurturing your relationship with Him and following His path? Or are you merely taking small, hesitant steps, saying, "Lord, I'll give this a try, but keep out of the rest of my life"? Your soul and your life require more than just a taste; they need to be fully nourished by the word of God daily. You should yearn for intimate time with God in prayer each day. Seek His daily provision for growth and sustenance. Remember, the posture of a true follower is reflected in their prayer life.

"Blessed are those who hunger and thirst for righteousness,
for they shall be satisfied" (Matthew 5:6).

CHAPTER 25

PRAY FOR FORGIVENESS

"And forgive us our debts, as we also have forgiven our debtors."
—Matthew 6:12

One Sunday, a pastor, weary of the discord in the church, initiated communion by asking, "How many of you have forgiven your enemies?" A few hands rose timidly. He then inquired, "How many of you desire to forgive?" This time, every hand in the congregation shot up, except one. Seated in the front row was the church's eldest member, Mrs. Lee, wearing a serene smile. Surprised, the pastor addressed her, "Mrs. Lee, are you unwilling to forgive those who have wronged you or extend peace to your adversaries?"

Mrs. Lee chuckled softly and replied, "Pastor, I have no enemies." Her response left the pastor astonished, prompting him to invite her onto the stage. He addressed the congregation, urging them to learn from Mrs. Lee's example of living without enmity and fostering harmony with others. Turning to Mrs. Lee, he asked, "At ninety-eight years old, how have you managed to live in this manner?"

With a radiant smile, Mrs. Lee responded, "It's simple, pastor. I outlived every last one of those ninnies."

Conflict is an unavoidable part of life. Sooner or later, we will all encounter it. However, the key to navigating conflicts lies in forgiveness. Why should we embrace forgiveness wholeheartedly? Because our relationships with others directly impact our relationship with our Heavenly Father. Our interactions, speech, and actions toward others here on earth not only have repercussions in eternity but also affect our vertical relationship with God. Therefore, it's crucial to demonstrate to others the grace and forgiveness we desire in our own lives.

SOWING AND REAPING

Consider these passages: God says forgive your brother so that you will be forgiven (Matthew 6:14–15). In Matthew 7:2, Jesus said with the same standard you judge others, you will be judged.

In Matthew 25:34–40, Jesus foretold an address to those who would inherit the kingdom prepared for them:

> Then the King will say to those on His right, "Come, you who are blessed of My Father, inherit the kingdom prepared for you from the foundation of the world. For I was hungry, and you gave Me *something* to eat; I was thirsty, and you gave Me *something* to drink; I was a stranger, and you invited Me in; naked, and you clothed Me; I was sick, and you visited Me; I was in prison, and you came to Me." Then the righteous will answer Him, "Lord, when did we see You hungry, and feed You, or thirsty, and give You *something* to drink? And when did we see You a stranger, and invite You in, or naked, and clothe You? When did we see You sick, or in prison, and come to You?" The King will answer and say to them, "Truly I say to you, to the extent that you did it to one of these brothers of Mine, *even the least of them*, you did it to Me."

Here's the point: you can't cultivate a deeper relationship with Jesus if you neglect your relationships with others! Forgiveness is one of the most potent tools in the kingdom of God. When we forgive, we reflect Jesus's forgiveness in our lives. However, forgiveness doesn't come naturally to us as fallen individuals, so we need to pray for this ability to forgive, as it's something Jesus desires to see in all who follow His teachings.

While salvation is a personal matter between you and Jesus, your spiritual growth is interconnected with others. Your progress in Christ is intricately linked to your relationships with others (see 1 Corinthians 12). That's why Jesus emphasizes that the way He relates to you is connected to how you relate to others. Therefore, strive to foster connections through forgiveness and the shared love we have in Jesus.

CONSIDER YOUR RELATIONSHIP WITH OTHERS

The Lord instructs His disciples to pray for several important aspects: peace within their church family, the strength to forgive others, and protection against the influence of the evil one, Satan, in their lives.

> Pray, then, in this way: "Our Father who is in heaven, hallowed be Your name. Your kingdom come. Your will be done, on earth as it is in heaven. Give us this day our daily bread. And forgive us our debts, as we also have forgiven our debtors. And do not lead us into temptation, but deliver us from evil. [For Yours is the kingdom and the power and the glory forever. Amen.] For if you forgive others for their transgressions, your heavenly Father will also forgive you. But if you do not forgive others, then your Father will not forgive your transgressions" (Matthew 6:9-15).

In the original language, evil is not a thing but a person. What is translated for us as evil is the devil, the tempter, *tou ponerou*—"the evil"— and is a title rather than a name. *Tou* is what is called a definite article in Greek, and we translate it as "the." Greek is similar to Spanish, where the ending of a word will tell you who it belongs to and whether it is a male or female word. In this case, "the" is owned by the word evil. The known nemesis of man is the devil. This doesn't necessarily mean that he personally tempts each individual, but he is the mastermind behind temptations carried out on earth. Satan is the tempter and deceiver of man. God is not carrying out the temptation. The prayer is asking God not to allow Satan to have success in tempting us.

The phrase "lead us not" doesn't imply asking God to prevent us from experiencing temptation or being placed in its path. Rather, it's a plea for God to shield us from embracing or succumbing to a lifestyle of temptation and sin. There is also a rhetorical understatement being said here in the form of a litotes, which is the use of two negatives to produce the positive. In this instance, "not" and "temptation" are the two negatives used because God would never lead us to temptation but to His perfect will and plan. It would be like eating someone's cooking, and when they ask how it tastes, you answer, "Not bad." The two negatives cancel each other out to reveal the "Good."

D. A. Carson emphasizes that the litote underscores God's protection of believers amidst temptation, highlighting His deliverance from the power of sin. Carson argues that the phrase, "Into temptation" is negated: Lead us, not into temptation, but away from it, into righteousness, into situations where, far from being tempted, we will be protected and therefore kept righteous. As the second clause of this petition expresses it, we will then be delivered from the evil one."[34]

Jesus is using a form of speech for His time to demonstrate that God always wants to lead us toward His perfect plan, and we should be in prayer for such guidance. The nuance of the original language can be overlooked here. God isn't guiding us into sin; instead, He's leading us away from it. This prayer urges God to intervene before we're engulfed by temptation, recognizing that yielding to temptation eventually leads to sin.

---

34. Carson, D.A. *The Sermon on the Mount: An Evangelical Exposition of Matthew 5-7*, (Grand Rapids, MI: Baker Books: 1987), 75, 76.

In prayer, we earnestly cry out against the struggle of temptation, pleading with God not to allow us to succumb to Satan's enticements, which lead to sin. This aligns with James's teaching that God does not tempt anyone (James 1:13).

It's crucial to understand that God doesn't tempt us or orchestrate situations of temptation; that's the work of Satan. When we pray, "lead us not into temptation," we're asking God to keep us from being ensnared by temptation and diverted from His path. Essentially, Jesus is instructing us on how to resist and overcome temptation through prayer.

UNFORGIVENESS AND DISUNITY HURTS OUR RELATIONSHIP

But why does Jesus speak about the devil in between praying and teaching about forgiveness? The Greek word *Opheilema* means both trespass, something done unintentionally, and debt, something withheld intentionally. Therefore, we are to forgive things done on accident and things intentionally withheld.

Luke 11 takes it further and says *sin*. Lord, forgive me of my sins, just as I have forgiven the people that have done wrong and sinned against me (Luke 11:4). This passage suggests that we have taken a page out of the Lord's book and forgiven like Jesus. Jesus on the cross looked at the people that had just nailed Him to it, the same people that had beat Him and whipped the flesh off His bones, and He prayed to God, "forgive them".

When we harbor unforgiveness, we stray from our identity as children of God and succumb to temptation. It's noteworthy that while many readily accept forgiveness, they struggle to extend it to others. This reluctance mirrors Gollum's attachment to the Ring in *The Lord of the Rings*, where despite recognizing its destructive nature, he clings to it, allowing it to corrode his soul. Similarly, holding onto anger and bitterness may offer temporary satisfaction, akin to Gollum's attachment to the Ring, but ultimately, it consumes and distorts us.

Many people adopt the stance that they cannot forgive others for the pain they've caused, adamant about holding onto grievances as a means of maintaining power or superiority. They resist the idea of granting forgiveness because it means relinquishing their ability to harbor resentment, gossip, or hold grudges. However, when they find themselves in the wrong, they often expect leniency, dismissing their own actions as trivial or unintentional. This double standard reveals hypocrisy, as they demand forgiveness for themselves while withholding it from others, contrary to the teachings of Jesus and the Bible, which emphasize the importance of forgiveness for all.

Holding onto bitterness not only harms us but also gives the evil one an opportunity to wreak havoc in our lives. "BE ANGRY, AND yet DO NOT SIN; do not let the sun go down on your anger, and do not give the devil an opportunity" (Ephesians 4:26–27).

Allowing unresolved anger to linger gives Satan a foothold in our lives. Unforgiveness not only damages relationships within the family of God but also disrupts the functioning of the body of believers. Most importantly, it creates a divide in our relationship with the Lord.

> For the body is not one member, but many. If the foot says, "Because I am not a hand, I am not a part of the body," it is not for this reason any the less a part of the body. And if the ear says, "Because I am not an eye, I am not a part of the body," it is not for this reason any the less a part of the body. If the whole body were an eye, where would the hearing be? If the whole were hearing, where would the sense of smell be? But now God has placed the members, each one of them, in the body, just as He desired. If they were all one member, where would the body be? But now there are many members, but one body. And the eye cannot say to the hand, "I have no need of you"; or again the head to the feet, "I have no need of you." On the contrary, it is much truer that the members of the body which seem to be weaker are necessary; and those members of the body which we deem less honorable, on these we bestow more abundant honor, and our less presentable members become much more presentable, whereas our

more presentable members have no need of it. But God has so composed the body, giving more abundant honor to that member which lacked, so that there may be no division in the body, but that the members may have the same care for one another (1 Corinthians 12:14–25).

Consider 1 Corinthians 12:21 for a moment. Just as the eye cannot say to the hand, "I don't need you," because the eye relies on the hand to carry out tasks, so too should we function in harmony within the body of Christ. If the hand were absent, the eye's ability to fulfill its purpose would be hindered. Likewise, the body of Christ works effectively when its members collaborate, rather than allowing conflicts to disrupt their unity and purpose.

When a part of the body is sick or dysfunctional, it disrupts the entire organism. The affected body part may cease to function properly, withdraw, or hinder the flow of the body's operations. The interconnectedness and relationships within the body of Christ are crucial; they impact the health and effectiveness of the entire church. In Matthew 6:12, Jesus emphasizes this interconnectedness by using the phrase "as we also have" in the prayer, highlighting the importance of forgiveness and reconciliation among believers. Our relationship with Jesus is intimately linked to our relationships with others in the body of Christ.

The phrase "as we" in the Lord's Prayer assumes that we have already forgiven others. By forgiving those who have wronged us, we release them from any debt we feel they owe us, including feelings of bitterness, anger, jealousy, or malice. When we pray, we are asking God to forgive us in the same manner that we have forgiven others.

Matthew's Gospel emphasizes this principle even more strongly, stating that if we forgive others, our heavenly Father will also forgive us. Conversely, if we do not forgive others, our Father will not forgive us. However, Jesus is not establishing a merit-based system here. Our forgiveness of others does not earn forgiveness for our sins before God; rather, it pertains to our relationships with others.

This passage is not about salvation but about relational dynamics within the community of believers.

In God's perspective, all sins have been paid for through Christ's sacrifice. Therefore, if you choose to hold a sin against a fellow believer, it displeases Him. One of the most poignant moments in Jesus's ministry is captured in the story of the woman caught in adultery (John 8). With no one remaining to condemn her, Jesus, the embodiment of holiness and justice, tells her, "I do not condemn you. Go, and sin no more" (John 8:11). This act of forgiveness and grace is grounded in John 3:17–19, which explains why Jesus took such a stance.

> For God did not send the Son into the world to judge the world, but so that the world might be saved through Him. The one who believes in Him is not judged; the one who does not believe has been judged already, because he has not believed in the name of the only Son of God. And this is the judgment, that the Light has come into the world, and people loved the darkness rather than the Light; for their deeds were evil (John 3:17–20).

God desires unity and peace within His family, not discord and conflict. He calls His people to emulate His stance of love rather than adopting a superficial role as judges. Love should characterize the family of God, not anger, bitterness, or quarrels. As Psalm 130:3–4 reminds us, if God were to hold our sins against us, we would be utterly condemned. Yet, He offers forgiveness abundantly through Jesus, demonstrating His immense power and mercy. Forgiveness is a manifestation of kingdom power and influence, so who are we to withhold it from others?

LIKE JESUS

"Let all bitterness, wrath, anger, clamor, and slander be put away from you, along with all malice. Be kind to one another, tender-hearted, forgiving each other, just as God in Christ also forgave you" (Ephesians

4:31–32). How did Jesus forgive you? Completely and unconditionally. He never holds our sins against us or brings them back up. In Jesus, our sins are forever gone, and His love for us remains steadfast. Christ calls us to release the burden of unforgiveness and the emotional baggage it carries.

> One day, two friends were lost in the desert, and they were struggling to find their way and began to get desperate. As they came down to the last few drops of water between them, the one friend saw a dessert fox wasting away in the sun; pitying the dying animal, he bent down and gave it their last bit of water. The other friend came up angrily and smacked him.
>
> The man immediately turned around and with his fingers wrote in the sand, "Today, my friend smacked me."
>
> They walked for a few more hours and there appeared water. Hoping that it was not a mirage, the one friend ran and jumped at it but, misjudging, he hit his head and began to drown. The other friend dove into the water and saved his sinking friend.
>
> When the man was revived, he saw a large stone by the water and using another stone he chiseled into it, "Today, my friend saved my life."
>
> The friend looked at him and said, "Today, when I smacked you, you wrote in the sand, and now that I saved you, you're writing on the stone, what's the deal?"
>
> The other friend looked at him and said, "When someone hurts you, you should always write it down in the sand where the winds of forgiveness can carry it away and erase it. But, when someone does good, you etch it in the stones where it remains."[35]

---

35. https://indianchild.com/sand_and_stone.htm.

The One who calls us friends has saved our lives, enabling us to inscribe our pains in the sands of forgiveness. This is the encouragement we find in this part of the Lord's prayer. When you pray, let forgiveness and the restoration of relationships infuse your prayer life, knowing that your forgiveness toward others directly impacts your relationship with the Father. Take a moment to pray a prayer of forgiveness now. If any hurt has surfaced as you read this chapter, take the time to release both the person and yourself from it.

CHAPTER 26

PRAY FOR DELIVERANCE FROM THE EVIL ONE

"And do not lead us into temptation, but deliver us from evil."
—Matthew 6:13

The concept of forgiveness and evil are intertwined. Lack of forgiveness is a temptation Satan uses to create division within the family of God. He detests unity and shared resolve, knowing that unforgiveness can fracture even the most steadfast believers and robust churches. However, forgiveness possesses the power to heal.

> Pray, then, in this way: "Our Father who is in heaven, hallowed be Your name. Your kingdom come. Your will be done, on earth as it is in heaven. Give us this day our daily bread. And forgive us our debts, as we also have forgiven our debtors. And do not lead us into temptation, but deliver us from evil. [For Yours is the kingdom and the power and the glory forever. Amen]" (Matthew 6:9–13).

A more accurate translation would be: "Do not allow us to be under the influence of or led by temptation, but deliver us from the evil one."

As we have seen, in the Greek, the phrase *ho ponerou* translated as *evil* is actually the title of the being responsible for temptation in our lives. The definite article *ho*, "the", denotes this *evil* as a specific title or name. Thus, the "evil one" refers to Satan, the tempter in our lives. It's important to understand that God is not the one tempting us; rather, Jesus instructs His disciples to ask God not to allow Satan to succeed in tempting them.

The Greek words for "the evil," *ho poneros*, from Matthew 6:13 are of particular interest. The Greek word *ho* is an article and in this case is a genitive, neuter, singular word which ties it into the main focus of the word *evil*, *poneros*, also a genitive, neuter, singular, yet in this case an adjective. The use of the article before the adjective makes it a noun. "Sometimes it functions with a participle…or an adjective to make it into a noun, even with words between them."[36]

In this context, both word endings, οῦ, bring the two words together. This indicates to whom the article belongs. According to grammatical rules, "Adjectives, including the article, agree with the nouns that they modify, in gender, number and case."[37] In this case, the NIV translation appears to have accurately rendered the words as "evil one," while the NASB and KJV translate it as simply "evil," which omits the definite article.

THE BAD GUY

Satan is *the* tempter and deceiver of man. God does not initiate temptation. "Here we have a 'Permissive imperative' as grammarians term it. Then, the idea is: 'Do not allow us to be led into temptation.'"[38]

---

36. William D. Mounce, *Greek for the Rest of Us: Using Greek Tools Without Mastering Biblical Greek* (Grand Rapids, MI: Zondervan, 2007), 96.
37. J. Gresham Machen, *New Testament Greek for Beginners* (NY, NY: The Macmillan Company, 1951), 35.
38. A. T. Robertson, *Word Pictures in the New Testament*, Vol. 1: *The Gospel According to Matthew* (Nashville, TN: Broadman Press, 1930), 55.

Christ's teachings are clear on the roles of the tempter and the tempted, and how individuals should respond to such situations. Therefore, in prayer, we petition the Lord to nullify the influence of Satan in our lives.

The expression "lead us not" is not a plea for God to refrain from tempting us or placing us in situations of temptation. Instead, it signifies our request for God's assistance in our weakness, asking Him not to allow us to be ensnared by or fall into a pattern of temptation and habitual sin. Once again, there seems to be a misunderstanding in translation. God is not guiding us toward sin; rather, He is aiding us and ensuring our success in life on earth and our flourishing in the future kingdom. The prayer instructs us to implore God to divert us from the path of sin before we are overcome by it. The term *temptation* carries significant meaning, indicating that we are being tempted and that there will be a subsequent outcome—sin is being conceived.

THE FATHER DOES NOT LEAD TO TEMPTATION

It is for the follower to cry out, "Do not let me fall into a life of Satan's temptation and sin." "Let no one say when he is tempted, 'I am being tempted by God'; for God cannot be tempted by evil, and He Himself does not tempt anyone" (James 1:13). God does not tempt any person, and He does not put temptation in their path.

> But each one is tempted when he is carried away and enticed by his own lust. Then when lust has conceived, it gives birth to sin; and when sin is accomplished, it brings forth death. Do not be deceived, my beloved brethren. Every good thing given and every perfect gift is from above, coming down from the Father of lights, with whom there is no variation or shifting shadow (James 1:14–17).

According to James, sin occurs when we yield to temptation through our own volition. However, according to Scripture, the Lord, in His grace, always offers an escape or rescue in the midst of temptation.

> No temptation has overtaken you but such as is common to man; and God is faithful, who will not allow you to be tempted beyond what you are able, but with the temptation will provide the way of escape also, so that you will be able to endure it (1 Corinthians 10:13).

WE LEAVE GOD'S PATH AND FOLLOW TEMPTATION

Let me be bluntly honest with you. Often, it's our own desire that leads us off the path of righteousness, away from following the example of Jesus, and towards embracing temptation. If we're truly honest with ourselves, most of the time, we actively seek out sin—it doesn't come looking for us.

When you fish, how do you catch a fish? You bait the hook and cast it out in front of the fish. If the fish doesn't bite, what do you do? Give up? No, you try different, more enticing bait until the fish takes it. Even when the fisherman finds the right bait, it's still the fish's choice to take it. A fisherman doesn't dive into the water and force the hook into the fish's mouth. Similarly, Satan doesn't compel you to sin; instead, he presents alluring temptations until you succumb. Consider the temptations he presented to Jesus.

Satan dangles the lure of temptation before you, and you're drawn to it because it's enticing. Like a fish, you go after the bait, following it off God's path with the single-minded thought, "I need that shiny lure." Once Satan has led you far enough astray, he grants you what you desired. But instead of satisfaction, it brings death—it ruins your relationship with God.

ASK THE FATHER TO HELP YOU STAY ON HIS PATH

Pray to God to keep you on His path of goodness and away from the path of sin. Humbly acknowledge your weaknesses and admit your need for help. Cry out for the strength of your Father to save you from the relational death that sin brings.

Listen, my friend. We are all sinners saved by grace. Some may pretend to be perfect, but in reality, we all have struggles. We falter in temptation: some battle with lust, while others struggle with coveting, gossiping, slandering, and lying. In short, believers can be very human. Pretending not to sin doesn't change the fact that we do. Instead of looking down on someone else's struggles, followers of Jesus should recognize this commonality among us and respond with empathy and love. It's through empathy and love that we can grow as a family.

When I was nine, I got very sick and had to be hospitalized. I had a stroke in the emergency room and nearly died a few times. After being in the hospital for a while, I was finally released to go back home, but my parents were not released of a massive debt laid upon them by the hospital. For the next four or five years, we lived on meager means. My dad awoke at 5 am to leave for work, and most nights did not get home until 8 pm. My four sisters, brother, and I depended on hand-me-downs for toys, shoes, and clothing. Almost every meal contained kidney beans. We had chili, red bean soup, and beans, rice, and cornbread. The exception was Fridays when my folks would make spaghetti. I loved the change Fridays brought! We kids did not know we were without, because our parents showered us with love to make up for the want.

My family had committed to do whatever was necessary to get me healthy and home. The doctors had told my parents that I was a goner as I lay on the hospital bed coming in and out. My mom stood there holding my little hand, and when I would be reawakened, I would tell her she needed to let me go home to be with Jesus. My dad stood in the back crying to God for mercy and that he would do anything to keep his youngest son. It was a struggle that made us close! But it was love that held us together.

In those times when the bills came piling in, when my parents did not eat so we could, when my mom had to work because my dad fell off a roof, we wanted to give up the struggle and fight, but *love* was the glue that held us together. We had two things as a family that drew us together: common struggle and common love.

In the family of Christ, we also have two commonalities:

1. Struggle--We all sin.
2. Love--We all have God's love.

The truth is that any man can commit any sin. Some are weaker to certain temptations than others, but no one is above any sin.

We all have struggles against sin, and the answer is Christ, but are we going to Him? Do you depend on Christ and His word to get you through the difficult times in your life? When hard times come, when life ebbs and flows, who are you calling out to? Who do you cry out to to save you?

Sin carries several consequences:

- It weighs heavily on you, draining your energy and wearing you down (Matthew 11:28–30).
- It ensnares you, binding you like a slave (John 8:34).
- It leads to spiritual death, creating a separation from God (Romans 6:23a). This doesn't imply a loss of salvation but rather erects a barrier between you and God.

CALL TO HIM

Jesus wants you to surrender the temptation, sin, and struggles to Him because you cannot handle them on your own. If we succumb to temptation, we risk becoming what we despise. This prayer serves as a crucial reminder to cry out in our moments of weakness, asking God to shield us from the struggles of temptation.

How do we remain on the path set by God? How can we stand firm and avoid stumbling, falling, and failing amid life's challenges and temptations? How do we resist the allure of the evil one and overcome our own weaknesses?

> ...fixing our eyes on Jesus, the author and perfecter of faith, who for the joy set before Him endured the cross, despising

PRAY FOR DELIVERANCE FROM THE EVIL ONE

the shame, and has sat down at the right hand of the throne of God. For consider Him who has endured such hostility by sinners against Himself, so that you will not grow weary and lose heart (Hebrews 12:2–3).

Let's cease dwelling on our past failures and allowing them to hinder our progress. Instead, let's keep our focus on moving forward, trusting in Christ and His plans for us. When we stumble, let's remember that each new day offers an opportunity to begin afresh. We must release the grip of past mistakes and embrace the forgiveness offered to us. As Jesus emphasized in Luke 9:62, looking back detracts from our present journey toward God's kingdom. Additionally, we mustn't lose heart in the face of adversity. Despite the challenges we face, we can persevere through the strength imparted by Jesus. Remember Philippians 4:13: "I can do all things through Him who strengthens me."

You need not allow sin to triumph over your frail flesh. "You have not yet resisted to the point of shedding blood in your striving against sin," as Hebrews 12:4 reminds us. Put up a fight! Do not surrender victory before the first round of the battle has even commenced.

As the great "theologian" Rocky would say, we're too quick to pass blame instead of standing firm:

> Let me tell you something you already know. The world ain't all sunshine and rainbows. It's a very mean and nasty place, and I don't care how tough you are, it will beat you to your knees and keep you there permanently if you let it. You, me, or nobody is gonna' hit as hard as life. But it ain't about how hard you hit. It's about how hard you can get hit and keep moving forward; how much you can take and keep moving forward. That's how winning is done!
>
> —Rocky Balboa[39]

---

39. Sylvester Stallone, Rocky Balboa, Metro-Goldwyn-Mayer (MGM), 2006.

"Submit therefore to God. Resist the devil and he will flee from you. Draw near to God and He will draw near to you. Cleanse your hands, you sinners; and purify your hearts, you double-minded" (James 4:7–8). To submit means to come under God's leadership and protection, and as a result, you can resist the evil one.

Are you willing to entrust your struggle to Him? Will you hand over the thing you cannot handle, or will you hold onto it? If you find yourself succumbing to temptation, allowing your flesh to lead you instead of the Spirit, pray for forgiveness. "If we confess our sins, He is faithful and righteous to forgive us our sins and to cleanse us from all unrighteousness" (1 John 1:9).

Either way, whether you find yourself sinning or struggling with temptation, pray for help. Call out for guidance. Call out for the hand to pull you out of the battle against sin. Call on your Father to stop the embrace of temptation. Christ will provide an escape. He will give you what you need for protection from the evil one's lure.

CHAPTER 27

FAST

"Whenever you fast, do not put on a gloomy face as the hypocrites do, for they neglect their appearance so that they will be noticed by men when they are fasting. Truly I say to you, they have their reward in full."

—Matthew 6:16

You may notice a recurring theme in Jesus's teachings: a call to genuine devotion and the shedding of any facade, pretense, or divisions that hinder your relationship with the Lord. As we search deeper, we'll see that these divisions can show up in various ways: through worry, doubt, or worldly desires such as fame, fortune, or material gain. They can also arise from carnal cravings like indulgence in sex, drugs, alcohol, lying, or cheating. Additionally, divisions may stem from religious obligations, where actions are driven by duty rather than love, or where serving, praying, singing, and congregating feel burdensome rather than joyful. We witness the dichotomy between acting out of a heart filled with the joy of the Lord, seeking His glory and eternal reward, and merely going through the motions out of obligation or tradition. Jesus refers to this divide as that between a hypocrite and a follower.

> When you fast, do not look somber as the hypocrites do, for they disfigure their faces to show men they are fasting. I tell you the truth, they have received their reward in full. But when you fast, put oil on your head and wash your face, so that it will not be obvious to men that you are fasting, but only to your Father, who is unseen; and your Father, who sees what is done in secret, will reward you (Matthew 6:16–18).

WHAT'S UP WITH FASTING?

In Matthew 9:14, John's disciples approached Jesus and the twelve, expressing their perplexity: "Why do we and the Pharisees fast, but Your disciples do not fast?" (Matthew 9:14). The disciples of John were in a somber state, aware of John's imprisonment and the imminent possibility of his death. Moreover, their expectations of the kingdom's arrival were not met with the triumphant victory they had anticipated over Rome and Herod.

According to tradition, fasting was associated with mourning. It involved sitting in ashes and donning coarse sackcloth as a symbol of sadness and repentance. John's disciples were observing a fast, reflecting on their dismal circumstances. Seeing Jesus and His disciples feasting while they themselves were fasting prompted them to seek clarification. They wanted to understand why John and his followers, along with the Pharisees and their disciples, adhered to fasting practices while Jesus and His disciples did not.

Jesus explained to them that His disciples were not fasting because they were in a time of celebration. They were joyfully celebrating Him as the bridegroom. This celebration was in anticipation of the future marriage, which the disciples may not have fully understood at the time, but Jesus was alluding to. In this time, the bridegroom would pay for the sin of His bride making her sinless, rendering the need for fasting as a means to demonstrate repentance needless (Ephesians 5:27). He referred to Himself as the bridegroom of the church. "But the days will come when the bridegroom is taken away from them, and then they will fast" (Matthew 9:15b). The time of sorrowful reflection would come when they would not want to eat, because they would think of the past and fasting would be for a connection with Him.

WHAT FASTING WAS

As mentioned, the traditional fasting practice was centered on reflecting on past mistakes, failures, and as a means of repentance. It often involved mourning or recalling moments of pain. However, Jesus's disciples were in a state of celebration while He was with them. Jesus further elaborates,

> But no one puts a patch of unshrunk cloth on an old garment; for the patch pulls away from the garment, and a worse tear results. Nor do people put new wine into old wineskins; otherwise the wineskins burst, and the wine pours out and the wineskins are ruined; but they put new wine into fresh wineskins, and both are preserved (Matthew 9:16–17).

Jesus conveyed that He wasn't here to merely patch up the Pharisees' system; He wasn't about refilling empty wine bags or fixing broken parts. He used the analogy of new patches on old clothing, illustrating that such patches would worsen tears when they shrink. Similarly, putting new wine into old wine skins would lead to bursting when the yeast expands. God's intention was to conclude the old system and initiate something entirely new, not to patch up the old one. His plan wasn't about refurbishing an outdated system but about establishing a superior, fresh approach. Jesus's sacrifice fulfilled the requirements of the old sacrificial system. His new way didn't involve the old practices of sacrifices, works, or dwelling on past guilt. Instead, it ushered in the new wine of grace, forgiveness, mercy, and love, which required new vessels.

Rather than patches that tear apart, Jesus offers a new coat—a covering of righteousness, as mentioned in Romans 3:21–22.

For the Pharisees and followers of John who still adhered to the Mosaic Law, fasting held significance as a time of enduring pain and deprivation. It served as a form of penitence, reminding individuals of the pain they caused God through their sins. Fasting involved self-denial, abstaining from food to express remorse for wrongdoing. Some would even wear rough, uncomfortable burlap clothing and apply ashes to their bodies instead of soothing oil, symbolizing their rejection of earthly comforts.

However, Jesus emphasized that His new message of grace required a fresh approach, incompatible with the old practices symbolized by "old wine skins" (Matthew 5:17). He did not intend to merely patch up the shortcomings of humanity and the Law. Nevertheless, Jesus didn't dismiss fasting altogether or deem it irrelevant. Instead, He provided guidance on how to fast appropriately within the context of their new life in Him.

WHAT FASTING IS

For Jesus's disciples, fasting held the potential to bring about new life, fostering a deeper reflection on the power and strength of Christ. It served as a means of seeking guidance and promoting growth in faith.

> When they came to the crowd, a man came up to Jesus, falling on his knees before Him and saying, "Lord, have mercy on my son, for he is a lunatic and is very ill; for he often falls into the fire and often into the water. I brought him to Your disciples, and they could not cure him." And Jesus answered and said, "You unbelieving and perverted generation, how long shall I be with you? How long shall I put up with you? Bring him here to Me." And Jesus rebuked him, and the demon came out of him, and the boy was cured at once. Then the disciples came to Jesus privately and said, "Why could we not drive it out?" And He said

> to them, "Because of the littleness of your faith; for truly I say to you, if you have faith the size of a mustard seed, you will say to this mountain, 'Move from here to there,' and it will move; and nothing will be impossible to you. ["But this kind does not go out except by prayer and fasting"] (Matthew 17:14–21).

Fasting transitioned into a faith-building practice, rather than a means of repentance or inducing sorrow. With faith, one can achieve great things, but it necessitates prayer and deep reflection on Christ. Fasting serves as a method for followers to intensify their focus on their spiritual journey.

> Now there were at Antioch, in the church that was there, prophets and teachers: Barnabas, and Simeon who was called Niger, and Lucius of Cyrene, and Manaen who had been brought up with Herod the tetrarch, and Saul. While they were ministering to the Lord and fasting, the Holy Spirit said, "Set apart for Me Barnabas and Saul for the work to which I have called them." Then, when they had fasted and prayed and laid their hands on them, they sent them away (Acts 13:1–3).

As evident here, fasting served as a tool to cultivate sensitivity to the Holy Spirit, enabling individuals to make sound decisions guided by divine wisdom.

HOW FASTING IS USED

In Acts 8, with the establishment of the church and the indwelling of the Holy Spirit in believers, the era of mourning has passed. Fasting was now embraced for fortification. As Paul and Barnabas embarked on their journey, they sought strength and guidance, not penance for past transgressions. Acts 14:23 reveals their reliance on fasting and prayer to discern critical decisions such as the appointment of church elders.

Fasting entails purposefully abstaining from physical indulgence to attain a spiritual objective. It involves denying the flesh to elicit a response from the Spirit and relinquishing the natural to invoke the supernatural. By saying "no" to oneself, distractions in life are cleared to focus on the task at hand.

When hunger strikes, we typically eat to alleviate it. However, during fasting, we prioritize the cry of our soul over the demands of our stomach. Fasting captures God's attention because it underscores the significance of nurturing the inner self above satisfying the outer self.

In various scenarios, individuals may forgo meals to prioritize other pressing matters. Salespeople may skip meals to focus on closing deals, while students might do the same during exam preparation. Similarly, professionals might skip lunch to meet deadlines. But what about focusing on the Lord? Is that worth skipping a meal?

Fasting shouldn't be associated with feelings of remorse for sins or characterized by gloominess. Contrary to the Pharisees' approach, as Jesus highlighted in Matthew 6, fasting should be about achieving spiritual clarity and fostering growth. Jesus introduced a new perspective on fasting, one that emphasizes joy through connecting with a powerful and magnificent Father in heaven. This joy extends to the union with Christ, the sense of belonging to His church, the experience of personal growth in Him, and the empowerment found in His strength.

There's a tale of two lumberjacks, one seasoned and the other younger. The younger one boasted of his ability to fell trees swiftly, confident he could outpace the older lumberjack. Despite the older lumberjack's renowned speed, he felt compelled to challenge the younger one. So, they agreed to see who could chop down the most trees in a single day.

As they began, the younger man relentlessly felled trees, refusing to pause. He was resolute, noting with some satisfaction that the older lumberjack would chop for only an hour before taking a fifteen-minute break. However, by day's end, the older lumberjack had cut down one-third more trees than his younger counterpart.

Perplexed, the younger man asked, "How did you manage to cut more than I did, despite taking breaks all day, while I chopped away tirelessly?" The older lumberjack replied, "It's quite simple. Every time I stopped to rest, I sharpened my ax."

Often, we find ourselves toiling tirelessly, yet puzzled as to why obstacles remain stubbornly in place. We attend church, engage in service, and study the Scriptures diligently, yet our spiritual growth seems stagnant. It's akin to chopping at trees with a dull axe and wondering why they won't fall.

The trees represent the challenges we face—hard times, temptations, sins, illness, and death—that take root in our lives. Faith, then, serves as the sharp ax that enables us to confront and overcome these obstacles. Just as sharpening the axe is crucial for felling trees efficiently, nurturing our faith through prayer, reflection, and spiritual disciplines is essential for overcoming life's challenges.

Fasting and prayer are all about sharpening the ax of the inner self to achieve spiritual victory. It's about refining our spiritual focus by eliminating life's distractions and building our faith while relying on the strength of the Lord.

Are you actively sharpening your ax? Are you seeking the laser accuracy and focus, the strength, and guidance from the Lord? Are you dedicated to strengthening your faith and relationship with Him? Don't continue chopping away with a dull ax.

Are you facing a significant decision, spiritual battle, or physical stronghold? Are you committed to growing in your walk with Jesus? It's time to sharpen your faith through prayer and fasting.

CHAPTER 28
TREASURES OF THE HEART

"But store up for yourselves treasures in heaven, where neither moth nor rust destroys, and where thieves do not break in or steal…"

—Matthew 6:20

Martyn Lloyd-Jones tells this story:

> One day, a farmer reported to his wife with great joy that his best cow had given birth to twin calves, one red and one white. He said, "You know, I have been led of the Lord to dedicate one of the calves to him. We will raise them together. Then when the time comes to sell them, we will keep the proceeds that come from one calf, and we will give the proceeds that come from the other to the Lord's work." His wife asked which calf he would dedicate to the Lord, but he answered that there was no need to decide that then. "We will treat them both in the same way," he said, "and when that time comes, we will sell them as I have said."

Several months later, the man entered the kitchen looking very sad and miserable. When his wife asked what was troubling him, he said, "I have bad news for you. The Lord's calf is dead." "But," his wife remonstrated, "you had not yet decided which was to be the Lord's calf." "Oh, yes," he said. "I had always determined that it was to be the white one, and it is the white calf that has died."[40]

The man's actions revealed his true intentions. When faced with the prospect of losing one thing, he deemed losing two, too great a sacrifice. It became clear that he was unwilling to make that sacrifice.

> Do not store up for yourselves treasures on earth, where moth and rust destroy, and where thieves break in and steal. But store up for yourselves treasures in heaven, where neither moth nor rust destroys, and where thieves do not break in or steal for where your treasure is, there your heart will be also (Matthew 6:19–21).

What does "treasure most in life" mean? The word *treasure* comes from the Greek word *thesauros*, which refers to stacking up treasure, like gold coins. It implies accumulating, laying aside, or attempting to build. Our treasures are a personal reflection of who we are on the inside. It's worth noting that "thesaurus" is derived from the same root.

This is not suggesting that accumulating wealth on earth or saving for the future is inherently wrong. Proverbs 13:22 advises that a wise person leaves an inheritance for their grandchildren. What Jesus is emphasizing is not to prioritize earthly possessions or achievements but to focus on the blessings of eternal life.

---

40. David Martyn Lloyd-Jones, *Studies in the Sermon on the Mount* (Grand Rapids, MI: Eerdmans Publishers, 1971), 2:95–96.

HEART ISSUES

The issue is not in storing treasure or what we view as treasure. The issue is: where is your heart?

> Watch over your heart with all diligence, for from it flow the springs of life. Put away from you a deceitful mouth and put devious speech far from you. Let your eyes look directly ahead and let your gaze be fixed straight in front of you. Watch the path of your feet and all your ways will be established. Do not turn to the right nor to the left; turn your foot from evil (Proverbs 4:23–27).

Our heart—its desires, its affections, and its manifestations—serves as a telling gauge of our priorities. Solomon recognized the danger of his son fixating on earthly treasures, which could leave him spiritually bankrupt. As Jesus teaches, "For where your treasure is, there will your heart be also" (Matthew 6:21). What we value ultimately governs our hearts and directs our thoughts. Jesus seeks to establish heavenly reign within our hearts. If your value is to get money at all costs and get a big house at all costs, what did you lose to gain it? You may have lost friends, kids, your spouse, and your relationship with Christ in the process.

> The good man out of the good treasure of his heart brings forth what is good; and the evil man out of the evil treasure brings forth what is evil; for his mouth speaks from that which fills his heart (Luke 6:45).

You safeguard what you treasure within the depths of your heart. It's stored securely in the vault of your being, influencing your actions and motivations.

Your values and the desires of your heart propel you towards your objectives. When your heart is committed to a goal, you'll pursue it relentlessly, finding every possible means to achieve it.

VALUING THINGS THAT ARE WORTHLESS

Jesus emphasizes the importance of prioritizing eternal values over transient ones and maintaining focus on Him. Jesus does not tell us our problem is that we do not want to work; many people overwork for things with little eternal value. His point is that we have a heart issue.

Like a skilled physician identifying the root cause of an illness, Jesus pinpoints our heart condition as the crux of our struggle. Just as a doctor recognizes symptoms, Jesus sees our life's focus as indicative of our spiritual health. Colossians 3:1–4 echoes this sentiment, urging us to set our minds on things above, echoing Jesus's teachings.

Jesus isn't discussing the actions required to earn rewards, nor is He suggesting that we should prioritize seeking rewards. His emphasis is on the sincerity of our motives and whom we ultimately serve. Many people engage in activities solely for financial gain, but where do their hearts truly lie? Similarly, the Pharisees mechanically fulfilled religious duties but lacked genuine devotion. Likewise, God desires heartfelt generosity, compassion, and worship, not mere clock-punching actions. Reading the Bible and praying shouldn't be approached as mere tasks to fulfill.

TRUE TREASURES LAST

We focus on treasure because of the joy and value associated with it. We recognize its benefits, its worth, and the effort required to attain it. We appreciate the immediate rewards of growth in the present while also acknowledging God's promise of eternal rewards.

Scripture points to this "eternal reward" for:

- Faithfully enduring persecution (Matthew 5:11–12; 2 Corinthians 4:16–18; 2 Timothy 4:8)
- Loving your enemies (Matthew 5:43–48)
- Praying in secret (Matthew 6:5–6)
- Serving the Lord and His people (Matthew 10:41–42; 1 Corinthians 3:8; Hebrews 6:10)

And as we have seen, Scripture points to eternal reward when:

- You give generously
- You pray and fast privately, not seeking public recognition
- You extend forgiveness to others
- You share the gospel message with others
- You love your enemies and those who oppose you
- You endure insults and persecutions for your faith

Real wealth is obtained by investing in "treasures in heaven." When the rich young ruler approached Jesus (Matthew 19:16–22), seeking abundant eternal life, reminiscent of the promise made to the children in verse 14, Jesus responds by highlighting the necessity of a shift in our perspective on earthly possessions and treasures. Attaining great rewards in heaven requires redirecting our focus away from earthly concerns. To have an abundant life takes heavenly focus.

In Matthew 6:19, we encounter a comparison between two types of rewards: the earthly ones that decay, get stolen, or are consumed and the heavenly ones that grow, endure, and last.

With the same sentiments, James states,

> Come now, you rich, weep and howl for your miseries which are coming upon you. Your riches have rotted and your garments have become moth-eaten. Your gold and your silver have rusted; and their rust will be a witness against you and will consume your flesh like fire. It is in the last days that you have stored up your treasure (James 5:1–3).

Jesus wants His followers to focus on what lasts, brings joy, and has an eternal value.

> A band of gangsters in France got away with more than $3.5 million. But the thieves had a problem. The loot was in French coins worth only about $2 each and weighing a total of 17 tons!

A Paris newspaper taunted the bandits with this statement: "You can't buy a chateau, a car, or even a pair of crocodile shoes with bags of change. And if you go out to celebrate your coup, the owner of the smallest cafe will become suspicious before you drop the tenth coin on the counter." The article continued, "Their punishment is included in their success. They will have to spend their loot franc by franc. They can buy millions of bottles of soft drinks. But what else?"

Those robbers had what might be called a wealth of poverty. Although they were rich, they couldn't spend their money for anything worthwhile. Their situation reminds me of people who spend a lifetime accumulating things while making no provision for eternity. They have material wealth but are spiritually poor. How much better to heed Jesus's words: "Lay up for yourselves treasures in heaven, where neither moth nor rust destroys and where thieves do not break in and steal" (Matthew 6:20). Anything else is just a wealth of poverty. [41]

—Richard De Haan

What drives you to do the things you do? If you lost it, would you still keep going?

When you are on your deathbed, your priorities shift away from material possessions like your 401k, bank account, or business. Instead, you find solace in moments spent with loved ones, connecting with your Savior, or cherishing the touch of someone dear to you for the last time.

Don't wait until death is imminent to recognize life's true treasures. Place worth on the intangible, enduring aspects such as friendships, family bonds, and your relationship with Christ. These are invaluable treasures beyond measure that are available on earth.

---

41. "A Wealth of Poverty!" *Runner for Christ*, https://runnerforchrist.wordpress.com/category/our-daily-bread/.

CHAPTER 29

CLEAR EYES

"The eye is the lamp of the body; so then if your eye is clear, your whole body will be full of light."

—Matthew 6:22

Seeing things clearly can help our headaches in life. If we truly had clear vision to see things, we could help our families, friends, co-workers, and acquaintances in things of eternal value. Let's not get distracted and let our vision be drawn to the shiny object that is here today and gone tomorrow.

Jesus warns us not to allow possessions to steal the place of God, and not to let position, success, and money blind our heavenly vision and stunt our affections for Christ.

> Then He said to them, "Beware, and be on your guard against every form of greed; for not even when one has an abundance does his life consist of his possessions." And He told them a parable, saying, "The land of a rich man was very productive. And he began reasoning to himself, saying, 'What shall I do, since I have no place to store my

crops?' Then he said, 'This is what I will do: I will tear down my barns and build larger ones, and there I will store all my grain and my goods. And I will say to my soul, "Soul, you have many goods laid up for many years to come; take your ease, eat, drink and be merry."' But God said to him, "You fool! This very night your soul is required of you; and now who will own what you have prepared?" So is the man who stores up treasure for himself, and is not rich toward God (Luke 12:15–21).

20/20 VISION

A follower of Jesus, committed to building a strong discipleship relationship with the Rabbi, must understand that earthly happiness is not the ultimate goal; rather, it's about finding contentment in Christ. This means emulating the Master by avoiding distractions like worldly praise, fame, and prizes, and instead focusing on heavenly priorities. Envy should not cloud our vision.

Are we accumulating wealth on earth or in heaven? Are our priorities earthly or heavenly? Merely possessing earthly riches doesn't equate to true wealth. While material possessions may satisfy our physical needs, they don't fulfill our eternal purpose. If we prioritize earthly acquisitions over spiritual growth, we'll find ourselves spiritually empty both now and in the future.

We must reflect on our motives: are we working diligently for the Lord and providing for our families, or are we driven by a desire for more possessions? When possessions become distractions, our focus shifts away from things with eternal value to temporary satisfactions of the world.

> Therefore if you have been raised up with Christ, keep seeking the things above, where Christ is, seated at the right hand of God. Set your mind on the things above, not on the things that are on earth (Colossians 3:1–2).

In this passage, we are instructed to focus our minds on heavenly things—those that hold eternal value and significance. Paul often draws from the teachings of Jesus in His writings as seen here. Jesus, as the ultimate teacher, emphasized the importance of heavenly perspective over earthly distractions. While earthly possessions, money, and fame hold no place in heaven, the souls we lead to Christ and the ways we glorify Him with our lives are everlasting treasures we can bring before the throne of God.

So why do we have this lack of focus? Jesus says it is a case of bad eyes:

> The eye is the lamp of the body; so then if your eye is clear, your whole body will be full of light. But if your eye is bad, your whole body will be full of darkness. If then the light that is in you is darkness, how great is the darkness! No one can serve two masters; for either he will hate the one and love the other, or he will be devoted to one and despise the other. You cannot serve God and wealth (Matthew 6:22–24).

The eye serves as the lamp for the body, because it influences what we treasure and where we direct our focus. Essentially, what we value shapes what we look at, and what we look at guides our actions and decisions.

FOR RED, DRY EYES

What does it mean if the eye is good or clear? In Greek, the original language of the New Testament, the word *good* translates to *single*. So, if we have a single focus, the whole body will be full of light. If you have a singular fixed view of God, you will succeed in pleasing the Lord here on earth. If your view is set on the treasures of heaven, where moth does not destroy, thieves do not break in and steal, and rust does not decay, your vision is good. If your treasures have a heavenly focus or a heavenly or spiritual drive, you have a clear vision and the right view of life. Having a good view of life, meaning how you should talk, live, and act makes life's path a clearer picture or as Scripture says, it will be straight.

A straight path does not mean it is free from ups and downs, debris to trip on in the road, and unseen threats. Walking on a straight path means you know how to react in moments based on the standard of living you have chosen by having a biblical life and heavenly view. With the single direction, or a single view, the course we take in life is set on one thing: "But seek first His kingdom and His righteousness, and all these things will be given to you as well" (Matthew 6:33).

On the flipside to seeking the kingdom with clear eyes, if your eye is focused on the earthly prize, the temporal value of things, and the sole benefit of what this world can give, then your eye is *poneros*—worse than bad; it is evil. Your vision is evil, and it is blinded by wickedness, wicked desire, and distractions of earth. In the Greek New Testament, this word was also used to describe a cloudy eye disease, so your eye can be seen as clouded by the distractions of worldliness. This does not make you an evil person, and it does not even mean the things that you are distracted by are terrible, but anything that can steal your gaze from Jesus, and anything that can rob your focus from grace and your freedom in Christ is wicked, because it distracts you from a single-minded focus on pleasing Jesus. You will trip and fall to temptations, because distractions of life are what drive you.

A man was looking at himself in the mirror. He had a potbelly, and his hair had traveled from his head to his shoulders, ears, and chest. He said to his wife, "Honey what happened to me? I used to be big and strong. I used to have such beautiful hair, and now it is gone!!!"

His wife, seeing he needed affirmation, said, "Oh…honey, at least you have great eyesight!"

Do you have good eyesight? "But a natural man does not accept the things of the Spirit of God, for they are foolishness to him; and he cannot understand them, because they are spiritually appraised. But he who is spiritual appraises all things, yet he himself is appraised by no one" (1 Corinthians 2:14–15).

A PROPER APPRAISAL

To appraise is to judge and value. A person with a spiritual view will judge and value spiritual things like a great treasure, and the one with the clouded eye will judge and value spiritual things as foolish, absurd, or wasteful. The person viewing things through the spiritual view assesses things by "how this is fulfilling God's will, or how this will help me grow in Jesus." They see things for their spiritual benefit. Jesus is calling His followers to appraise life on what has spiritual benefit. He wants to be our sole focus, desire, reward, and vision.

Remember the song by the Flamingos?

> My love must be a kind of bling love
> because I can't see anyone but you
> Are the stars out tonight, I don't know if it's cloudy or bright…
> I only have eyes for you….[42]

God wants us to have a clear singular vision fixed to godly gain, not earthly satisfaction, staying focused on Him, and not distracted by the things we see on the right or left.

Any other focus causes our life to slip into moral decay. "But if the eye is bad, the body will be full of darkness" (Matthew 6:23). How you view your purpose on earth and what you view as treasure determines whether you are in the dark or not. Do you consider your life as your own or Christ's?

If you are looking at these as gains for self and not for Christ, you are not walking in the light. Your eye is clouded and dark. Your view on things is temporal and foolish.

How do we keep clear vision and focus on the eternal value? How can we be content in this life? I think the answer is found in nature.

---

42. The Flamingos, *I Only Have Eyes*, Flamingo Serenade, Roulette Records, 1959.

Have you ever watched sunflowers throughout the day? If you plant sunflowers in a central location, something very neat happens. At the start of the day, the flowers will be pointing east with the rising of the sun. By midday, they will be pointing straight because the sun is straight overhead, and by sunset, they will be looking west with the setting evening sun. Why? Because sunflowers need to soak in the sun to grow. The way to make leaves, the way to get tall, and the way to grow flowers and seeds is to soak in the sun. The sun provides the life-giving qualities to the root, to the stem, and to the flower.

> In Him was life, and the life was the Light of men. The Light shines in the darkness, and the darkness did not comprehend it. There was the true Light which, coming into the world, enlightens every man (John 1:4–5, 9).

Jesus, the Son of God, is our light, and we are looking to soak in the Son. He is the Son who gives us the life-giving qualities to grow and produce. Spending time with Jesus helps us to develop. It allows us to live right, to speak proper, to think straight, and encourages us to share with others. "Then Jesus again spoke to them, saying, 'I am the Light of the world; he who follows Me will not walk in the darkness, but will have the Light of life'" (John 8:12).

Jesus is our sun. He is what keeps us from staying in the shadows of unproductive darkness. Why? Well, let us go back to the sunflower. Why does the sunflower follow the sun? The plant follows the sun to maximize its growth in life. Sunflowers are considered annuals, meaning they are only around a few times a year. They do not live all year because winter kills them. So, for this tiny seed to grow anywhere from six to twenty feet tall and produce beautiful flowers and seeds, they need to work a lot harder than a plant that lives all year and grows very slowly. Think about it. Trees grow about six to twelve inches a year, but a sunflower grows six to twenty feet in 180 days. Why? Because their life is short, and because their life is short, it is devoted to growing in the short time it has. The sunflower absorbs the light, and it follows the source of light—the sun. It treasures each drop of sun and stores the sun's energy to use to become the giant beautiful sunflower.

When you treasure the light of Jesus and grab onto it to grow, it streams out of your life, produces, and multiplies. The sunflower's focus is getting light to grow, and the life of a believer's focus should be to grab the Light and grow. A tiny line between two numbers represents our life on earth: the day we are born and the day we die. While you are here, keep focused.

Are you storing up the Son and all He has to give in mercy, love, and grace? Are you embracing the relationship He wants to have with you? Do you see things with a clear eye of spiritual profit? Soak in the Son. Store up things of true value. Assess yourself by asking: How is this fulfilling God's will? How will this help me grow in Jesus?

If you start to feel discouraged and distracted by this world when your eyes begin to get cloudy, take a moment to inventory your treasures. Like the song says, "Count your blessings. Name them one by one. Count your many blessings. See what God has done."[43]

---

43. Johnson Oatman, Jr., *Count Your Blessings*, 1897.

CHAPTER 30

WORRY

"Do not worry then, saying, 'What will we eat?' or 'What will we drink?' or 'What will we wear for clothing?'"
—Matthew 6:31

[I]t turns out that 85 percent of what subjects worried about never happened, and with the 15 percent that did happen, 79 percent of subjects discovered either they could handle the difficulty better than expected, or the difficulty taught them a lesson worth learning. This means that 97 percent of what you worry over is not much more than a fearful mind punishing you with exaggerations and misperceptions.[44]

---

44. Don Joseph Goewey, "85 Percent of What We Worry About Never Happens," *Achnet*, https://www.achnet.com/content/85-percent-of-what-we-worry-about-never-happens.

Let's ponder that statistics and our own lifetime of fears. The monster under the bed is probably a vegetarian. Your eyes getting stuck crossed from the flash during a picture, mom's creepy clown coming to life, Jaws breaking into the deep end of your pool—none of those will happen. I recognize that the things listed are the irrational fears of our childhood, but we still have irrational fears as adults. As adults, the things we fear, we just relabel as worry.

WORRY?

What is worry? In Matthew 6, Jesus warns us three times (as the chapter closes) not to worry. But what does it mean to worry?

> *For this reason I say to you, do not be worried about your life, as to* what you will eat or what you will drink; nor for your body, as to what you will put on. Do not worry then, saying, 'What will we eat?' or 'What will we drink?' or 'What will wear for clothing?' So do not worry about tomorrow; for tomorrow will care for itself. Each day has enough trouble of its own (Matthew 6:25, 31, 34)**.**

The word *worry* in Greek is *merimnao,* which is really two different Greek words: *merizo,* which means to divide, and *nous,* meaning mind. In other words, it means we have a divided mind. As we get older, our worries and fears are based on a divided mind. We want to focus on Christ, but earthly values and possessions stay swirling in our heads. The fear of losing worldly possessions and prestige is overwhelming one's mind and taking the focus from Christ.

> Now as they were traveling along, He entered a village; and a woman named Martha welcomed Him into her home. She had a sister called Mary, who was seated at the Lord's feet, listening to His word. But Martha was distracted with all her preparations; and she came up to Him and

said, "Lord, do You not care that my sister has left me to do all the serving alone? Then tell her to help me." But the Lord answered and said to her, "Martha, Martha, you are worried and bothered about so many things; but only one thing is necessary, for Mary has chosen the good part, which shall not be taken away from her" (Luke 10:38–42).

In this passage, Mary chose the treasure of being at the feet of Jesus. Her sister, Martha, was so distracted by life that she failed to see what was of the most value, because worrying about details got the best of her.

Likewise, we tend to get worried and distracted by everyday life when Jesus is saying, "Sit at My feet. Spend time with Me. That is your number one priority."

The word used for *worry* in Matthew 6 and Luke 10 is the same *marimanao*, divided mind. You are too worried about tasks, position, success, food, money, and the future. Rather than looking to the Lord as the provider of your needs, you are looking to your needs to provide you peace and comfort. James talks about the person that lives in this way and how they should pray for wisdom.

> But if any of you lacks wisdom, let him ask of God, who gives to all generously and without reproach, and it will be given to him. But he must ask in faith without any doubting, for the one who doubts is like the surf of the sea, driven and tossed by the wind. For that man ought not to expect that he will receive anything from the Lord, being a double-minded man, unstable in all his ways (James 1:5–8).

If Jesus tells us to stop doing a particular thing and we continue to do it, then we are willfully sinning. Worrying occurs in our lives when circumstances control and dictate our well-being.

Having a divided mind is a consequence of having a bad eye, as we discussed in the previous chapter. If you have a singular, fixed view of

God, you will succeed in pleasing the Lord here on earth. If your view is set on the treasures of heaven—where moth does not destroy, thieves do not break in and steal, and rust does not decay—then your vision is good.

KINGDOM FOCUS OR FOCUS ON LOSS

If your treasures are oriented towards heavenly pursuits or spiritual fulfillment, your vision remains sincere and clear. This unwavering focus guides you along a straight path. When your gaze is fixed on one thing, distractions fade away.

However, if your eye is fixated solely on earthly rewards, on the fleeting pleasures and material gains of this world, your vision becomes clouded. It becomes obscured by the allure of wicked desires and the distractions of earthly pursuits. Why does this happen? Because when value is placed on earthly treasures over heavenly worth, clarity is lost.

When your focus is on earthly possessions and the transient offerings of this world, your mind becomes entangled in the fear of loss. What once diverted your attention from laboring for the Lord's favor and eternal reward now dominates your thoughts with apprehensions of loss. Your mind is besieged by what-ifs.

What if a thief breaches your home's security, if a fire engulfs your apartment, or if a colleague usurps your client? These what-ifs fracture your focus, hijack your thoughts, and redirect them away from heavenly pursuits to safeguarding earthly possessions. Christ beckons His followers not to succumb to these distractions.

According to Dr. Joseph Goldberg on *Web*MD, worry and stress brings on health problems: heart attacks, stroke, cancer, early death, early aging, asthma, obesity, diabetes, headaches, depression and anxiety, gastrointestinal problems, and Alzheimer's disease.[45] Worry can kill you and rob from your life or happiness. Worrying doesn't

---

45. Joseph F. Goldberg, "10 Health Problems Related to Stress That You Can Fix," https://www.webmd.com/balance/stress-management/features/10-fixable-stress-related-health-problems.

add anything positive to your life. In fact, it often detracts from it, consuming your energy and peace of mind without offering any solutions or benefits in return.

> And why are you worried about clothing? Observe how the lilies of the field grow; they do not toil nor do they spin, yet I say to you that not even Solomon in all his glory clothed himself like one of these. But if God so clothes the grass of the field, which is alive today and tomorrow is thrown into the furnace, will He not much more clothe you? You of little faith! Do not worry then, saying, "What will we eat?" or "What will we drink?" or "What will we wear for clothing?" For the Gentiles eagerly seek all these things; for your heavenly Father knows that you need all these things (Matthew 6:25–32).

Why do you allow yourself to be consumed by concerns about your appearance? No matter how splendid Solomon's attire, it paled in comparison to the beauty of the flowers that adorn the fields. Is fretting over appearance truly worthwhile?

You're caught up in the incessant cycle of providing for yourself, constantly thinking, "I need to ___." Yet, in the midst of this distraction, you fail to recognize that your Heavenly Father sees, hears, and knows all. He is fully aware of your needs and is committed to providing for them.

Unlike the pagan or unbeliever who lacks knowledge of God's provision, you have the assurance of a loving Father who cares for you. Trust in Him, for He will fulfill all your needs.

OUR PRESCRIPTION FOR WHAT HURTS

Jesus offers us keys to overcome fear and anxiety. In Matthew 6:34, He reminds us that each day presents its own tasks and challenges. Tomorrow will bring its own concerns, so there's no point in dwelling on them excessively. The God who provides is firmly in control.

Consider His words in Matthew 6:26. Birds don't toil or store food, yet they always find sustenance when they search. Whether in the soil or on a bush, provision awaits. Jesus is teaching us that God understands our needs and knows how to care for His people. So, there's no need to fret that God won't provide.

When we worry excessively about our possessions, they start to possess us. Instead, we should recognize that our life, love, finances, influence, and time all originate from God. We must acknowledge the source of these blessings and appreciate how fortunate we are to have them.

Remove resource thinking from your mindset. It's a mindset that arises when you fail to acknowledge the Provider and believe that things will inevitably run out. When you succumb to resource thinking, material possessions take precedence in your studies and life. You become consumed with acquiring more, making it the focus of your dreams and goals, all the while neglecting to recognize that these things are merely provisions bestowed by God.

Listen:

- Your job does not provide you money; it is the route God has chosen to provide you finances.
- Your friends do not provide you companionship; they are means by which God chooses to let you know you are not alone.
- Popularity does not dictate your importance; it is a platform God has given you to use for Him. Your importance was shown when Jesus died for you.
- Your family is not your source of love; they are just who God uses to demonstrate and illustrate what He feels for you.

When God is your source, there's no need to fret about resources. Even if they seem to falter, He always finds a way to replenish and sustain you. Therefore, you can focus diligently on your tasks, trusting that God will handle the outcomes and provide for your needs, both today and tomorrow.

LOOK AROUND--NATURE DOES NOT WORRY

Jesus references the birds of the air and the grass of the fields in Matthew 6 to highlight a profound truth. These elements of nature fulfill their God-given purpose on earth without worrying about anything else. They simply follow their natural cycle: seeds are sown, roots spread, growth occurs, and blooms flourish, all under the watchful care of God.

Jesus uses birds as an example. Birds effortlessly find their worm, berry, or twig for nest-building. They stay busy seeking what the Lord has provided for them. You won't find lazy birds pondering, "Where will I find a home and food for my five eggs?" No, birds actively gather twigs to construct their nests. They instinctively know where to look because they trust in their Creator's ability to provide.

Birds don't passively wait with open mouths for food to drop from the sky. Instead, they venture out, fully aware that God has meticulously provided every bug in the dirt, every berry on the bush, and every seed for their sustenance. They don't worry about finding the same provisions tomorrow; their focus is on living and thriving in the present moment, following the design intended for them.

The grass and flowers don't concern themselves with the rain watering their roots or the sun facilitating photosynthesis. They don't fret over bees pollinating or the wind scattering seeds. Their minds are not divided by doubts. Instead, they rest in the knowledge of their Creator. God has intricately programmed them to trust in His provision.

He orchestrates the growth of their roots through nutrient-rich soil, provides rain from the clouds, enables photosynthesis with the sun's rays, ensures pollination by bees, and disperses seeds through the wind. The flowers live as a testament to God's faithful provision, devoid of doubt or worry.

What the Lord is saying in this, is while you are waiting for His provision, live out your purpose. While you wait for the seed, keep busy doing what He made you to accomplish. Your purpose is to seek His kingdom first. So, do not let worry starve you out of your view of God. Do not let doubt distract you from living what He has called you to.

Even if you're faithfully living out God's purpose and design for your life, fear may still linger. You might be progressing forward yet find yourself entangled in the webs of what-ifs, shadows of doubt, and the grip of anxiety, all obscuring your vision of Christ.

But here's God's prescription for facing your fears: "Be anxious for nothing, but in everything by prayer and supplication with thanksgiving let your requests be made known to God. And the peace of God, which surpasses all comprehension, will guard your hearts and your minds in Christ Jesus" (Philippians 4:6–7). Through prayer, gratitude, and surrendering your worries to God, His peace, beyond all understanding, will envelop you, safeguarding your heart and mind in Christ Jesus.

First and foremost, this passage from Philippians issues a direct command in the Greek imperative: "Be anxious for nothing." Following this command, the Philippians are instructed on how to deal with their anxiety or worries.

The first step outlined in this passage is prayer. To conquer anxiety, turn to the God who provides for the birds of the air and clothes the fields. Pray earnestly.

Next, make supplication. Supplication entails expressing precisely what you need, lack, or desire. Thus, God instructs us to pray and to be specific in our requests.

The final step is thanksgiving. This entails praising Him, expressing gratitude, and rejoicing in Him because you acknowledge that He is able and is the source of all things. So, along with prayer and supplication, cultivate a heart of thanksgiving, acknowledging God's provision and sovereignty in your life.

> And Jesus answered and said to them, "Truly I say to you, if you have faith and do not doubt, you will not only do what was done to the fig tree, but even if you say to this

mountain, 'Be taken up and cast into the sea,' it will happen. And all things you ask in prayer, believing, you will receive" (Matthew 21:21–22).

Do not let fear, doubt, and anxiety cast a shadow on your tomorrow. Instead, address the God who is fully capable. Engage in prayer, supplication, and thanksgiving, trusting in His ability to provide and sustain you through every challenge and uncertainty.

CHAPTER 31

SEEK

"But seek first His kingdom and His righteousness, and all these things will be added to you."

—Matthew 6:33

Have you ever experienced the sensation of time slipping away, feeling like you're constantly struggling to keep up with the demands of each passing day? It's as if every ounce of effort is dedicated to merely surviving the present moment. And when you factor in the pressures of tomorrow—whether it's responsibilities like school, marriage, children, or other obligations—it can all feel overwhelming, leaving you wishing for a reprieve.

But amidst the chaos and madness that the world thrusts upon us, there is a solution—an antidote to the anxiety and stress that threatens to engulf us. We've delved into the importance of maintaining the right focus and perspective on things of genuine value. In this chapter, we'll explore even further what it means to embody this focused mindset in our daily lives.

> But seek first His kingdom and His righteousness, and all these things will be given to you as well. Therefore do not worry about tomorrow, for tomorrow will worry about itself. Each day has enough trouble of its own (Matthew 6:33–34).

How can we relinquish our worries and fully entrust everything to God? How do we maintain a steadfast focus on Him amidst life's distractions? Let's be candid: often, we're too preoccupied to recognize what truly holds significance. Our time on this earth is fleeting; our life expectancy pales in comparison to the vast expanse of eternity. The dash on our headstone represents but a fraction of time against the backdrop of eternity.

The challenge we confront is that we often live as if this temporary life is all there is, when in reality, we should be living with eternity in mind.

THE POWER IN ONE WORD

Jesus offers profound guidance on how to live our dash on the headstone to the fullest. He teaches us how to embrace the present and make the most of our fleeting lives. His instruction? "Seek."

Now, seeking may not initially sound like a game-changer, but its significance runs deep. In Greek, *seek* comes from the word *zēteite*, which implies not just a casual search, but a diligent inquiry, investigation, and a pursuit of reaching a binding, final, or terminal conclusion. Essentially, Jesus is urging us to give God the first place in our lives. He desires to be our foremost authority, the primary source of guidance, counsel, and wisdom. To put it succinctly, seek Him first.

Yet, the biggest hurdle many face is prioritizing the opinions, advice, and approval of others, or even seeking worldly wisdom, before turning to the One who holds the universe together. We often seek out the guidance and validation of friends, ourselves, or worldly sources like Dr. Phil before seeking God's wisdom.

Seeking God is not merely a quest for knowledge or understanding; it's an intimate closeness, a worshipful act. To the Hebrew audience Jesus addressed (remember, He was instructing His disciples with a large group of onlookers present [Luke 6:17-20]), seeking God was synonymous with worship. Jesus calls them—and us—to actions of heavenly focus, urging us to prioritize seeking God above all else.

> So I say to you: Ask and it will be given to you; seek and you will find; knock and the door will be opened to you. For everyone who asks receives; he who seeks finds; and to him who knocks, the door will be opened (Luke 11:9-10).

STOP AND SEEK

In essence, we're urged to let go of worries, to cease fretting over trials, challenges, and impending pains. Instead, let's center our attention on what transcends the present moment. Let's fixate on what endures beyond countless tomorrows, far into the future. Let's prioritize seeking and honoring the One who extends beyond the day we're laid to rest. Let's concentrate on the worship we share with Christ, on cultivating a life and a bond with Him. As Jesus said:

> And He said to His disciples, "For this reason I say to you, do not worry about your life, as to what you will eat; nor for your body, as to what you will put on. For life is more than food, and the body more than clothing. Consider the ravens, for they neither sow nor reap; they have no storeroom nor barn, and yet God feeds them; how much more valuable you are than the birds! And which of you by worrying can add a single hour to his life's span? If then you cannot do even a very little thing, why do you worry about other matters? Consider the lilies, how they grow: they neither toil nor spin; but I tell you, not even Solomon in all his glory clothed himself like one of these.

> But if God so clothes the grass in the field, which is alive today and tomorrow is thrown into the furnace, how much more will He clothe you? You men of little faith! And do not seek what you will eat and what you will drink, and do not keep worrying. For all these things the nations of the world eagerly seek; but your Father knows that you need these things. But seek His kingdom, and these things will be added to you. Do not be afraid, little flock, for your Father has chosen gladly to give you the kingdom. Sell your possessions and give to charity; make yourselves money belts which do not wear out, an unfailing treasure in heaven, where no thief comes near nor moth destroys. For where your treasure is, there your heart will be also (Luke 12:22–34).

A mind divided loses its heavenly focus, its godly drive, its Christ-centeredness. The anxieties of wealth have hijacked your thoughts. Yet, you can banish worry from your life by directing your attention to your true treasure and safeguarding it where it's beyond reach.

In Luke 12:29, Jesus exhorts: "Do not keep worrying." He expands on this lesson further. The Greek term for "keep worrying" (*meteorizo*) gives rise to the English word *meteor*. It conveys the idea of being lifted up or suspended in the air. It's a word often used to depict a ship tossed to and fro, up and down by waves. It's like conversing with someone who seems distracted—physically present but mentally elsewhere, lost in reverie. Yet, Jesus calls His followers to resist being tossed into the whirlwind of doubts, to refuse succumbing to worry that leaves them suspended in midair, ensnared by distractions and fears.

SEEK HIS KINGDOM

"But seek first the kingdom of God and His righteousness, and all these things will be added to you" (Matthew 6:33). When we prioritize seeking the kingdom, we're pursuing God's reign in our lives. In seeking His righteousness, we strive for His standards and His will for us. We must place Him first, not as an afterthought or a last resort, if we're to break free from worry. Focus on what enriches our lives, brings eternal joy, and fosters contentment today. Concentrate on living for the Lord in the present moment. How can my life honor the Lord right now? How can I store up treasures in heaven today? Live with a heavenly perspective.

That's why, following His discourse on worry, Jesus immediately warns in Luke 12 about the necessity of readiness for His return: "You also must be ready, for the Son of Man is coming at an hour you do not expect" (Luke 12:40). Why? Because while you were divided in mind, distracted, and preoccupied with comfort, you might have missed the opportunity to prepare your life for the Master's return. Life is too fleeting to overlook chances to glorify God.

KINGDOM FOCUS

So, let's live with our focus squarely on His kingdom. "Therefore, since we receive a kingdom which cannot be shaken, let's show gratitude, by which we may offer to God an acceptable service with reverence and awe" (Hebrews 12:28).

As followers, our gaze should be fixed on what endures—the unshakeable kingdom that remains impervious to decay, impervious to destruction by moths, impervious to theft by thieves, and impervious to corrosion by rust. Let your focus be such that you become the world's introduction to God's grace, love, and mercy here on earth. As 1 Peter 2:11 suggests, we should live as strangers, aliens to this world. Paul further emphasizes in 2 Corinthians 5:20 that we are ambassadors of Christ, essentially delegates to the kingdom of God. If we are indeed ambassadors or foreign representatives of heaven, then the church serves as the embassy—so conduct yourselves as if you're representing His homeland while residing in this foreign territory. "For here we do not have a lasting city, but we are seeking the city which is to come" (Hebrews 13:14).

In simple terms, this world is not our permanent residence; we are merely passing through. And while we traverse this earthly realm, our hearts yearn for His kingdom. But, you may ask, what exactly is this kingdom we're striving for?

> ...then comes the end, when He hands over the kingdom to the God and Father, when He has abolished all rule and all authority and power. For He must reign until He has put all His enemies under His feet. The last enemy that will be abolished is death. For HE HAS PUT ALL THINGS IN SUBJECTION UNDER HIS FEET. But when He says, "All things are put in subjection," it is evident that He is excepted who put all things in subjection to Him. When all things are subjected to Him, then the Son Himself also will be subjected to the One who subjected all things to Him, so that God may be all in all (1 Corinthians 15:24–28).

The kingdom we long for is the kingdom of Christ, the kingdom of heaven, the kingdom of God. In this kingdom, Jesus will sit on the throne of David, will rule Israel and the whole world, with the church as citizens.

> Then I saw the thrones, and those seated on them had been given authority to judge. And I saw the souls of those who had been beheaded for their testimony of Jesus and for the word of God, and those who had not worshiped the beast or its image, and had not received its mark on their foreheads or hands. And they came to life and reigned with Christ for a thousand years. The rest of the dead did not come back to life until the thousand years were complete. This is the first resurrection. Blessed and holy are those who share in the first resurrection! The second death has

no power over them, but they will be priests of God and of Christ, and will reign with Him for a thousand years (Revelation 20:4–6).

When we pray for "Thy kingdom come," we're petitioning for the establishment of the kingdom where the One who conquered sin and death reigns from the throne of David in Jerusalem. We're longing for God's original intention, thwarted by Adam's sin—human dominion over a world free from the curse. This prophetic vision unfolds in Isaiah 11, where the descendant of David, the root of Jesse, rules with righteousness (Isaiah 11:1–5). It's a realm where the lion and the calf peacefully coexist, where the wolf and the lamb lie down together (Isaiah 11:6–7), devoid of predator and prey dynamics (Isaiah 11:8). Even babies will play fearlessly with venomous snakes (Isaiah 11:8).

Isaiah 2:4 paints a picture of such abundance that implements of war are repurposed into tools for agriculture. And for millennia, there will be no demons, no Devil, and no wars.

THE WORLD WANTS JESUS

This is the time Jesus teaches His followers to pray for in the statement "thy kingdom come," and it is what every believer should pray for and earnestly seek. But this is not just something the believer and devoted follower of Jesus is seeking. Scripture says the earth longs for it and grumbles for it as well.

> For the anxious longing of the creation waits eagerly for the revealing of the sons of God. For the creation was subjected to futility, not willingly, but because of Him who subjected it, in hope that the creation itself also will be set free from its slavery to corruption into the freedom of the glory of the children of God. For we know that the whole creation groans and suffers the pains of childbirth together until now. And not only

this, but also we ourselves, having the first fruits of the Spirit, even we ourselves groan within ourselves, waiting eagerly for our adoption as sons, the redemption of our body (Romans 8:19-23).

The world cries out, pleading, "Lord, free us from corruption and sin, eradicate the evil, the suffering, diseases, and cancer." But until that awaited day arrives—until the moment we draw our final breath or are summoned in the rapture—we have a mission to fulfill. This is precisely what Jesus conveyed in Matthew 6. Lord, we yearn for that promised time, and we desire to play a role in it. Yet, if we must endure in waiting, let me live out Your will. Scripture affirms that the saints will reign upon His return (2 Timothy 2:12, Revelation 20:4-6, Luke 19:17-19, Revelation 5:10, Daniel 7:26-27, 1 Corinthians 6:1-3, Galatians 3:29, and Romans 8:17).

SEEK AND ACT

Before delving deeper into this chapter's profound teachings, let's revisit Matthew 6:33: "But seek first His kingdom and His righteousness, and all these things will be added to you."

Jesus emphasizes the surpassing nature of righteousness in Matthew 5:20: "For I say to you that unless your righteousness surpasses that of the scribes and Pharisees, you will not enter the kingdom of heaven." He doesn't merely want us to be part of His Millennial Kingdom; He desires our righteousness to transcend superficiality. We're called to seek His kingdom, but the Bible also instructs us to pursue His standard for it. After all, it's His kingdom, and if we represent it, His standards must be upheld. Jesus makes this point, because the originally designated representatives of the nation Israel, the Levites, and priests, had distorted the Lord's standard. Consequently, they embodied what Jesus referred to as whitewashed tombs. The Pharisees, appearing outwardly holy and righteous, were nevertheless doomed. This is why Jesus likened them to whitewashed tombs—appearing pristine on the outside, perhaps adorned with flowers and emitting pleasant scents, but inwardly concealing death. Even a meticulously maintained tomb houses decaying flesh and lifeless bones.

So, why does Jesus insist that the righteousness of His followers must exceed that of the revered holy men of Israel, the scribes and Pharisees?

> Woe to you, scribes and Pharisees, hypocrites! For you are like whitewashed tombs which on the outside appear beautiful, but inside they are full of dead men's bones and all uncleanness. So you, too, outwardly appear righteous to men, but inwardly you are full of hypocrisy and lawlessness. Woe to you, scribes and Pharisees, hypocrites! For you build the tombs of the prophets and adorn the monuments of the righteous, and say, "If we had been living in the days of our fathers, we would not have been partners with them in shedding the blood of the prophets." So you testify against yourselves, that you are sons of those who murdered the prophets. Fill up, then, the measure of the guilt of your fathers. You serpents, you brood of vipers, how will you escape the sentence of hell? (Matthew 23:27–33)

He indeed did not mince words when addressing the "holy men" of His time, labeling them hypocrites, snakes, evil, and devoid of compassion and love. He concludes by posing a sobering question: how can one escape Gehenna when their righteousness is nothing but a facade? The so-called holy men of Jesus's era, much like some today, presented themselves as sinless and pure externally, yet internally harbored corruption. Jesus likened them to whitewashed tombs—clean on the outside but containing decay within. He suggested they be cast out like worthless refuse until they recognize their shortcomings, repent, and undergo transformation.

Ultimately, we will all stand before the consuming fire of our great God to give an account and receive reward based on our deeds (1 Corinthians 3:12-13, 2 Corinthians 5:10, Hebrews 12:29).

Apart from Jesus, apart from being in Him, worshipping Him, and being in His grace, your actions mean nothing. Our words, works, and actions are nothing without Jesus. Without Jesus, they are like clean tombs with rotting corpses inside. Isaiah starkly contrasts our best efforts to God's standard (Isaiah 64:6), likening them to used menstrual rags. However, believers are clothed in Christ's righteousness.

> More than that, I count all things to be loss in view of the surpassing value of knowing Christ Jesus my Lord, for whom I have suffered the loss of all things, and count them but rubbish so that I may gain Christ, and may be found in Him, not having a righteousness of my own derived from *the* Law, but that which is through faith in Christ, the righteousness which *comes* from God on the basis of faith, (Philippians 3:8-9).

Jesus makes us righteous, and living a life of love for Him and others is His standard of righteous living He calls us to and rewards. When you live out love, when your heart is filled with love for God and love for your fellow man, you are living the righteousness in Him and have surpassed the scribe and Pharisee.

A deeper explanation is indeed warranted for the words "you will not enter the kingdom of heaven" (Matthew 5:20). Does this mean that works are necessary for eternal life? No. It's crucial to remember that Jesus's primary audience was His disciples. Therefore, His teachings were primarily directed towards them, much like a pastor tailors a message to address the specific needs, struggles, or encouragements of their congregation. However, this doesn't exclude others from listening or participating.

The disciples, already believers in Jesus as the Messiah, weren't being encouraged in works for salvation, because they had already placed their faith in Him. Salvation, as preached by Jesus, was consistently presented as a matter of belief.

However, Jesus often emphasized discipleship, inheritance, and reward as active pursuits requiring effort. For instance, He repeatedly emphasizes that eternal life comes through belief (John 3:1, John 6:4), and Paul reiterates that entry into the kingdom of heaven is through belief (Colossians 1:13–14).

So, what was Jesus conveying by the phrase "enter the kingdom"? It seems that He was instructing them on the posture of discipleship. He was teaching them His standard for living as followers and learners. "But seek first His kingdom and His righteousness, and all these things will be added to you" (Matthew 6:33). This is a call for a grand entrance of an inheritor claiming their prize. Jesus's standard is for us to seek Him, His kingdom, and His righteousness, with the assurance that the greatness of the kingdom will be bestowed upon us.

CHAPTER 32
JUDGING

"Do not judge so that you will not be judged."
—Matthew 7:1

A small-town baker bought his butter from a local farmer. After weighing his butter, he concluded the farmer had been reducing the amount in the packages but charging the same. Therefore, the baker accused the farmer of fraud. In court, the judge asked the farmer, "Do you have measuring weights?" "No sir," replied the farmer. "How then do you manage to weigh the butter that you sell?" The farmer answered, "When the baker began buying his butter from me, I thought I'd better get my bread from him. I have been using his 1-pound loaf as the weight for the butter I sell. If the weight of the butter is wrong, he has only himself to blame." [46]

---

46. Henry Bosch, "Bread and Butter," *Our Daily Bread*, April 16, 1998.

This story beautifully illustrates a profound truth that Jesus often emphasized in His teachings. Just as the baker accused the farmer of fraud based on his own measuring standard, only to realize he himself was being judged by that same standard, so too do we face the consequences of our own judgments and measures. Jesus's words in Matthew 7:2 echo this principle: "With what judgment you judge, you will be judged; and with the measure you use, it will be measured back to you."

GIVE OUT THE MERCY YOU WANT

What we desire to receive from God and from others—love, grace, mercy, and forgiveness—we must freely give ourselves. It's a matter of paying it forward to receive it. Therefore, we must demonstrate to those around us the very qualities we wish to see reflected in our own lives.

God instructs us to forgive others so that we ourselves may be forgiven (Matthew 6:14-15). Jesus further emphasizes in Matthew 7:2 that the same standard by which we judge others will be applied to us. Additionally, in Matthew 25:34-40, Jesus illustrates that the kingdom of God will be characterized by acts of compassion and kindness towards others: feeding the hungry, clothing the naked, and quenching the thirst of the thirsty. He explains that when we extend such care to others, we are doing it unto Him.

These verses make it clear that nurturing our relationship with Jesus is inseparable from how we relate to others. The path of discipleship involves engaging with and caring for others. God has placed us in a world with billions of fellow human beings to interact with, learn from, and serve for the sake of the gospel.

Your salvation is indeed a deeply personal journey, a relationship between you and Jesus. However, your growth in Christ is intricately connected to your relationship with others. Jesus emphasizes the significance of our interactions with others, teaching that the way we relate to them reflects how we relate to Him. This is why Paul, in 1 Corinthians 12, describes us as members of one body, highlighting the interconnectedness of believers.

JUDGING

At the core of our interactions with others lies our patience, forbearance, and the grace we extend—or withhold. These qualities not only shape our relationships with fellow believers but also contribute to our spiritual growth in Christ.

> Do not judge so that you will not be judged. For in the way you judge, you will be judged; and by your standard of measure, it will be measured to you. Why do you look at the speck that is in your brother's eye, but do not notice the log that is in your own eye? Or how can you say to your brother, "Let me take the speck out of your eye," and behold, the log is in your own eye? You hypocrite, first take the log out of your own eye, and then you will see clearly to take the speck out of your brother's eye (Matthew 7:1-5).

Jesus's measure is grace. His standard is love. His judgment is mercy. When a believer goes beyond these, they go beyond His teaching and His example. The way you judge a situation will come back on you. The same heart of unforgiveness will happen to you. It's not that God refuses to forgive you. Bitterness is sin. Unforgiveness is a sin, and sin affects your relationship with the Lord. But when you forgive and get rid of bitterness, your relationship stays together.

Jesus puts this in stronger terms: "For if you forgive men when they sin against you, your heavenly Father will also forgive you. But if you do not forgive men their sins, your Father will not forgive your sins" (Matthew 6:14-15). It's crucial to understand that Jesus wasn't establishing a merit system. Our forgiveness of others could never earn God's forgiveness for our sins. This isn't about salvation; it's about relationships. In God's eyes, all sins have been atoned for, so when we choose to hold a grudge against a fellow believer, it grieves Him.

IF GOD FORGIVES, WHO ARE WE TO KEEP REMEMBERING?

"If You, LORD, should mark iniquities, O Lord, who could stand? But there is forgiveness with You, That You may be feared" (Psalm 130:3–4). If God were to hold every "speck" of wrongdoing against us, we would be utterly condemned. We'd stand convicted, humiliated, embarrassed, and sentenced. However, in Jesus, we find forgiveness for everything and anything we could ever do. Without love, grace, and mercy as our guiding principles, we will inevitably encounter problems. These virtues serve as our barometer, guiding us in our interactions and decisions.

A man wanted to get his dog trained, so he dropped him off and after a few months went back to get his dog. The trainer brought the dog out without a leash and said, "sit." Amazingly the rambunctious pup sat and didn't move a muscle. The trainer proceeded to teach the owner the commands, and the dog acted upon each function. He threw a ball and yelled "fetch," and the dog ran and got the ball. He said "paper," and the dog got the newspaper, "shoes" and the dog got his shoes, "mail" and the dog opened the mailbox, shut it, and brought the mail, "breakfast" and the dog fried eggs, made toast, and plated them. The dog was so well behaved and trained that at the end of the demonstration, the *crème de la crème* was when the man commanded "taxes," and the dog prepared the taxes and filed them with the IRS! This dog was remarkable, to say the least. But the owner, always being one to find a problem, looked at the dog and trainer and said, "he can't swim." Some people will always find something wrong.

> And He also spoke a parable to them: "A blind man cannot guide a blind man, can he? Will they not both fall into a pit? A pupil is not above his teacher; but everyone, after he has been fully trained, will be like his teacher. Why do you look at the speck that is in your brother's eye, but do not notice the log that is in your own eye? Or how can you say to your brother, 'Brother, let me take out the speck that is in your eye,' when you yourself do not see the log that is in

your own eye? You hypocrite, first take the log out of your own eye, and then you will see clearly to take out the speck that is in your brother's eye (Luke 6:39–42).

In this passage, Jesus highlights that our words and actions reveal whom we learn from and what truths we internalize. Therefore, the journey of discipleship leads away from judgment and toward embracing love, grace, and mercy.

THE HEART OF A JUDGE

The way we judge others reflects what's inside us and whom we choose to follow (Luke 6:41–42). If we are followers of Jesus, then grace, mercy, and love should be the standards by which we judge and interact with people. Our hearts are revealed through our judgments.

In Jesus's time, this parable likely served as a critique aimed at the Pharisees. They emphasized strict adherence to the minutest details of the Law but lacked compassion for those who were suffering and struggling to survive each day. Their blindness to God's goodness, grace, and mercy meant they couldn't impart these qualities to their followers. They were unable to see the grace of God, and consequently, they couldn't guide others to find it either.

Jesus exhorts His followers to move beyond merely knowing Scripture for the purpose of condemning others, urging them instead to apply it for personal growth and to benefit others. He urges us to cease judgment and embrace grace.

The Pharisees, on the other hand, were notorious for nitpicking the faults of their neighbors while disregarding the deeper issues within themselves. They hypocritically referred to others as "brother" while harboring a false sense of superiority. Unfortunately, since they lacked personal experience of God's mercy, they couldn't effectively teach their disciples how to be gracious or merciful.

In battle, soldiers are trained to administer first aid to themselves before assisting others. This principle applies spiritually as well: if we are wounded, we must attend to our own healing before attempting to aid others. If we neglect our own wounds, we'll be ineffective in helping others, potentially putting them at risk. Similarly, if we're embroiled in our own struggles, we'll be unable to provide proper care and support to those around us.

It's not that Jesus doesn't want us to remove the specks from the eyes of our brothers and sisters. He does, and He wants us to help each other and see to each other's wounds. But He also knows we won't be able to help them heal in any meaningful way until we allow the Great Physician to heal us. And we cannot be healed if we ignore our wounds or even worse, conceal them. I know it hurts, but we have to trust Him and each other with our vulnerabilities. With our frailties, any wounded animal's instinct is to cover up its wounds, but that's how infection sets in. An injury can only be cleaned and bandaged if we expose it to the light, where it can be clearly seen and the remedy more easily identified.

A SYSTEM BASED ON ME

The problem in passing judgment is that we become the standard-bearer of perfection.

> And He also told this parable to some people who trusted in themselves that they were righteous, and viewed others with contempt: "Two men went up into the temple to pray, one a Pharisee and the other a tax collector. The Pharisee stood and was praying this to himself: 'God, I thank You that I am not like other people: swindlers, unjust, adulterers, or even like this tax collector.'" (Luke 18:9–10).

The term *Pharisee* carries a negative connotation in modern times, often associated with contempt, vilification, and hypocrisy. However, in the context of Jesus's time, being a Pharisee signified being at the pinnacle of the religious hierarchy. It meant dedicating oneself to studying and understanding God's laws, and it implied standing on a

JUDGING

moral high ground. The perception of Pharisees has evolved over time, but during Jesus's era, they were regarded as leaders and experts in matters of religious law and practice.

In Luke 18:9-10, Jesus presents a stark contrast between the Pharisee and the tax collector. During that time, tax collectors working for Rome were despised by the Jewish people, because they were seen as traitors to their own community as opposed to the ones working for the temple who were seen as loyal to Israel. Roman tax collectors were Jewish individuals who collaborated with the Roman authorities and collected taxes from their fellow Jews, often exploiting them for personal gain. In the eyes of the Jewish society, tax collectors were considered even worse than Samaritans or pagans because of their betrayal.

The Pharisee in Jesus's parable demonstrates this attitude of self-righteousness and superiority. He thanks God that he is not like the tax collector, boasting about his own perceived moral superiority and adherence to religious laws. However, in doing so, he fails to recognize his own need for repentance and forgiveness.

He comes to God, seeing himself above everyone else. He lists his accomplishments and tells God why he should be liked above everyone else. He makes a list of why he feels God owes him. God, this is why I am so good and so righteous. "I fast twice a week; I pay tithes of all that I get" (Luke 18:12). "God, it must be so good to know me." It's as if he is saying, "God if I weren't praying in here right now, you would have to listen to that guy, the tax collector."

Look at the tax collector's prayer. "But the tax collector, standing some distance away, was even unwilling to lift up his eyes to heaven, but was beating his breast, saying, 'God, be merciful to me, the sinner!'" (Luke 18:13). The tax collector is broken; he doesn't bother to look up out of shame; he doesn't try and get close to the altar of God. The verse says he stands far off. Some say he may even be in the outer temple where Gentiles could enter. He beats his chest as if to say, "I hate this sinful flesh", and says, "God, I am the sinner." No mention of other people, no mention of his good actions, just a prayer of forgiveness. God was at work in the life of a man stuck in sin.

Listen to the pain in his voice, not mentioning a single person, not a hint of comparison to another. He says, "forgive me the sinner" as if he were the only one in the sea of sinners. That statement is true remorse; it is seeing God as the Most High and all-powerful and seeing yourself for who you are.

The Pharisee was praying to God for a pat on the back. God, you owe me for all I do for you. The Pharisee in Jesus's parable arrogantly boasts before God, claiming his own goodness and holiness. He exudes an air of self-righteousness, cloaked in the outward appearance of holiness, yet beneath the facade lies the reality of human imperfection. He fails to recognize his own need for redemption and remains blind to his own sinfulness, considering himself superior to others.

On the other hand, the tax collector approaches God with humility and honesty. He doesn't parade his righteousness or religious attire but stands before God acknowledging his sinfulness and his need for redemption. His prayer reflects a posture of repentance and dependence on God's mercy: "God, I am a sinner; You are the redeemer of sinners."

GRADING ON GRACE

When I was in middle school, I never did well in math, and usually when midterms came out, I was between a C- or a D+, and by the time report cards came out, I would even out to a solid C. I remember I would wait to show my parents my progress report until my brother had shown his. Why? Because I knew my brother was doing horribly in all his classes. So, by the time they looked at his C's, D's, and F's, they were happy to see A's, B's, and one C. Having my brother do terribly lightened the blow for me. Eventually, they stopped asking for his grades, and that's when it got more challenging for me. But for three semesters, I was happy to be next in line.

JUDGING

Many of us are guilty of comparing ourselves to others who we perceive as struggling more than we are. This behavior stems from a desire to feel better about ourselves in light of the mistakes and failures of others. Similarly, we appreciate grading curves because they often elevate our performance relative to others.

However, when it comes to evaluating our sins, we mustn't rely on comparisons. Instead, we should acknowledge our own need for salvation and extend compassion to others, recognizing that we are all sinners in need of God's grace. Rather than judgment, our forgiveness should be rooted in compassion, grace, love, and mercy.

Jesus exemplifies this standard of grace. He who was sinless bore our sins on the cross so that we might be made righteous in Him. This profound act emphasizes the importance of extending grace to others as we have received from Him.

His standard is love.

> Owe nothing to anyone except to love one another; for the one who loves his neighbor has fulfilled *the* Law. For this, "YOU SHALL NOT COMMIT ADULTERY, YOU SHALL NOT MURDER, YOU SHALL NOT STEAL, YOU SHALL NOT COVET," and if there is any other commandment, it is summed up in this saying, "YOU SHALL LOVE YOUR NEIGHBOR AS YOURSELF." Love does no wrong to a neighbor; therefore love is the fulfillment of *the* Law (Romans 13:8–10).

If we desire to make a meaningful impact in this world, it's essential to demonstrate the values we uphold—such as grace, love, and mercy—rather than focusing solely on what we oppose. By embodying these virtues in our actions and interactions, we can inspire positive change and foster understanding and compassion in our communities. Instead of being known for our opposition, let us strive to be recognized for the values we champion and the love we extend to others.

CHAPTER 33

PEARLS OF WISDOM

"Do not give what is holy to dogs, and do not throw your pearls before swine, or they will trample them under their feet, and turn and tear you to pieces."

—Matthew 7:6

Many people would not consider making spaghetti in a wedding dress, wearing a suit to do an oil change, or using fine China for BBQ or pizza. Certain activities are typically associated with particular attire or settings. In many cases, we reserve our best attire or possessions for special occasions or activities that we consider more formal or significant. This is a common social convention and reflects our desire to maintain a sense of appropriateness and respect for the occasion. Ultimately, it's a matter of personal preference and cultural norms. While some individuals might feel comfortable breaking from tradition and using fine China for casual meals or wearing formal attire for mundane tasks, others may prefer to adhere to established customs and reserve special items for specific occasions.

In Matthew 7, Jesus urges us to exercise discernment in sharing our most cherished and sacred possessions or truths with those who may not value or understand them. He warns, "Do not give what is holy to dogs, and do not throw your pearls before pigs, or they will trample them under their feet, and turn and tear you to pieces" (Matthew 7:6). This cautionary advice underscores the importance of wisely stewarding our spiritual treasures and not exposing them to those who may disregard or misuse them, leading to potential harm or conflict.

This passage brings back memories of my childhood. My dad, a master carpenter and skilled builder, constructed a treehouse for my brother and me. We eagerly "helped," handing him tools as he expertly worked. Amidst the construction, he took the time to teach us how to use the tools, emphasizing their importance in enabling the work. When the treehouse was complete, we excitedly employed our newfound skills and tools to fashion furniture from the leftover wood scraps.

However, in our youthful enthusiasm, we neglected to properly care for our tools. Left outside in Miami's humid and rainy climate, they quickly succumbed to rust. Our tools, which we viewed as toys, bore the weight of disappointment when we realized their diminished condition. While to us they seemed insignificant, mere accessories to our play, to my dad, they were instruments of livelihood, deserving of respect and care.

Through this experience, my brother and I learned a valuable lesson, amidst a sore tush: the true value of tools lies not just in their material worth, but in their ability, in capable hands, to transform and create.

Similarly, Jesus uses symbolism to teach about the things of God. He starts by warning against giving what is sacred to dogs. In Jesus's era, dogs weren't regarded as domesticated companions but rather as untamed, scavenging creatures often linked with negative connotations (see 1 Kings 21:22-25). They were employed in hunting, combat, or guard duties, and were often left to scrounge for sustenance, subsisting on scraps and remnants.

When Jesus advises against giving what is holy to dogs, he refers to the sacred offerings made in Jewish religious customs. These sacrifices, such as oxen, bulls, goats, sheep, or birds, were consecrated to God, with a portion allocated to the priests and the remainder burned as an offering (Deuteronomy 18:1-8). Thus, bestowing something sanctified and designated for God upon a creature known for scavenging and disregarding sacred items would be inappropriate.

In this context, the term *dogs* symbolizes religious leaders who have rejected Jesus as the Messiah. They believe their own offerings and rituals surpass the significance of Jesus's sacrifice. Just as a dog fails to comprehend the importance of the offering, these leaders fail to grasp the true value and significance of Jesus's sacrifice.

> Finally, my brothers *and sisters,* rejoice in the Lord. To write the same things *again* is no trouble for me, and it is a safeguard for you. Beware of the dogs, beware of the evil workers, beware of the false circumcision; for we are the *true* circumcision, who worship in the Spirit of God and take pride in Christ Jesus, and put no confidence in the flesh, although I myself *could boast as* having confidence even in the flesh. If anyone else thinks he is confident in the flesh, I *have* more *reason:* circumcised the eighth day, of the nation of Israel, of the tribe of Benjamin, a Hebrew of Hebrews; as to the Law, a Pharisee; as to zeal, a persecutor of the church; as to the righteousness which is in the Law, found blameless (Philippians 3:1–6).

Paul cautions against religious individuals who perform deeds without genuine meaning. They consume acts of kindness and engage in reading the Scriptures, but their motivations are similar to a dog devouring food merely to sate its hunger, devoid of appreciation for flavor or culinary craftsmanship. These individuals lack reverence in their actions, as their study of Scripture, acts of charity, fasting, prayers, and songs of praise are driven by self-serving desires rather than awe for the Lord. Paul's advice echoes Christ's teachings: he advises not to invest time and energy in such individuals.

It's akin to serving hot dogs on silver platters—misplacing value where it doesn't belong. The word of the Lord is intended for those who seek spiritual growth and honor God through their actions, not for those who seek personal gratification.

ABOUT PIGS

Who are the pigs in Matthew 7:6? Pigs, also known as swine, were unclean animals; they were seen as unfit to eat and unfit to sacrifice. When they get very hungry, they will bite and attack their handlers until they get what they want. In the passage, unbelievers were paralleled as pigs.

Pearls are a reference to wisdom in Scripture (Job 28:18), and Jesus says the kingdom of God is like finding the rarest of pearls (Matthew 13:45–46). Jesus says do not cast the wisdom of the kingdom and of the word before swine. Why? Because Jesus says two things happen when an unbeliever hears the word of God: "they will trample them under their feet and turn and tear you to pieces." They care less about what the believer sees as precious, and because you did not give them what they wanted to eat, they turn on you and attack.

The world doesn't care about Christian morals and standards. They want you to feed them what they want, or they will turn on you. When believers stand on truth of Scripture that benefits unbelievers, they herald them as heroes. But when they take a stance against the accepted worldview, they are seen as the enemy, and the same hand they heralded as a hero is bitten.

Paul put it this way: "For the word of the cross is foolishness to those who are perishing, but to us who are being saved it is the power of God" (1 Corinthians 1:18).

> But a natural person does not accept the things of the Spirit of God, for they are foolishness to him; and he cannot

understand them, because they are spiritually discerned. But the one who is spiritual discerns all things, yet he himself is discerned by no one (1 Corinthians 2:14–15).

Paul encourages believers to adopt a mindful approach to life. In every situation, whether at work, home, or among family and friends, believers should ask themselves, "How can I grow from this? How can I honor God in this situation? How might He use this moment?" Consulting God's word for guidance is integral to this approach.

Conversely, unbelievers often view engaging with Scripture and contemplating its teachings as pointless. They may disregard its significance, treating it with disdain or indifference, akin to trampling upon it.

Peter puts it this way: "It has happened to them according to the true proverb, 'A DOG RETURNS TO ITS OWN VOMIT,' and, 'A sow, after washing, *returns* to wallowing in the mire'" (2 Peter 2:22). This passage discusses the tendency of individuals to revert to religious rituals and self-righteous deeds in pursuit of salvation. This behavior parallels Peter's actions in Acts 10 when he challenged the Lord's directives regarding what is clean and holy, as if presuming to know better than God, so he is speaking from a place of understanding the ease of falling back to tradition. Dogs go back to their vomit, meaning they go back to their own understanding; they go back to their tradition and their own righteousness. For Peter, the usage is for a believer struggling with traditions, and for Jesus, it speaks of individuals locked into tradition and not appreciating the glorious truths taught by Jesus. With people using this pattern and thinking, it is a waste to argue with the holy things, especially the word of God. If they do not care to listen, it is just more table scraps to them and not something special.

A pig doesn't take comfort in being clean, just like an unbeliever does not take comfort in the Lord. A pig finds solace in the mud and muck, even if it contains their own waste.

Although some passages in the Bible may be challenging to accept, and following Jesus's call to self-sacrifice may demand effort, there is freedom in understanding Scripture. By living out its teachings and applying them in our lives rather than succumbing to inaction or delusion, we can experience liberation from condemnation. Through prayer and diligent study of God's word, we can continually grow in knowledge and understanding, embracing a life marked by freedom and growth.

> All Scripture is inspired by God and profitable for teaching, for reproof, for correction, for training in righteousness; so that the man of God may be adequate, equipped for every good work (2 Timothy 3:16–17).

DEALING WITH THE WORLD

For an unbeliever that could care less, the pig in our passage, a dog, or someone thinking they can justify themselves aside from Christ, this does not mean we do not share the love of Jesus with them. It's essential to remember that this passage primarily addresses discerning the appropriate approach when offering judgment and sharing wisdom, not discouraging outreach to the lost. Its essence lies in refraining from attempting to rectify the lives of sinners who have yet to encounter the Savior. Let's examine the passage in its entirety for a comprehensive understanding.

> Do not judge, so that you will not be judged. For in the way you judge, you will be judged; and by your standard of measure, it will be measured to you. Why do you look at the speck that is in your brother's eye, but do not notice the log that is in your own eye? Or how can you say to your brother, "Let me take the speck out of your eye," and look, the log is in your own eye? You hypocrite, first take the log out of your own eye, and then you will see clearly to take the speck out of your brother's eye! Do not give what is holy

to dogs, and do not throw your pearls before pigs, or they will trample them under their feet, and turn and tear you to pieces. Ask, and it will be given to you; seek, and you will find; knock, and it will be opened to you (Matthew 7:1–7).

To the one you call brother, do not judge unfairly and harshly because that will come back to you. Instead, employ Jesus's standard—a measure of grace, love, and mercy. It's appropriate to accept correction from someone who cares for you and shares a mutual journey with you as discussed in verses 1-5. However, refrain from attempting to judge, correct, or establish standards with unbelievers, as outlined in verse 7. The wisdom and guidance you offer out of love and concern may seem nonsensical to them.

In essence, it's not productive to admonish an unbeliever for behaviors like premarital sex or drunkenness when they haven't encountered Jesus. Attempting to explain the Lord's teachings on issues like lust or greed is similarly futile before someone has found salvation. The priority should be leading the person to salvation first, rather than focusing on their moral character. When evangelizing, begin with the foundational message of God's love for the world, as in "For God so loved the world," rather than delving into specific moral injunctions like "whoever looks at a woman with lust in his eyes."

It's crucial to prioritize their eternal well-being over critiquing their sinful lifestyle. Saving souls takes precedence over trying to prompt immediate changes in their behavior.

CHAPTER 34

ASK

"Ask, and it will be given to you; seek, and you will find; knock, and it will be opened to you."

—Matthew 7:7

Have you ever considered that when you pray, you're communicating with the creator of the entire cosmos? You're conversing with the One who spoke, and galaxies materialized. Think about it: God is so vast and mighty that His mere words brought entire worlds into being. And when you talk to Him, you have the undivided attention of the One who scattered the stars across the heavens and sculpted humanity from the dust of the earth.

Moreover, when you open the pages of the Bible, you're immersing yourself in the very thoughts, desires, love letters, and wisdom of God Himself. It's a profound realization, isn't it?

So, why is our communication with God often so sporadic and infrequent? Perhaps it's time we reflect on the magnitude of who God is and the privilege we have in conversing with Him.

A diver drifted ten kilometers with the tide in Canada as dozens of people desperately searched for him. He died, in part, because his friends delayed calling for help. His partners in the dive boat waited an hour and forty-five minutes to call for help after he was swept away in a strong ebb tide.

"They tried to search for him themselves," said marine controller Marc Proulx. "Maybe they were embarrassed. I don't think they are his best buddies now."

The Canadian Coast Guard had some strong words of advice after the incident. "Call us quickly, the quicker it is the better," said Proulx.

Calling for help as soon as possible is always a good idea, especially when it comes to spiritual matters. Why is prayer usually our last resort instead of our first option? How far do we have to "drift" before we call on God to help us?[47]

Why do we wait to cry for help until the seashore is so far away we can't see it? Why, when the waves are too overwhelming, do we start to swim with urgency? Why, when we sought peace out at sea, do we wish for the comfort of company?

As we navigate through life, we often find ourselves gradually losing strength, losing sight of our goals, and sinking under the weight of our struggles. Each day becomes a battle to stay afloat. In such times, it only makes sense to cry out to the one who can rescue us. But for that rescue to take place, we must actively seek help, strive towards the safety of the shore, and genuinely desire the comfort that another can provide.

In Matthew 7:7–11, Jesus emphasizes the importance of redirecting our focus. Rather than expending our wisdom on harsh judgment and comparisons, we are encouraged to channel our energy towards seeking

---

47. From Fresh Illustrations, http://www.freshministry.org/illustrations.html.

the Lord and nurturing our personal relationship with Him. This passage underscores several key points. Firstly, prayer requires action—it's not merely a passive endeavor. And secondly, it highlights the nature of God as a loving Father who not only listens to our cries but also delights in taking action on our behalf.

> Ask, and it will be given to you; seek, and you will find; knock, and it will be opened to you. For everyone who asks receives, and he who seeks finds, and to him who knocks it will be opened. Or what man is there among you who, when his son asks for a loaf, will give him a stone? Or if he asks for a fish, he will not give him a snake, will he? If you then, being evil, know how to give good gifts to your children, how much more will your Father who is in heaven give what is good to those who ask Him! (Matthew 7:7–11)

TALK OFTEN

The idea here is to communicate frequently, sincerely, and intimately with our heavenly Father. Jesus emphasizes persistence—continually praying, asking, seeking, and knocking. In the original Greek, each of these actions—asking, seeking, and knocking—is in the present tense, suggesting ongoing, continuous engagement. This implies a dynamic and growing prayer life.

As followers of Jesus, we're encouraged to approach the throne room of the Father with persistence and constancy. We should keep asking, keep seeking, and keep knocking, recognizing that our Father in heaven hears us, cares for us deeply, and is ready to respond.

ASK

In Greek, the term for *asking, gar ho auteo*, carries the connotation of making a request, petitioning, or even begging. It depicts the posture of someone who recognizes their own limitations and appeals to someone with greater power for assistance. For us, this aspect of prayer resembles confessing our dependence on God. It's an acknowledgment that we are unable to accomplish certain things with our limited abilities, but we trust that God, with His unlimited power, can bring about the outcomes that is best for us.

C. S. Lewis once wrote, "as a friend of mine said, 'we regard God as an airman regards his parachute; it's there for emergencies but he hopes he'll never have to use it?'"[48] Indeed, we shouldn't treat God as a mere emergency escape; He is the source of power in our moments of inability. That's precisely why He identifies Himself as the good Father in this context. We're encouraged to ask the good Father for what we cannot achieve on our own—to intervene on our behalf, to influence outcomes in our favor, to soften hearts, move obstacles, accomplish the impossible, and lift burdens too heavy for us to bear. In essence, we're invited to ask Him to do what we cannot.

However, this isn't merely about repeating the same request over and over. As we persist in asking, we're also called to continue seeking. Part of this seeking involves discerning God's will in the matter, often through His word. God prepares our hearts before placing things into our hands. Sometimes, we become so preoccupied with earthly treasures that we lack the capacity to receive what God desires to give us. Let's not lose sight of the treasures awaiting us in His kingdom and the eternal goals that truly matter amidst the fleeting pleasures of this life.

SEEK

The next thing Jesus says in our passage is to seek or be seeking, *ho zeteo*. This implies a stronger desire for guidance. This is searching for answers. Jesus says we should seek first His kingdom, actively in all we do, and in our prayer be seeking.

When we ask in prayer, we are to be seeking Him through His word and looking for the obvious answer through His revealed will or promises written in Scripture. We are not sitting passively and idly. We

---

48. C. S. Lewis, *The Problem of Pain* (NY, New York: MacMillan Co., 1947), 84.

are not waiting lazily for God's answer. We are actively searching in His word. We actively ask, and we actively seek. "Come close to God and He will come close to you. Cleanse *your* hands, you sinners; and purify *your* hearts, you double-minded" (James 4:8).

KNOCK

The last action in prayer is knocking. Knocking is for communion—to be in one's presence. Knocking, *ho krouonti*, implies a greater sense of urgency. The concept of "knocking" implies more than just a gentle request; it signifies a persistent and earnest pursuit of communion with God. When we knock on God's door, we are actively seeking His presence, desiring His counsel, and longing for a deep relationship with Him.

In Revelation 3:20, Jesus illustrates this idea by portraying Himself as standing at the door of believers' lives, knocking for communion and fellowship. Our role is to respond by inviting Him in, walking alongside Him, and enjoying fellowship with Him.

Knocking represents a posture of intimate fellowship with our Savior. It signifies that certain situations require more than simply asking for something; they necessitate a persistent and determined effort to seek God's presence. It's not just a single tap on the door; it's a continuous pounding, a fervent desire to be heard and to enter into His presence.

In Matthew 7:10, we're assured: "For everyone who asks receives, and he who seeks finds, and to him who knocks it will be opened." It's noteworthy that the outcomes corresponding to each action—asking/receiving, seeking/finding, and knocking/opening—are also expressed in the present tense. This underscores the ongoing nature of these principles.

These imperatives convey that when we ask, seek, and knock, God the Father not only hears our prayers but is also inclined to respond to His children, for He is a good Father who delights in giving good gifts. When we take active steps, God acts on our behalf, opening doors, revealing truths, and bestowing blessings in accordance with His will and our genuine needs.

BEING HEARD

By consistently practicing the disciplines of asking, seeking, and knocking, we break the pattern of relegating prayer to a mere option or reserving it solely for moments of crisis. Instead, we cultivate an ongoing and open line of communication with our heavenly Father. Prayer becomes more than just a recourse for midnight emergencies; it becomes a constant dialogue with our Father.

Our passage in Matthew 7:7 emphasizes the promise that God will respond when we ask, seek, and knock. Jesus assures us: "Ask, and it shall be given to you; seek, and you shall find; knock, and it shall be opened to you." This reflects the heart of God the Father, who desires to please and care for His children, responding to their needs and desires with love and generosity.

In a complementary passage, Luke provides further insight into how God comforts us:

> So I say to you, ask, and it will be given to you; seek, and you will find; knock, and it will be opened to you. For everyone who asks, receives; and he who seeks, finds; and to him who knocks, it will be opened. Now suppose one of you fathers is asked by his son for a fish; he will not give him a snake instead of a fish, will he? Or if he is asked for an egg, he will not give him a scorpion, will he? If you then, being evil, know how to give good gifts to your children, how much more will your heavenly Father give the Holy Spirit to those who ask Him? (Luke 11:9–13)

A good Father doesn't spoil their child by granting every whim or desire. However, like a loving and wise Father, God hears our requests and discerns what we truly need. His responses are aligned with His perfect wisdom and our ultimate well-being.

As we delve deeper into Scripture and cultivate a richer prayer life, our focus naturally shifts towards spiritual matters, spiritual requests, and spiritual growth. We begin to recognize the significance of aligning our desires with God's will and seeking His guidance in all aspects of our lives, including our material needs and spiritual aspirations.

The context suggests that God encourages His children to regularly seek His assistance. However, He doesn't abandon us to our limited understanding. Instead, He provides the Holy Spirit to intercede on our behalf, conveying our needs accurately to the Father. This aligns with Paul's message in his letter to the Romans:

> For you have not received a spirit of slavery leading to fear again, but you have received a spirit of adoption as sons *and daughters* by which we cry out, "Abba! Father!" The Spirit Himself testifies with our spirit that we are children of God, and if children, heirs also, heirs of God and fellow heirs with Christ, if indeed we suffer with *Him* so that we may also be glorified with *Him.* Now in the same way the Spirit also helps our weakness; for we do not know what to pray for as we should, but the Spirit Himself intercedes for *us* with groanings too deep for words; and He who searches the hearts knows what the mind of the Spirit is, because He intercedes for the saints according to *the will of* God (Romans 8:15–17 and 8:26–27).

Likewise, the passage encourages us to persist in asking, seeking, and knocking. It assures us that God will continue to respond, we will keep discovering, and doors will remain open. God doesn't hide Himself or His answers from us; rather, He invites us to keep our hearts and mouths open in prayer and to diligently search for answers in His word while remaining in His presence.

CHAPTER 35
THE GOLDEN RULE

"In everything, therefore, treat people the same way you want them to treat you, for this is the Law and the Prophets."
—Matthew 7:12

The concept of treating others as you would want to be treated has ancient roots. Hillel, a rabbi during the time of Christ, commented on the Law of Moses, saying, "That which is hateful to you, do not do to your fellow. That is the whole Torah; the rest is the explanation; go and learn."[49] Jesus expands on this principle, presenting His standard that surpasses earthly interpretations and recommendations. He says, "In everything, therefore, treat people the same way you want them to treat you, for this is the Law and the Prophets" (Matthew 7:12).

---

49. Babylonian Talmud, Shabbat 31a.

THE SUMMARY OF THE LAW IS LOVE GOD AND LOVE PEOPLE

Just as Jesus often challenged conventional thinking, He does so again here. He suggests that this principle encapsulates the essence of the Law, what God intended for His people all along: to live in peace with everyone. Jesus goes beyond mere outward religious observance, because He desires hearts turned toward Him rather than deceived by self-righteousness.

In our relationship with Jesus, it's not merely about fulfilling a checklist of actions. Rather, He calls us to act, think, and live out of gratitude for what He has done for us—out of love, grace, and mercy.

JESUS'S LAW IS LOVE AS AN ACTION

Jesus takes it beyond the law, beyond a summary from a rabbi, and beyond you must do.

> This is My commandment, that you love one another, just as I have loved you. Greater love has no one than this, that a person will lay down his life for his friends. You are My friends if you do what I command you. No longer do I call you slaves, for the slave does not know what his master is doing; but I have called you friends, because all things that I have heard from My Father I have made known to you. You did not choose Me but I chose you, and appointed you that you would go and bear fruit, and *that* your fruit would remain, so that whatever you ask of the Father in My name He may give to you. This I command you, that you love one another (John 15:12–17).

In this passage, Jesus emphasizes the transformative power of love in our interactions with Him and others. His command isn't about blind obedience to Sabbath laws or traditions. Instead, He calls us to active love, sometimes requiring us to step out of our comfort zones to uplift others.

Love involves sacrifices—going without to provide for others, holding back our words to build others up. As we grow in this new relationship with Jesus, He invites us to become close to Him as friends and partners in His work.

LEARN THE LAW OF LOVE

"For the whole Law is fulfilled in one word, in the statement, 'YOU SHALL LOVE YOUR NEIGHBOR AS YOURSELF'" (Galatians 5:14). Jesus, as the fulfillment of the Law (Matthew 5:17–18), emphasized the centrality of love to His disciples. Paul reaffirms this focus later in his writings (Romans 13:8–10, Galatians 5:14).

Jesus contrasted His teachings with the burdensome interpretations of the Law by the rabbis and Pharisees, describing His yoke as easy and light (Matthew 23:4, 11:28–30). Love is universally desired and sought after. Paul asserts that love is the essence of the Law, while Jesus teaches in Matthew 7 that if you want love, you must give it. Love, therefore, becomes the defining characteristic of following Jesus. But what does this love look like in practice?

THE LOOK OF LOVE

> Brethren, even if anyone is caught in any trespass, you who are spiritual, restore such a one in a spirit of gentleness; each one looking to yourself, so that you too will not be tempted. Bear one another's burdens, and thereby fulfill the law of Christ. For if anyone thinks he is something when he is nothing, he deceives himself. But each one must examine his own work, and then he will have reason for boasting in regard to himself alone, and not in regard to another. For each one will bear his own load (Galatians 6:1–5).

In this passage, Paul addresses how to handle sensitive situations within the Christian community. He isn't presenting hypothetical scenarios but rather offering guidance for when a fellow believer faces struggles with sin or encounters hardships in life.

It's important to note that Paul doesn't equate sins with life's burdens. He isn't suggesting that personal struggles are a result of sin. Sometimes, people wrongly assume that difficulties arise from personal failings, such as attributing illness or misfortune to moral shortcomings. Paul emphasizes that both sins and life's challenges are common experiences for everyone, and they shouldn't be conflated.

By addressing both sin and life's trials together, Paul highlights how both can have a profound impact, leading to feelings of isolation and loneliness. Whether grappling with temptation or facing life's adversities, individuals can feel overwhelmed. Paul's aim is to provide support and guidance for navigating these difficult circumstances within the Christian community.

LOVE COMES ALONGSIDE

Let's delve into Galatians 6:1, where Paul addresses how to handle a fellow believer's sin: "Brethren, even if anyone is caught in any trespass, you who are spiritual, restore such a one in a spirit of gentleness; each one looking to yourself, so that you too will not be tempted."

What exactly is a trespass? In modern terms, we often use signs that say, "Private Property, No Trespassing," indicating ownership and a boundary not to be crossed.

In the New Testament, a trespass (*paraptōmati*) carries a similar notion. It signifies a false step, wrongdoing, or sin. Paul advises those who are spiritually mature to assist a fellow believer who has stumbled into sin. But how should this be done? Not with harshness or condemnation, but with a spirit of love and gentleness.

Paul then transitions to discussing burdens, which are heavy weights or obstacles in life. These burdens can take various forms: financial struggles, health issues, loss of a loved one, or distressing news that consumes one's thoughts. We are called to help bear these burdens for one another, providing support and relief.

In light of Jesus's commandment in Matthew 7:12 to treat others as we would like to be treated, bearing one another's burdens in Galatians 6 is an expression of love—a fulfillment of the law of Christ.

THE GREAT COMMAND PLUS ONE

> One of the scribes came and heard them arguing, and recognizing that He had answered them well, asked Him, "What commandment is the foremost of all?" Jesus answered, "The foremost is, 'HEAR, O ISRAEL! THE LORD OUR GOD IS ONE LORD; AND YOU SHALL LOVE THE LORD YOUR GOD WITH ALL YOUR HEART, AND WITH ALL YOUR SOUL, AND WITH ALL YOUR MIND, AND WITH ALL YOUR STRENGTH'" (Mark 12:28–30).

This foremost command quoted by Jesus from Deuteronomy is known to the Jews as the Shema. It declares that there is no god but the true God, and He is to be loved with every ounce of one's power and being.

So, what does it mean to love the Lord with all? It's akin to a marriage. Initially, there's a physical attraction, then intellectual connection. Eventually, there's engagement, leading to an intimate union where nothing is held back—financially, physically, mentally, or even locationally. Jesus desires this level of profound intimacy in our relationship with Him, likening it to marriage (Ephesians 5:21–31).

But Jesus takes it a step further by emphasizing that this application isn't merely a matter of law or tradition. He adds, "The second is this, 'YOU SHALL LOVE YOUR NEIGHBOR AS YOURSELF.' There is no other commandment greater than these."

Consider this: The second most crucial thing a person can do to please God is to love their neighbor. This echoes Paul's sentiment in Galatians 6. The key to understanding this entire passage lies in verse 1 and is further elaborated in verses 3–5.

Let's examine them side by side.

> ...you who are spiritual, restore such a one in a spirit of gentleness; each one looking to yourself, so that you too will not be tempted (Galatians 6:1b).
>
> For if anyone thinks he is something when he is nothing, he deceives himself. But each one must examine his own work, and then he will have reason for boasting in regard to himself alone, and not in regard to another. For each one will bear his own load (Galatians 6:3-5).

It's the spiritually mature who are tasked with restoring a brother as indicated in Galatians 6:1. The mature believer, as defined in Galatians 6:3-5, is one who considers others and regularly checks their own behavior to ensure they're not causing harm or engaging in gossip.

Galatians 6:3-5 reveals the consequence of seeking assistance from the immature. Instead of offering genuine help, the immature tend to boast about their own virtues while highlighting others' struggles in sin or life. Anytime one feels compelled to divulge someone else's shortcomings to boost their own self-esteem, whether related to sin or life challenges, it amounts to gossip and indicates immaturity. Mature believers, however, find their confidence in Christ and don't require such validation, enabling them to provide genuine assistance to others.

When you need surgery, you don't turn to a plumber, do you? Similarly, when you're feeling low, don't seek out gossip or bad advice from the immature. Instead, seek help from someone who can truly lift you up and restore you—a person who has spent time at the feet of Jesus and can offer love and grace.

Why turn to the immature for advice that could lead to further problems? Seeking counsel from those who only tell us what we want to hear often results in negative outcomes, whether it's in marriage, dealing with sin, or facing challenges at work. The advice of the immature or unbelieving world can be damaging and unhelpful.

Just as you wouldn't visit a mechanic for a tooth extraction, it's important to seek guidance from mature believers who can provide genuine support and wisdom. Those who are spiritually mature should extend love and compassion to those in pain or struggling with sin. And for those who are struggling, it's essential to turn to the mature for help in bearing their burdens. Ultimately, we should treat others with the same love, respect, and care that we desire for ourselves.

CHAPTER 36
THE GATE

"For the gate is small and the way is narrow that leads to life, and there are few who find it."

—Matthew 7:14

The Bible presents a unified message regarding salvation: it is through faith in Christ alone. However, there are passages that emphasize the importance of works for learning and growth in the Christian walk.

At times, passages such as those found in the Olivet discourse and upper room may seem to suggest that salvation is maintained by a believer's actions. In reality, these passages are emphasizing discipleship and the ongoing growth that comes from the believer's choices. The invitation to enter the narrow gate in Matthew 7:13-14 is connected to the narrow life that follows, highlighting the commitment and dedication required in discipleship.

It's important to understand that passages that may cause confusion are not questioning our salvation but rather challenging us to assess whether we are truly on the path of discipleship. This is because our choices and actions reflect the paths we choose to follow in life.

GOOD START WITH A BAD FINISH

What will Nadab and Abihu be remembered for? They were Aaron's sons, wicked priests who were consumed by God's fire (Leviticus 10). Solomon, renowned as the wisest man, ended his days turning to the demon gods of his foreign wives and concubines, his heart not wholly devoted to the Lord (1 Kings 11:4), committing evil in God's sight. The Corinthian church was notorious for drunkenness, pride, and discord, acting immaturely despite their faith (1 Corinthians 3:1), even tolerating a member involved in incest (1 Corinthians 5:1). Ananias and Sapphira will forever be remembered for attempting to deceive not only the apostles but the Holy Spirit Himself (Acts 5:1–13). Peter, too, had his share of missteps: cutting off a man's ear, denying the Lord, and succumbing to hypocrisy (Matthew 26:51, Luke 22:61, Galatians 2:11–13). Hymenaeus and Alexander are remembered for derailing their spiritual growth (1 Timothy 1:20).

Each of these individuals, among many others, experienced significant failures in their lives. Despite their shortcomings—momentary lapses in judgment, moral failings, or sinful behavior—they are now in the presence of the Lord, saved in heaven. Their stories serve as reminders of the consequences of folly, leading to pain, heartache, and sometimes physical death. Yet, even in their failings, they stand as examples of God's grace and forgiveness, demonstrating that no mistake is too great for His redemption.

CHOOSE THE RIGHT PATH

The reality is that every moment, every day, we are faced with a choice: Will we prioritize our own desires, or will we align ourselves with the will of the Lord? Will we insist on following our own path, or will we submit to God's way?

> Trust in the LORD with all your heart and do not lean on your own understanding. In all your ways acknowledge Him, And He will make your paths straight. Do not be wise in your own eyes; Fear the LORD and turn away from evil (Proverbs 3:5–7).

Walk in His ways. Acknowledge Him in all your ways. Seek His guidance, direction, and growth through His word, which provides instruction on how to navigate life, finances, circumstances, work, family, and friendships. When we do trust in the Lord, our path is straight. It's clear. We can see the direction.

"And He was saying to *them* all, 'If anyone wants to come after Me, he must deny himself, take up his cross daily, and follow Me'" (Luke 9:23). Jesus's call to discipleship is simple, "Follow Me." We see it repeatedly and know it is a direct call to believers to enter into an intimate relationship of growth and change. Scripture says that when the disciples heard this call, they forsook all and followed. Meaning they rejected all other options, opinions, desires, calls, and ties to life and literally followed the path, footsteps, and teaching of Jesus.

Following Jesus means allowing Him to guide our path, making it straight and free from distractions. Both paths ultimately lead to the same destination, but one may be filled with more pain and distractions, while the other is more direct.

In this analogy, we see two tracks, each representing a choice, leading to the same city. One path may seem easier to walk due to fewer obstacles, but it may also be filled with distractions that divert us from our ultimate goal. The other path may present greater challenges and risks, but it offers fewer distractions and a more direct route to our destination.

Vans, trucks, and SUVs have two places in the wheels that are required to be adjusted in order to align them properly. You can get away with adjusting it in only one spot for it to go for a little while. But to make the van, SUV, or tuck drive straight, it takes proper alignment.

And what is true for cars, vans, trucks, and SUVs is true for life.

We require the hand of the Master to align us properly, not just for a straightforward adjustment. This alignment is crucial in various aspects of our lives. We don't desire our journey to proceed straight for a brief period only to veer off course into a ditch. Our aim is to succeed in reaching our destination, but this necessitates being aligned with Him.

THE EXTRA MILE

In the Sermon on the Mount, Jesus instructs His disciples on how to align with Him in prayer, fasting, attitude, and character. He desires them to attain the correct alignment so that their path is clear, enabling them to make the right choices along the way.

TWO PATHS INTO ONE CITY

"Enter through the narrow gate; for the gate is wide and the way is broad that leads to destruction, and there are many who enter through it. For the gate is small and the way is narrow that leads to life, and there are few who find it" (Matthew 7:13–14).

Rice, Edwin W. A pictorial commentary on the Gospel according to Mark. (1881).

The passage presents the choices between the path of the flesh and the path of discipleship. Many biblical scholars believe that the narrow gate refers to the "needle gate" Jesus mentioned in Matthew 19:24:

> "And Jesus said to His disciples, 'Truly, I say to you, only with difficulty will a rich person enter the kingdom of heaven. Again I tell you, it is easier for a camel to go through the eye of a needle than for a rich person to enter the kingdom of God.' When the disciples heard this, they were greatly astonished, saying, 'Who then can be saved?' But Jesus looked at them and said, 'With man this is impossible, but with God all things are possible'" (Matthew 19:23–26).

Here, Jesus isn't saying that rich people cannot be saved eternally. Instead, He's discussing the challenges associated with growth, sanctification, salvation, or the transformation of one's lifestyle.

THE GATE

Understanding this passage requires considering its historical context. In ancient cities like Jerusalem, the main entrance faced the well-traveled Roman Road, bustling with commerce, tourists, delegates, and various unsavory characters. This main gate was a hub of activity, with merchants, money changers, prostitutes, and thieves vying for attention. To reach the city, one had to navigate through these distractions along the paved road, which, while visually appealing, paved nice and flat, and usually barring a wide path, posed significant moral hazards.

In addition to the main gate, there were other entrances to the city, such as the sheep gate for temple sheep, the water gate for cleansing, the dung gate for waste disposal, and the Al-Buraq or funeral gate. Unlike the wide main gate, these side gates were narrow and often overlooked. They typically consisted of a single door and were accessed via bumpy, sometimes overgrown dirt paths, offering a less conspicuous but more challenging route into the city. The narrow entrances around the city would not have the merchants, money changers, hotels, brothels, and fanfare to distract the weary traveler.

THE COST OF TRAVEL

> Then Jesus said to His disciples, "If anyone wants to come after Me, he must deny himself, take up his cross, and follow Me. For whoever wants to save his life will lose it; but whoever loses his life for My sake will find it. For what good will it do a person if he gains the whole world, but forfeits his soul? Or what will a person give in exchange for his soul? For the Son of Man is going to come in the glory of His Father with His angels, and WILL THEN REPAY EVERY PERSON ACCORDING TO HIS DEEDS (Matthew 16:24–27).

The term *soul* (*psuches*) in this context refers to the spirit or essence of a person, akin to someone with great spirit representing their personality. On the other hand, *pneuma* typically denotes spirit, such as the Holy Spirit or one's eternal spirit. What benefit is there if wealth, fame, and worldliness compromise your personality, rationality, and true self? You may amass worldly possessions and riches but forfeit your genuine identity in the process.

This concept finds further exploration in 1 Corinthians 3:

> Now if anyone builds on the foundation with gold, silver, precious stones, wood, hay, *or* straw, each one's work will become evident; for the day will show it because it is *to be* revealed with fire, and the fire itself will test the quality of each one's work. If anyone's work which he has built on it remains, he will receive a reward. If anyone's work is burned up, he will suffer loss; but he himself will be saved, yet *only* so as through fire (1 Corinthians 3:12–15).

When examining Scripture, it's crucial to grasp the nuances of the words used in the text. In Matthew 7:13, the term *destruction* isn't synonymous with hell or judgment; rather, it originates from the Greek word *apoleian*, which suggests loss. Entering through the narrow gate entails experiencing loss.

As mentioned, Jerusalem boasted numerous gates, each with its own level of popularity and foot traffic. The main entrance was grand and spacious, attracting many travelers and visitors. However, it was also bustling with distractions, as sellers, merchants, and money changers crowded the area. But distractions come with a price.

The main gate always had soldiers to police the area, check bags, make sure no armies were smuggling in, and no goods were brought in without tax. The side gates did not have guards, because they were so narrow that no elephant could make it in, and a donkey or camel caravan would not fit with their goods on their backs. All the taxable items, the spices, money, cups, and jewelry would have to be removed to enter the side gates. To enter through the narrow side gates, merchants had to unload their bags, leaving them vulnerable outside while they led their animals through the gate, then reload afterward. This risked theft but prioritized entering the city over preserving earthly possessions.

Jesus likened this sacrifice to the effort needed to enter the narrow gate of discipleship. Wealthy individuals, attached to material possessions, struggle to make this sacrifice, as it demands shedding worries, fears, luxuries, and worldly gains. In Matthew 6, Jesus urges disciples to prioritize heavenly treasures, secure from theft, over earthly possessions.

CHOOSE THE HARD PATH OF DISCIPLESHIP

When Jesus instructs to take the narrow road in Matthew 7, He isn't referring to the path to heaven; He means the road of discipleship. This path is narrow and challenging; you'll have to forsake worldly possessions. You'll leave behind the caravan, but the path of discipleship avoids the temptations the world has to offer.

Some people are enticed by the attractions of the city, its lights, and nightlife, while others prefer a quieter life with fewer consequences and headaches. To resist the allure of sin means embracing the path of Jesus, the way of discipleship.

The narrow way serves as the gateway to discipleship, but it comes with its costs. Not everyone chooses this road, because it is more demanding. Consider the demands of discipleship: one must prioritize their love for Jesus over their life and family (Luke 14:26), practice self-denial (Luke 9:23), be willing to leave work, home, and family behind (Luke 18:28), endure humiliation and suffering (Luke 14:27), and face rejection and persecution (Luke 10:16).

The words spoken by Jesus in Matthew 7 reflect the choices presented to the nation of Israel as they entered the Promised Land, this after getting there and having to wonder forty years for refusing to enter the first time (Deuteronomy 30). They faced a crucial decision: to embrace an abundant life, drawing near to the Lord and forsaking the grumbling of the desert, the golden calf, and the false gods of Egypt, or to succumb to grumbling and accept the false gods, along with the ensuing consequences. Although they were in the land either way, the choice of lifestyle was theirs to make.

> See, I have set before you today life and goodness, as well as death and disaster. For I am commanding you today to love the LORD your God, to walk in His ways, and to keep His commandments, statutes, and ordinances, so that you may live and increase, and the LORD your God may bless you in the land that you are entering to possess (Deuteronomy 30:15–16).

Listen to the rest of what Jesus taught about the eye of the needle in Matthew 19:

> Then Peter responded and said to Him, "Behold, we have left everything and followed You; what then will there be for us?" And Jesus said to them, "Truly I say to you, that you who have followed Me, in the regeneration when the Son of Man will sit on His glorious throne, you also shall sit upon twelve thrones, judging the twelve tribes of Israel. And everyone who has left houses or brothers or sisters or father or mother or children or farms on account of My name, will receive many times as much, and will inherit eternal life. But many *who are* first will be last; and *the* last, first" (Matthew 19:27–30).

My aspiration is to hear those words from Him when I stand before Him: "Well done, my good and faithful servant." I desire my earthly life to have significance, even if it means foregoing life's distractions. How about you? Are you inclined towards the entrance filled with distractions and pain, or the one requiring hard work that yields eternal rewards? Align yourself correctly and walk the path of a disciple for a fulfilling relationship now and an abundant life later.

CHAPTER 37
FRUIT OF FALSENESS

"So then, you will know them by their fruits."

—Matthew 7:20

A substantial number of individuals are employed to inspect fruit and vegetables, a vital service considering the significant amount of produce imported into the United States.[50] With over half of fresh fruit and nearly a third of vegetables being imports, the role of fruit inspectors becomes even more crucial.[51] Their diligence is essential for safeguarding public health, as contaminated produce can lead to illness and even fatalities. It's alarming to think that millions of people fall ill, and thousands die each year due to tainted fruit.[52] The importance of rigorous inspection measures to guarantee the safety of the food supply chain cannot be overstated.

---

50. https://www.brandeis.edu/investigate/food-health/foodborne-illness/who-monitors-food.html.
51. https://www.fda.gov/about-fda/fda-basics/fact-sheet-fda-glance.
52. https://www.cdc.gov/foodborneburden/index.html.

LOOKS CAN DECEIVE

One might assume that spotting a bad fruit is straightforward, right? Avoid the green strawberries, steer clear of the brown apples, and don't touch the yellowing zucchini. The issue isn't with the eye test; it's easy to identify rotting fruit. The challenge arises when producers and sellers deliberately disguise the bad as good. They might dye zucchini and cucumbers green, inject watermelons with red dye, or spray chemicals on strawberries to make them appear ripe. This is why we need trained individuals who can discern the difference. Even though the produce looks, smells, and tastes fine, it could still make you very sick.

This reality extends to our spiritual lives as well. Take a moment before concluding this chapter and consider all the famous pastors, TV evangelists, and others who have experienced moral failures. For many of them, their misconduct came as a surprise. They seemed to have all the outward appearances of doing things right. I'm not suggesting we judge or condemn them, but it's worth reflecting on how challenging it was to detect their issues.

Why? Because outward appearances can be deceiving. Success can be deceiving. Fruitful ministries can be deceiving. Flowery words can be deceiving. How do we discern what is spiritually sound? How can we know if teachers, pastors, bands, singers, writers, and speakers are genuinely good or if they are hiding behind a facade of tainted fruit? The answer isn't found in the FDA; it's found in the word of God.

THE WORD

"Now these were more noble-minded than those in Thessalonica, for they received the word with great eagerness, examining the Scriptures daily to see whether these things were so" (Acts 17:11).

The Bereans were a commendable group who verified what they heard against the Scriptures. Their eagerness for faith led them to pursue growth actively, integrating daily Scripture study into their lives.

The Bible emphasizes that genuine transformation comes through Scripture (Romans 12:2, James 1). Changing our lifestyles and thought patterns occurs through immersion in God's word. Distinguishing truth from falsehood requires knowledge and study of the Scriptures. As 2 Timothy 2:15 advises, "Be diligent to present yourself approved to God as a workman who does not need to be ashamed, accurately handling the word of truth."

Be prepared and vigilant; ensure nothing is overlooked in seeking God's approval for your life. The phrase "be diligent" (*spoudazo*), connoting earnestness and diligence, implies prompt and purposeful action toward a desired goal. It suggests focused and persistent effort. *Spoudazo*, in the aorist imperative, commands immediate and effective action. There's no time to waste; demonstrate fervent dedication to fulfilling the Lord's will for your life.

Understand how to live, speak, work, and relate based on God's word and its application to life. Accurately handling it means not just reading or knowing it but living it out. Let it be your anchor in all situations—source of wisdom, comfort, love, joy, and guidance. As 1 Thessalonians 5:21–22 advises, "Examine everything carefully; hold fast to that which is good; abstain from every form of evil."

To avoid false teachings and sinful living displeasing to God, test everything against the standard of Scripture. Examine it through the lens of God's word.

TEST BY THE WORD, NOT LOOKS

The goal isn't to become fruit inspectors, passing judgment on others' salvation based on their outward appearances of fruitfulness. Saying, "That person isn't saved; they lack enough fruit," or "That person is saved; look at all the fruit," is presumptuous. Who has the authority to determine the sufficient quantity of fruit, or whether God prefers apples over oranges? He might prefer figs and olives anyway. The real aim is to safeguard yourself from false teachings and the deceptive allure of counterfeit fruit presented by false teachers. Rather than focusing on fruit inspection, prioritize message inspection.

Jesus cautioned about the presence of wolves who would deceive and mislead people. Similarly, Paul warned about false teachers who would infiltrate and disrupt the flock. These deceivers often appear genuine, with a substantial following and seemingly righteous actions. The only effective way to identify a false teacher is by immersing yourself in the Word, studying and comparing texts diligently.

Consider Jesus's admonition in Matthew 7.

> Beware of the false prophets, who come to you in sheep's clothing, but inwardly are ravenous wolves. You will know them by their fruits. Grapes are not gathered from thorn *bushes* nor figs from thistles, are they? So every good tree bears good fruit, but the bad tree bears bad fruit. A good tree cannot produce bad fruit, nor can a bad tree produce good fruit. Every tree that does not bear good fruit is cut down and thrown into the fire. So then, you will know them by their fruits (Matthew 7:15–20).

In this passage, Jesus warns about the presence of false prophets who claim to speak on behalf of God. He emphasizes that relying solely on outward appearances is insufficient, likening false teachings to counterfeit fruit that may look genuine. But like we discussed, fruit can be artificially enhanced with dyes or chemicals, so they look the part.

In fact, in Matthew 7:15, Jesus describes them as "wolves in sheep's clothing," implying that they outwardly resemble genuine believers and reputable teachers. He uses the analogy of a wolf, because their primary concern is self-interest, often manifested as financial gain, popularity, or recognition. By relying solely on outward appearances, one might be deceived, as Jesus suggests that they appear as harmless as a sheep's fleece.

A FRUITFUL FAKE

Matthew 7:16–19 teaches that merely observing outward appearances such as fruit won't suffice, because false teachers can appear to produce spiritual goodness. They may lead large congregations, enjoy financial success, and publish books on spiritual matters, presenting themselves as genuine followers of God. Despite their outward appearance, false teachers may still deceive, even using Christian language convincingly. In today's context, many can manipulate crowds with persuasive speech (2 Timothy 4:3). So, what can believers do when wolves hide among the flock? What can they do when the apple looks ripe, but it is poisoned? Listen carefully.

TEST WHAT YOU HEAR WITH THE WORD

Jesus tells us that to truly test is not based on the eyes but the ears. It is all based on what you hear and what you personally have studied and know. The passage that helps us understand Matthew 7:15–20 is Matthew 12.

> Either make the tree good and its fruit good, or make the tree bad and its fruit bad; for the tree is known by its fruit. You brood of vipers, how can you, being evil, speak what is good? For the mouth speaks out of that which fills the heart. The good man brings out of *his* good treasure what is good; and the evil man brings out of *his* evil treasure what is evil. But I tell you that every careless word that people speak, they shall give an accounting for it in the day of judgment. For by your words you will be justified, and by your words you will be condemned (Matthew 12:33–37).

If someone claims to teach with divine knowledge, their fruit isn't measured by the size of their following, financial success, or material accomplishments. For a teacher, it's about how they handle the word of God. As 2 Timothy 2:15 states, it's about "accurately handling the word of truth." The true fruit of a teacher is the accuracy and integrity of their teaching.

KNOWN BY THEIR TEACHING, NOT THEIR CROWDS

A wolf in sheep's clothing reveals itself through its words. The rotten fruit of a corrupt tree is false teaching that contradicts the Bible. The leader's appearance, success, or eloquence are irrelevant. What truly matters is whether their teachings align with the Scriptures. Is it biblical? Is it God's truth? Does it withstand the scrutiny of His word? By seeking answers to these questions, you are diligently studying to know, be approved, and sanctified by God's word.

A good tree is known by its words. Jesus emphasized the purity of God's word, so as believers and followers, our purity is upheld by immersing ourselves in the truth of His word. "Sanctify them in the truth; Your word is truth" (John 17:17). Only the gospel truth and the cleansing power found in studying God's word can truly grow and purify us.

To follow Jesus and be His disciple means engaging with His word through study and application. "So Jesus was saying to those Jews who had believed Him, 'If you continue in My word, then you are truly disciples of Mine; and you will know the truth, and the truth will make you free.'" (John 8:31-32). Continuing in His word involves practicing the grace revealed in Jesus's teachings and living out love for God and others. Jesus encourages us to read, study, act, and follow His word personally, rather than relying solely on the teachings of others. You cannot sustain your soul and relationship with God by feeding off someone else's spiritual nourishment. It requires you to feast on God's word yourself.

I want to leave you with this analogy: When the FBI and CIA train their agents to detect counterfeit currency, they don't focus on showing them fake bills. Instead, they immerse them in the authentic currency, teaching them its characteristics, textures, and scents. Why? Because when you're intimately familiar with the real thing, it becomes much easier to identify a counterfeit.

Similarly, immerse yourself in God's word because that's how you'll discern the truth. Memorize it to maintain purity. Live by it to actively follow the Master. Knowing God's word is the surest defense against deception.

CHAPTER 38
LORD, LORD!

"Not everyone who says to Me, 'Lord, Lord,' will enter the kingdom of heaven, but he who does the will of My Father who is in heaven will enter."

—Matthew 7:21

Have you ever wondered when someone cries out, "Good Lord" or "Oh, God," if they are genuinely calling for Jesus? Or are they just uttering phrases out of habit or frustration?

My mom spent many years working at Eckerd Pharmacy before CVS bought the company. Among her colleagues was Sheri (not her real name), who had a habit of using the Lord's name in vain. Whenever things didn't go her way, Sheri would exclaim "God" or "Jesus Christ" in frustration.

One day, my mom had enough. When she made a mistake while typing, she decided to confront Sheri's habit head-on. With a burst of courage, my mom loudly exclaimed, "Sheri, dang it!" Sheri paused, giving my mom a puzzled look, but my mom played it cool and continued working.

Later, when Sheri's computer froze, she exclaimed, "Jesus!" My mom rushed over and jokingly asked, "Where? I'm ready for the rapture!" Sheri chuckled, catching on to the reference. Sensing an opportunity, my mom gently told Sheri, "If you don't know Him, please stop using His name." Surprisingly, Sheri laughed and agreed.

It's a common occurrence for people to use the name of Jesus without intimately knowing Him.

CAN SOMEONE CLAIM JESUS BUT NOT BELIEVE?

Mahatma Gandhi, a devout Hindu, credited Jesus, particularly the Sermon on the Mount, as one of the greatest influences on his life and way of living. He famously remarked, "A man who was completely innocent, offered himself as a sacrifice for the good of others, including his enemies, and became the ransom of the world. It was a perfect act."[53] However, Gandhi's appreciation for Jesus and His teachings does not imply that he was a Christian. Despite practicing fasting, love, and prayer based on Jesus's sermon, Gandhi did not view Jesus as his Savior. Following Jesus's teachings does not necessarily equate to belief in Him as Savior.

Jesus Himself spoke of those who perform works in His name and emulate His interactions with others, yet have not placed their trust in Him as Savior (Judas Iscariot being an example). Note the proof of why they should be saved is not belief in Christ but their works or actions.

> Not everyone who says to Me, "Lord, Lord," will enter the kingdom of heaven, but he who does the will of My Father who is in heaven *will enter*. Many will say to Me on that day, "Lord, Lord, did we not prophesy in Your name, and in Your name cast out demons, and in Your name perform many miracles?" And then I will declare to them, "I never knew you; DEPART FROM ME, YOU WHO PRACTICE

---

53. https://bemagazine.org/gandhi-christ-and-christianity/.

LAWLESSNESS." Therefore everyone who hears these words of Mine and acts on them, is like a wiseman who built his house upon the rock (Matthew 7:21-24).

Jesus discusses eternal life, which is bestowed freely upon all who believe (John 6:47). Additionally, He refers to the earthly kingdom as an integral aspect of this eternal inheritance (Revelation 20:6).

NOT EVERYONE SEES JESUS LIKE YOU

We shouldn't presume that everyone who claims to be a Christian is truly living for Jesus, as illustrated by the parables in Luke 15, which demonstrate how believers can stray and live apart from Christ. Similarly, we shouldn't assume that all individuals leading upright lives and performing good deeds are believers. Not everyone who lives like Jesus necessarily believes in Him or acknowledges Him as their Savior, despite His sacrifice being for all. This debate has persisted since the time of Jesus.

> Now when Jesus came into the district of Caesarea Philippi, He was asking His disciples, "Who do people say that the Son of Man is?" And they said, "Some say John the Baptist; and others, Elijah; but still others, Jeremiah, or one of the prophets" (Matthew 16:13-14).

As Jesus walked along, He asked His followers, "Who do people say I am?" Their responses echoed a trend that persists today. Many regarded Him as a godly man, a wise teacher, or a prophet of God—sentiments still commonly heard today. However, they failed to recognize Him for who He truly is: the Savior, the Lord, and God with us.

The issue with those alternative views is that if Jesus isn't God, then He must be considered a madman. Consider these statements: "I and the Father are one" (John 10:30) and "Jesus said to them, 'Truly, truly, I say to you, before Abraham was born, I am'" (John 8:58). The term "I

Am" comes from the Greek word *eimi,* meaning to be or to exist, which parallels the Hebrew *Yahweh,* the self-existing one.[54]

Jesus claimed to be Yahweh, the one true God. He cannot simply be a good teacher, a prophet, or a godly person while also being insane or deceitful. He unequivocally claimed to be God. Either He is God or He isn't. If Jesus isn't God, then He can't be regarded as a good teacher, a godly man, or a prophet because He would be a delusional liar. If He is God, then He deserves reverence and exaltation. Yet, sadly, many today depict Jesus as something other than who He claimed to be.

WHO HE IS

"He said to them, 'But who do you say that I am?' Simon Peter answered, 'You are the Christ, the Son of the living God'" (Matthew 16:15–16). Peter's response holds profound significance: Jesus is acknowledged as the Christ, the anointed Messiah, and as the Son of the living

---

54. The conversation and tension with the Pharisees, highlighting the strength of Jesus's claims, begin in John 7 when Jesus identifies Himself as "Living Water" (John 7:38). He further asserts His identity in John 8:12 as the "Light of Life." When Jesus uses phrases like "I am" or "I am He," He is alluding to the term *"Ani, Ani Hu"* from Hebrew, emphasizing His divine identity. This connection is significant because during the Feast of Booths, three main ceremonies are observed: the lighting ceremony, the water pouring ceremony, and the theological affirmations of 'Sukkot', to remind Israel how God delivered His people out of Egyptian bondage and provided for them in the wilderness. Jesus's declarations of being the Light and the Water are not merely symbolic of the celebrations but assert His role as the reason for celebration. This prompts the religious leaders to inquire about His identity, asking both about His father and who He claims to be. Jesus's statements claim deity, drawing from passages in Isaiah and Deuteronomy (e.g., Isaiah 41:4; 43:10, 13; 46:4; 48:12; 52:6; Deuteronomy 32:39) where God declares Himself as "I am He." The pivotal moment occurs in John 8:58 when Jesus states, "Before Abraham was, I am," prompting the leaders to seek His death for equating Himself with God. This phrase echoes God's declarations in Isaiah (Isaiah 41:4; 43:10, 13; 46:4; 48:12; 52:6), using the emphatic form *ego eimi* in Greek, meaning "I am that very One." In the Septuagint, various forms of Hebrew phrases like *ani hu* and *anokhi,* and *anokhi hu* are consistently translated in the emphatic *ego eimi* autos (The I am), emphasizing Jesus's claim to be the divine figure from the Old Testament scriptures. In John 8, the use of *ego eimi* in Greek grammar serves to emphasize His identity, akin to how God's name is referenced in the Septuagint translations of Isaiah and Deuteronomy. This demonstrates Jesus's deliberate assertion of His deity, culminating in claims that align Him with the divine declarations of the Old Testament and the reason Israel exists, is maintained, and was celebrating.

God, God incarnate. Salvation hinges on believing in Jesus. God, in human form, came, died, and rose again for the forgiveness of sins, redeeming all the wrongs and transgressions committed. "And Jesus said to him, 'Blessed are you, Simon Barjona, because flesh and blood did not reveal this to you, but My Father who is in heaven'" (Matthew 16:17). Let us earnestly pray for the enlightenment of those who are spiritually blind that they may recognize Jesus for who He truly is, the Savior of the world, and place their trust in Him for eternal life (John 3:14-18, 1 Corinthians 15:1-4).

KINGDOM VERSUS ETERNITY

"Not everyone who says to Me, 'Lord, Lord,' will enter the kingdom of heaven." The portion of the passage is hard to consider, and yet, in light of a discipleship and non-salvific view, it comes into a clearer focus.

> "And there is salvation in no one else; for there is no other name under heaven that has been given among mankind by which we must be saved" (Acts 4:12).

Many people may acknowledge Jesus as Lord, but mere acknowledgment does not ensure entry into heaven. Even Judas, among others, referred to Jesus as Lord, yet their hearts remained unchanged. The Pharisees and Sadducees also addressed Him with titles of respect, but their acknowledgment did not translate into genuine belief in Him as Savior and Lord.

As stated previously, Gandhi revered Jesus's teachings, considering Him an exemplary figure, yet he did not embrace Jesus as his personal Savior. Similarly, acknowledging Jesus's moral teachings does not equate to accepting Him as the only path to salvation.

Jesus emphasized that salvation is exclusively through faith in Him as the Son of God, who died and rose again for our sins. Good deeds alone cannot secure entry into heaven; it is only through faith in Christ that one can be saved.

For God so loved the world, that He gave His only Son, so that everyone who believes in Him will not perish, but have eternal life. For God did not send the Son into the world to judge the world, but so that the world might be saved through Him. The one who believes in Him is not judged; the one who does not believe has been judged already, because he has not believed in the name of the only Son of God" (John 3:16–18).

LORD VERSUS SAVIOR

In ancient biblical times, if someone committed a shameful act toward their rabbi, the rabbi would declare a *neziphah*, a temporary form of excommunication for a day or event. This action could be triggered by misapplying the rabbi's teachings, offending him, or engaging in inappropriate behavior. When the rabbi pronounced "I do not know you," it signified that the individual's actions were unrecognizable, indicating a departure from the teachings and values imparted by the rabbi. This declaration conveyed that the student's behavior was inconsistent with the teachings they had received and that the rabbi did not recognize their conduct as reflective of their teachings. A rabbi could declare a *neziphah* on a person in the temple congregation or a student, causing them to miss the sabbath, be removed from readings, or not allowed in a holy day celebration.[55] These punishments increased from a single day or event to a month or until repentance was found.[56]

In Matthew 10:25, Jesus emphasizes that a disciple's aim is to mirror their master. As Christians, our lives should reflect Jesus, bearing His name with honor and respect. This aligns closely with the teaching that a wise person builds their life on the foundation of

---

55. Lynn Kaye, "Lay People's Advocacy and Resistance in Talmudic Adjudication Narratives," *Yale Journal of Law & the Humanities*, 32:1 (2021), 78–118.
56. J. Dwight Pentecost, *The Words and Works of Jesus Christ* (Grand Rapids, MI: Zondervan, 1981), 290–91.

Christ's word. Ultimately, we will be called to give an account for our actions, and some may hear the sobering words, "I do not recognize myself in your actions."

It is a privilege to know Jesus as our Savior and to grow in Him as our Lord. This is what it truly means to follow Him, to take His yoke and carry His burden as outlined in Matthew 11:29–30. Embrace the joy of discipleship, as Paul encourages, even sharing in the joy of Christ's sufferings (Philippians 3:10).

CHAPTER 39
THE WISEMAN BUILDS

> *"Therefore everyone who hears these words of Mine and acts on them, may be compared to a wise man who built his house on the rock."*
>
> —Matthew 7:24

It is fitting that Jesus ends His teaching on what a commitment to follow Him looks like in everyday thoughts, actions, speech, and attitude, by stating wisdom is application of His teaching. Every day, we have a decision to make on how we will act, react, talk, and interact. Jesus wants us to interact with love as His representatives here on earth (Matthew 5:16, 43). He does not force people to obey; instead, each person must choose to follow in obedience, or choose to do it their own way. We can follow Him and His word or go to the world and its pleasures as our means of satisfaction.

> Therefore I urge you, brethren, by the mercies of God, to present your bodies as a living and holy sacrifice, acceptable to God, *which is* your spiritual service of worship. And do not be conformed to this world, but be transformed by

the renewing of your mind, so that you may prove what the will of God is, that which is good and acceptable and perfect (Romans 12:1–2).

Let the word of God change your thoughts and mind so you are living right. Conform to the standards of the word of God. His word can keep you from sin; likewise sin can keep you from His word.

THE EFFECTS OF WHO YOU FOLLOW

Decisions come with consequences, whether good or bad. Jesus offers guidance on decision-making and highlights the outcomes. He presents believers with two paths to choose from in life (Matthew 7:13–14), emphasizing how obedience to His word can shield them from life's pitfalls.

> "Therefore, everyone who hears these words of Mine, and acts on them, will be like a wise man who built his house on the rock. And the rain fell and the floods came, and the winds blew and slammed against that house; and *yet* it did not fall, for it had been founded on the rock. And everyone who hears these words of Mine, and does not act on them, will be like a foolish man who built his house on the sand. And the rain fell and the floods came, and the winds blew and slammed against that house; and it fell— and its collapse was great." When Jesus had finished these words, the crowds were amazed at His teaching; for He was teaching them as one who had authority, and not as their scribes (Matthew 7:24–29).

Jesus presents two audiences, two types of people who hear His teachings but choose differently, resulting in distinct outcomes. One audience consists of those who hear His words and heed them, embracing His teachings and incorporating them into their lives. The other audience includes those who hear but disregard His teachings, opting for their own paths or interpretations instead. These two groups experience divergent consequences based on their responses to Jesus's teachings.

A WISE FOLLOWER

A wise follower of Jesus is characterized by two key actions: hearing and acting. Many people may hear or even admire Jesus's teachings, but according to Jesus Himself, true wisdom lies in obeying His words. Those who not only listen but also put His teachings into practice are likened to someone who builds their life on a solid foundation, like rock.

In Matthew 7:25, the imagery of wind, rain, and floods symbolizes the inevitable challenges and trials of life. Only those who live out Jesus's teachings will find themselves able to withstand the storms that come their way. Mere familiarity with His teachings won't suffice when faced with adversity; it's the application of His words that provides stability in the midst of life's uncertainties.

To build on the rock, which is Christ and His teachings, is to establish a firm foundation that can withstand whatever storms may come. By embodying His teachings in our actions, we fortify ourselves against the trials of life, finding security and strength in our faith.

THE FOOLISH BELIEVER

The fool hears but doesn't obey (Matthew 7:26-27). Just like the wise man, Scripture acknowledges that the fool hears. They attend Bible studies, Sunday school, church services, and read the Scriptures, but the crucial difference lies in their lack of commitment to living out what they learn.

Just recently, my keyboard wasn't working properly on my computer. After ten or fifteen minutes of use, every other letter typed would not appear on the screen. This had happened before, so it seemed like an easy fix: replace the batteries. I flipped the keyboard over, put in the new batteries, and continued typing. There was no response. I turned on and off the Word doc I had been working on, figuring something would trigger a response. And…still no response. I restarted my computer…no response. Then I realized I had forgotten to press the reset button on the keypad. Sometimes that needs to be done, so I pushed it…still no response. My keypad was obviously broken. I had worked so hard and done so many obvious solutions to fix the problem, but still there was no response. Then I took a second to look at everything calmly and saw that the batteries were not properly put in and were not making a good connection.

Reflecting on this, I realized how often our spiritual lives resemble this scenario: God is reaching out to us, attempting to establish a connection, but we fail to respond to His call.

> Therefore, putting aside all filthiness and all that remains of wickedness, in humility receive the word implanted, which is able to save your souls. But prove yourselves doers of the word, and not merely hearers who delude themselves. For if anyone is a hearer of the word and not a doer, he is like a man who looks at his natural face in a mirror; for once he has looked at himself and gone away, he has immediately forgotten what kind of person he was. But one who looks intently at the perfect law, the law of liberty, and abides by it, not having become a forgetful hearer but an effectual doer, this man will be blessed in what he does (James 1:21–25).

When you read the Bible, listen to a message, or encounter something prompting action but don't act upon it, you're deluding yourself.

THE TRICKED PERSON

The Bible warns about the possibility of self-delusion. The Greek word *paralogizomai* implies being tricked by falsehood. When you're deluded, you have a false understanding, often leading to a state of no response. James 1:21–25 explains how this occurs: You engage with God's word but fail to act upon it.

The key lies in our action, which is application. People often remember only a fraction of what they read, see, or hear. So how can we truly grow from God's word by merely studying it? In my school days, I studied for tests just to pass them, and once the test was over, it felt like my memory was wiped clean.

But our God is amazing and knew that we would have a sort of "Bible ADD." His word is full of verbs—words that convey action. In other words, it's about doing something. "Therefore, prepare your minds for action, keep sober in spirit, fix your hope completely on the grace to be brought to you at the revelation of Jesus Christ" (1 Peter 1:13). God is telling us to get ready to do something, to apply His word. He's teaching us through action because it's through living it, acting upon it, and trying it that we truly learn about Jesus.

When I used to swim competitively, we would all get on the dive blocks in a crouched position, feet staggered, fingers gripping the edge of the diving board. That was the "get set" moment just before the go or gunshot. It might seem mundane, tedious, and annoying, but it's a crucial time in the race. Being in the set position prepares you for the dive into the water, and with the right "set," you can get a great start ahead of the competition.

But for some swimmers, sitting still is a challenge, and they end up with a false start. There was a kid on my team, the fastest freestyle swimmer around, but he had lousy starts. Despite usually lapping the competition, he was disqualified from half of our matches and couldn't swim in districts and counties because of it. In all my competitions, finals, and heats, I've never seen someone freeze in the set position when it's time to go. It's usually the opposite—they're anxious to leap out and go.

What applies to swimming competition applies to believers. We need to "get set," get prepared, and get ready on the springboard, because we're about to leap into action. Sadly, some Christians get tired from too many emotional false starts in their spiritual life, and they never finish what God wants them to do. For others, they never leap into action; they don't even want to climb the diving board, because they don't care about the race. Jesus says they're being foolish, and James says they're deceived.

THE IDEA: AVOID PAIN

> Therefore, everyone who hears these words of Mine, and acts on them, will be like a wise man who built his house on the rock. And the rain fell and the floods came, and the winds blew and slammed against that house; and *yet* it did not fall, for it had been founded on the rock. And everyone who hears these words of Mine, and does not act on them, will be like a foolish man who built his house on the sand. And the rain fell and the floods came, and the winds blew and slammed against that house; and it fell— and its collapse was great" (Matthew 7:24–27).

This is not just a plea from Jesus to obey Him in order to not miss out on the life He offers. This is also a warning. The last part of the verse says, "and that house fell, and great was its fall." You compare these two men, and they have similarities and differences. They both hear Jesus's words, but only one does them. Only one takes His words to heart in such a way that he lives by them.

Jesus is telling us how to avoid harsh consequences and avoid pitfalls and pain. In Luke 6, Jesus directly says, "Don't call Me 'Lord'", meaning "Don't call Me your head, the one that calls the shots, guides your life, and takes your hand in instruction, if you refuse to listen." Listen, it's the same teaching.

> Now why do you call Me, "Lord, Lord," and do not do what I say? Everyone who comes to Me and hears My words and acts on them, I will show you whom he is like: he is like a

man building a house, who dug deep and laid a foundation on the rock; and when there was a flood, the river burst against that house and *yet* it could not shake it, because it had been well built. But the one who has heard and has not acted *accordingly* is like a man who built a house on the ground without a foundation; and the river burst against it and it immediately collapsed, and the ruin of that house was great (Luke 6:46–49).

The Bible and its application help us avoid sin, but sin, in turn, can hinder us from reading and applying Scripture. The wise person opts for the best for their life, which is found in Christ's plan. So, heed the teachings of Jesus. A wise individual acts on His words and remains stable and prosperous amidst life's pressures. As Romans 8:28 assures us, "And we know that God causes all things to work together for good to those who love God, to those who are called according to His purpose."

Given these reflections, it's essential to consider how we think and behave in our daily interactions, whether at home, work, or school. If others were to hear our words, observe our actions, or discern our intentions, would they perceive that we are aligning our lives with Christ and His teachings? Would they recognize us as faithful representatives of Him here on earth? Is Christ evident in our conduct?

CHAPTER 40
OUR RESPONSE

What should be our response to Jesus's Sermon on the Mount? Is it applicable for today? Is it a writing just to the Jews? Should we view this as a writing for another time?

The Gospels and the Epistles maintain continuity in distinguishing between salvation and discipleship. We must remember that the writers are explaining to us the teachings of Jesus for application and growth. In essence, everything one reads in the New Testament originated from the mouth of Christ. Consider Paul's articulation of salvation in passages like Ephesians 2:8–9, 4:7; Romans 5:15–17, 6:23, 11:6. In these passages, Paul employs language such as "free gift," "given," "by grace," and "abundance of grace" to emphasize the unmerited nature of salvation. This is very similar to Jesus's teaching of salvation being based on His finished work on the cross expressed in the book of John. Nowhere in these verses does Paul associate a cost with belief in Jesus. Instead, when Paul speaks of cost, it is linked to the concept of reward (see 1 Corinthians 9:25, 1 Timothy 6:11–19, 2 Timothy 4:1–8).

In each of the cited verses, Paul highlights that the struggle and associated cost are aimed at achieving specific rewards: an imperishable crown, the accumulation of future treasure, and the anticipation of a future crown of righteousness. This distinction highlights that while salvation is freely given through faith in Jesus Christ, discipleship involves a commitment to follow Christ wholeheartedly, which may entail struggles and sacrifices in pursuit of eternal rewards. This verbiage is nearly identical to what Jesus uses in the Sermon on the Mount.

Other indications that the growth of a believer is not necessarily tied to their initial salvation can be found in Paul's address to the Corinthians, where he describes them as needing milk, because they were not yet able to handle solid food (1 Corinthians 3:2). Despite this, Paul still referred to them as brethren, indicating their status as believers. Similarly, the author of Hebrews urges the readers to move beyond elementary teachings (Hebrews 6:1), suggesting that spiritual growth is an ongoing process. The writer also expresses the expectation that the readers, who had been believers for a considerable time, should have progressed to the point of being teachers (Hebrews 5:12–14).

Paul's relationship with Timothy further stresses the importance of growth and development in the faith. Paul referred to Timothy as his "son in the faith," implying a special investment in Timothy's spiritual maturity (1 Timothy 1:2).

In the post-Christ era, the cost of discipleship became increasingly evident. Believers faced persecution from Jewish leaders and later from the Roman authorities. As Earl Radmacher points out, Jesus Himself indicated that persecution would be a hallmark of discipleship: "Persecution will come upon them because they are identified with Jesus whom the world hates without cause."[57] When examining the path of discipleship as outlined by Jesus and the apostles, it's evident that a believer's public declaration of faith in Christ often led to immediate

---

57. Gary Derickson and Earl Radmacher, *The Disciplemaker: What Matters Most to Jesus* (Salem, OR: Charis Press, 2001), 32.

discipleship. We must see that there are clear costs associated with following Jesus, exemplified by the martyrdom of Christ and His early followers. So, what insights can we derive from Jesus and the apostles regarding the journey of discipleship?

Firstly, Jesus's teachings emphasize the radical nature of discipleship, requiring wholehearted commitment and surrender. He challenges His followers to count the cost, acknowledging that discipleship involves denying oneself, taking up the cross, and following Him (Matthew 16:24-26).

Secondly, the apostles' lives exemplify the sacrificial nature of discipleship. They endured persecution, hardship, and even martyrdom for the sake of Christ, demonstrating unwavering devotion to His cause (Acts 5:41, 2 Timothy 4:6-8).

Furthermore, the apostolic writings emphasize the transformative power of discipleship. Believers are called to be conformed to the image of Christ, growing in maturity and holiness through the indwelling presence of the Holy Spirit (2 Corinthians 3:18, Galatians 5:22-23).

In essence, the path of discipleship entails embracing the radical call to follow Christ wholeheartedly, enduring the inevitable challenges and costs that come with it, and experiencing transformation and growth as we walk in obedience to His teachings.

DISCIPLESHIP IS COSTLY

Jesus had a mission while He was on earth. He said, "For the Son of Man has come to seek and to save that which was lost" (Luke 19:10). His objective was to single-handedly redeem the entire world with His death, burial, and resurrection (John 3:16; 1 Corinthians 15:1-4, 55-57; 1 Timothy 4:10). While on earth, He used His time to gather followers to Himself. He shared the message of Messiah and verified the message through His miracles (John 2:23). Yet, Jesus realized His message needed to be broadcast beyond Himself. There needed to be people to pass the baton with the good news of the gospel, and so with few words, Jesus chose twelve men He would disciple and said, "Follow Me" (Matthew 4:19). These men became His disciples, and He became their teacher, and it was to them He entrusted the responsibility to spread the good news after He ascended to the Father.

Over the span of three years, Jesus trained the twelve for the task of sharing His message. As Earley and Dempsey point out in their work, *Disciple Making Is*, "Jesus was a Jewish Rabbi, or teacher, who used a rabbinical method for disciple making. [B]uilt on progressive level of commitment, trust, obedience, and learning. At each step He demanded greater commitment, which gave His followers greater impact."[58] For the men to grasp the seriousness of their future task, Jesus would require total commitment as these men would carry on His message and be foundational in the launch and building of the church.

Jesus consistently emphasized the radical nature of discipleship, calling on followers to deny themselves, take up their cross, and follow Him (Matthew 16:24). He stressed the need for total commitment, even if it meant forsaking worldly possessions and relationships (Luke 14:26-27, 33). Moreover, Jesus highlighted the importance of love, humility, and servanthood as essential qualities of His disciples (John 13:34-35, Matthew 20:26-28).

The apostles echoed these teachings, emphasizing the necessity of perseverance amidst trials and suffering (2 Timothy 3:12, James 1:2-4, 1 Peter 4:12-14). They urged believers to walk in righteousness, pursue holiness, and remain steadfast in faith (2 Peter 3:11-12, Hebrews 12:1-2, Ephesians 4:1). Additionally, they encouraged mutual edification and accountability within the body of Christ (Hebrews 10:24-25, Galatians 6:1-2).

In essence, the writings of Jesus and the apostles portray discipleship as a demanding yet deeply rewarding journey characterized by self-sacrifice, perseverance, love, and a steadfast commitment to following Christ's example. "The decision to follow a rabbi meant total commitment. They would have to memorize His words and replicate

---

58. Dave Earley and Rod Dempsey, *Disciple Making Is...: How to Live the Great Commission with Passion and Confidence* (Nashville, TN: B & H, 2013), 58.

His lifestyle."[59] Jesus would do the same with His disciples, and yet His words were different than those of contemporary rabbis.

Jesus condemned the modern rabbis because they exasperated their pupils with rules, laws, and traditions that they could not even keep (Matthew 23:4). It is estimated that there are 613 laws Jewish people need to maintain, and depending on the rabbi's interpretation, there could be a dozen other traditions and rules associated with each law. Jesus said not to follow these men, because they are unfair hypocrites and should not be followed (Matthew 23:6–14). Jesus described the yokes of these hypocrites as heavy burdens on the shoulders of men, yet He described His yoke of teaching as "easy" and "light" (Matthew 11:30). His call was to release themselves of the other rabbis' unobtainable teachings (Matthew 11:28) and "Take My yoke upon you and learn from Me" (Matthew 11:29).

Jesus's teaching would be surrounded by the four-letter word *love*. Love God (Mark 12:30), love others (Mark 12:31), love each other (John 13:34–35), and love your enemies (Matthew 5:44). It would be up to Jesus's disciples to share His message and engage others to do the same. In fact, this was His main concern after His resurrection when He said, "All authority has been given to Me in heaven and on earth. Go therefore and make disciples" (Matthew 28:18b–19a). His last instruction was for His learners to make learners.

"FOLLOW ME" IS DISCIPLESHIP

As we've observed, the call to discipleship has remained consistent throughout the centuries. When Jesus called the twelve disciples (Matthew 4:18–20), He used the phrase "Come, follow Me." This phrase, "Follow me" (LECH AHARAI), was a technical term in Hebrew for becoming a disciple. Even before Christ, the Hebrew people used this terminology to call individuals into a mentorship relationship. As a rabbi in His ancient context, Jesus employed the same language to invite His followers into a similar role. Similarly, Paul used the call to follow,

---

59. Dave Earley and Rod Dempsey, *Disciple Making Is*, 68.

though he extended it to a broader audience (1 Corinthians 11:1). Having been trained under the renowned rabbi Gamaliel, Paul would have been intimately familiar with this concept of following as a disciple. "If the rabbi thought the student could make the cut, he extended an invitation to follow him until the age of thirty, which was when most rabbis began their own ministries. Three prominent first-century rabbis were Hillel, Shammai, and Gamaliel."[60]

Paul's approach to discipleship mirrored that of Christ's; he prioritized the transmission of knowledge (2 Timothy 2:2). Advising his mentee Timothy, Paul emphasized the importance of discernment in choosing disciples. Similar to Jesus, Paul dedicated substantial time to his disciples, engaging in ministry alongside them. Paul took Timothy nearly everywhere he went: "Timothy had the opportunity to see Paul in action for a three-year period as he did evangelism and discipleship."[61] This was Timothy's time to be invested in by Paul, much like Jesus did with His disciples. And like Jesus, Paul sent out his disciples to do ministry without him. Jesus sent the seventy-two to spread the message of the kingdom (Luke 10), and Paul had Silas and Timothy stay in Athens after he left to "run the ministry there in his absence (Acts 17:14)."[62] The goals were the same: hands-on training and application. Lastly, Paul impressed on Timothy that ministry should not be driven by self-interest or internal concerns.

THE CALL FOR ALL

This call to follow Jesus is universal and timeless, extending across generations. God doesn't choose based on human qualifications; instead, He equips those whom He calls. Consider Peter as an example: his past as a fisherman, marked by stubbornness and roughness, made him precisely the kind of "fisher of men" that Jesus desired. Despite Peter's

---

60. Robby Gallaty, *Rediscovering Discipleship*, 34.
61. Dave Earley and Rod Dempsey, *Disciple Making Is*, 161.
62. Ibid., 162.

imperfections, Jesus saw in him the potential to bring glory to God.

Reflecting on John Wesley's evangelistic revivals, a captivating story emerges. Wesley's methodology involved organizing series of preaching nights, where pastors from nearby regions would deliver sermons. This approach sought to integrate new believers into local churches, nurturing a sense of community and solidarity in their spiritual growth. It exemplifies how the call to discipleship transcends individual interactions, encompassing a wider community of believers collaborating to propagate the message of Jesus.

One time, a pastor from a nearby farming village was preaching from a text in Luke 19:21 talking of the talents,

> "Lord, I feared Thee, because Thou art an austere man" (KJV). Not knowing the word *austere*, he thought the text spoke of "an oyster man."
>
> He explained how a diver must grope in dark, freezing water to retrieve oysters. In his attempt, he cuts his hands on the sharp edges of the shells. After he obtains an oyster, he rises to the surface, clutching it "in his torn and bleeding hands." The preacher added, "Christ descended from the glory of heaven into...sinful human society, in order to retrieve humans and bring them back up with Him to the glory of heaven. His torn and bleeding hands are a sign of the value He has placed on the object of His quest."
>
> Afterward, 12 men received Christ. Later that night, someone came to Wesley to complain about unschooled preachers who were too ignorant even to know the meaning of the texts they were preaching on. The Oxford-educated Wesley simply said, "Never mind. The Lord got a dozen oysters tonight."[63]

---

63. Cindy Kasper, "Oyster Man," *Our Daily Bread*, April 9, 2008, https://odb.org/US/2008/04/09/the-oyster-man.

Follow, answer His call, use what you have, where you are, and let Him work out the rest. Jesus called tax collectors, fishermen, and men that were uneducated and uninspiring. "And He was saying to them all, 'If anyone wishes to come after Me, he must deny himself, and take up his cross daily and follow Me'" (Luke 9:23).

Following means a commitment to taking someone's guidance and instruction; it is a total commitment with no hesitations or excuses. Let's compare two men in Luke 9 who are both called to follow Jesus. "As they were going along the road, someone said to Him, 'I will follow You wherever You go.' And Jesus said to him, 'The foxes have holes and the birds of the air have nests, but the Son of Man has nowhere to lay His head'" (Luke 9:57–58). Look at this first man. Matthew 8:19 says he is a scribe. He tells Jesus he is going to follow Jesus wherever He goes. Jesus responds by giving him a warning that following Him is tough, because you may have to do without when you put Jesus first.

"And He said to another, 'Follow Me.' But he said, 'Lord, permit me first to go and bury my father.' But He said to him, 'Allow the dead to bury their own dead; but as for you, go and proclaim everywhere the kingdom of God.'" (Luke 9:59–60). Look at this second man. Jesus calls him to follow, and he says let me bury my father. Now a lot of people get confused when we read this. Christ's response causes readers to believe Jesus is showing a lack of compassion to a man who just lost his father. But the Jewish tradition was to bury the dead immediately following death. "In the East, burial followed so immediately on death that the former would hardly have involved more than the delay of a few hours. In the latter case, the request was, in fact, a plea for indefinite postponement."[64] This person was saying, "Jesus, I will follow you once my dad dies and I get my inheritance. Wait until my dad passes away." His dad was not dead yet. The son was selfish and only thinking about his inheritance. Jesus then said to the first man that offered to follow Him

---

64. C. J. Ellicott, *A Bible Commentary for the English Reader: The Four Gospels* (New York, NY: Cassell and Co., 1878), 48.

to go tell everyone about Him. Jesus saw no need for him to physically follow, because he was ready to serve Jesus where he was. He could sense this man was ready and willing to put Jesus and others first before his own needs, unlike the second man.

LOOK AHEAD

Reflecting on missed opportunities can hinder your current path like creating a zigzag in your journey, causing you to stumble over unseen obstacles. Instead of fixating on what could have been, focus on the present and keep moving forward with clarity and determination. This way, you can navigate your path effectively and avoid unnecessary setbacks. "But Jesus said to him, 'No one, after putting his hand to the plow and looking back, is fit for the kingdom of God'" (Luke 9:62). A follower needs to be looking straight ahead at Christ's path, not at what could have been.

In Jesus's time, the cross symbolized death, so when He urged His followers to take up their cross daily, He essentially called them to embrace a daily surrender of self. This commitment demands effort, as worthwhile endeavors often do, and entails facing pain and struggle.

The call to believers today resonates similarly. It's a call to live paradoxically: to dwell on earth while keeping a heavenly perspective. The Sermon on the Mount serves as a guide for discipleship, instructing on prayer, fasting, generosity, community, ethical conduct, and mindset. These teachings equip believers to live in the present with an eye toward eternity, encouraging them to embrace a life that reflects the values of God's kingdom.

Choosing to heed this call means embracing a life of distinction, aiming for the ultimate commendation of "well done. . . enter the joy of your master" (Matthew 25:23). It entails letting go of selfishness, pride, and self-promotion, and instead, living as vessels for bringing glory to Jesus. In this journey, Jesus uses our imperfections, experiences, and past to shape us into the disciples He envisions, but the decision to respond to His call rests squarely with us. We should view Matthew 5-7 as instruction on how to live the abundant life He offers to all who are willing to live out His words. What will be your response to the call to follow His legacy and go the extra mile?

IN SUMMARY

Christ's teachings on the mountainside were profound and transformative, designed to guide His followers toward a life of righteousness and compassion. He imparted wisdom on matters of the heart, relationships, integrity, and devotion to God. My hope and prayer for you is that you would embrace these teachings wholeheartedly, allowing them to shape not only your beliefs but also your actions and attitude.

May you embody the love, grace, and humility that Jesus exemplified, demonstrating kindness and compassion in your interactions with others. Let His words resonate deeply within you, influencing every decision you make and every word you speak. May your life be a reflection of His teachings, inspiring others to seek truth, love, and righteousness.

As you journey through each day, may you continually seek to live in alignment with the principles of Christ, drawing strength and guidance from His timeless words. And may your life serve as a beacon of light and hope in a world that desperately needs the transformative power of His love.